SCC



# Indian Youth in a Transforming World

# Indian Youth in a Transforming World

## Attitudes and Perceptions

*Edited by*

**Peter Ronald deSouza**
**Sanjay Kumar**
**Sandeep Shastri**

CSDS

Konrad Adenauer Stiftung

SAGE www.sagepublications.com
Los Angeles • London • New Delhi • Singapore • Washington DC

*First published in 2009 by*

**SAGE Publications India Pvt Ltd**
B1/I-1 Mohan Cooperative Industrial Area
Mathura Road, New Delhi 110 044, India
*www.sagepub.in*

**SAGE Publications Inc**
2455 Teller Road
Thousand Oaks, California 91320, USA

**SAGE Publications Ltd**
1 Oliver's Yard, 55 City Road
London EC1Y 1SP, United Kingdom

**SAGE Publications Asia-Pacific Pte Ltd**
33 Pekin Street
#02-01 Far East Square
Singapore 048763

Published by Vivek Mehra for SAGE Publications India Pvt Ltd, typeset in 11/13 pt AGaramondPro by Star Compugraphics Private Limited, Delhi and printed at Artxel, New Delhi.

**Library of Congress Cataloging-in-Publication Data Available**

**ISBN:** 978-81-321-0171-0 (PB)

**SAGE Production Team:** Rekha Natarajan, Sejuti Dasgupta, Amrita Saha and Trinankur Banerjee

# CONTENTS

# Acknowledgements

We are most happy to place on record our gratitude to the Konrad-Adenauer-Stiftung for initiating and commissioning this study on 'Youth Attitudes' in India. Here we will like to convey our special thanks to Mr. Jörg Wolff from KAS for his continuous support and involvement at various levels of deliberations from the very beginning of the project.

The project has been possible because of the institutional support that we received from the Centre for the Study of Developing Societies, Delhi.

We are also grateful to the members of the Advisory Board, Coordination Committee and the International Advisory Board for their expert suggestions and review comments during the initial conceptualisation of the study till its finalisation.

Our special acknowledgement also goes to Prof. Suhas Palshikar, Co-Director Lokniti for his inputs throughout the project and to Prof. Pradeep Chibber from University of California, Berkeley, who was specially invited by the Steering Committee of the project for his expert comments on the data analysis.

We would also like to give special thanks to Prof. N. Jayaram from Institute for Social and Economic Change, Bangalore and Coordination Committee member Prof. Sasheej Hegde for their detailed review of all the Case Studies commissioned under the KAS-CSDS Youth Study.

We would also like to thank the Research Team at Lokniti (CSDS), Lokniti Network members, and the data analysis team of CSDS. Finally, we thank those who helped us with layout designing and provided us with administrative support, at every stage.

# The Big Story

- Young men are more fashion conscious as compared to young women.
- Young rural men are more supportive of promotion of greater gender equality by the government as compared to their urban counterparts.
- Small town youth are more satisfied with the existing educational facilities in comparison to those from villages and big cities.
- Young women in cities are least supportive of reservation for women in parliament.
- Corruption, illiteracy and terrorism are not primary national concerns among the Indian youth.
- Dalit and Tribal youth have higher aspirations in life as compared to those from Forward Castes and OBCs.
- For Indian youth, guarantee of employment should be first priority for the nation followed by provision of quality health care and educational facilities.
- More than two-third of the Indian youth consider alcohol consumption to be unacceptable.
- Urban youth favour improved friendly relations with Pakistan as compared to rural youth.
- Youth from small towns have the highest levels of aspirations in life as compared to those from metropolitan cities and villages.
- Poverty is seen as the major concern of national importance among all sections of the youth in India.
- Youth from towns are more optimistic about their future as compared to those from villages and cities.

# Executive Summary

The executive summary of the findings of this youth study are presented below. The report indicates that in significant ways the youth in India mirror continuity with change. On significant parameters they think very much like the older generations. In many other critical areas, they have chosen to tread a different path. The study has also found that the youth in India mirror many of the goals, aspirations and attitudes of youth across the world. The study also reports that in select areas the attitude and choices of the Indian youth vary significantly from those of the younger generation the world over. The study has been divided into seven thematic chapters and each section below reports the major findings of the seven chapters.

## Trust and Circles of Belonging

Youth appeared to voice the flavour of the changing times in terms of their levels of inter-personal social trust and circles of belonging even while reflecting the 'social environment' that shapes the reality and the times that they live in. In social interactions that they nurture and nourish, Indian youth have pushed traditional boundaries. The youth demonstrate a moderate level of inter-personal trust in those they interact with. The intensity of trust is significantly higher among those who are a part of their 'immediate social circle'. Youth reported limited experience of being discriminated against. Critical differences in trends are produced by three important variables—access to higher education, improved socio-economic status and exposure to urban life. These cause important and significant variations in the nature of social transactions that the Indian youth are exposed to and are a part of.

## Family and Social Networks

The study developed an Index of Parental Authority and an Index of Family Values to understand what influences the way youth think and act in their personal and social domains. The nature of parental authority is both a by-product of a set of value preferences and also something that shapes the world view that youth tend to develop on matters linked to family life and social relationships. It is clearly apparent that tradition and modernity play out in multiple ways in the lives of young people in India. The nature of the social structure and the dynamics of social relationships that the youth are exposed to, appear to shape their family values in particular and their social values in general.

### Leisure and Lifestyle

The study analysed the leisure habits of the young in India. They are intrinsically linked to their socio-economic status, educational levels and place of stay. Television is a crucial source of entertainment and an important leisure activity for most youth, especially those residing in urban areas and those who are educated. Internet use is largely limited to the cities and almost exclusively among those who have had the benefit of higher education. Wearing fashionable clothes is important for a large segment of the youth. This often reflects an aspiration rather than a fact of life.

## Politics and Democracy

The study finds that the youth in India buck the global trend of declining interest in politics. The youth not only show a high level of interest in politics. There is no decline in this interest across generations. There is a reasonably high level of participation in all forms of politics—direct, indirect, formal or non-formal—as well among the youth. Their trust in democracy is also significantly high. Educational levels and media exposure appear to clearly influence their reflections on democracy and politics.

## Governance and Development

The youth identified unemployment and poverty as the two major challenges that people faced. When it comes to other issues of national importance and what the priority of the government should be, the youth are in favour of the government tackling the problem of HIV/AIDS as the first priority followed by maternal health and reducing child mortality rates. Ensuring greater gender equality too is given high priority by the youth. Women seem to lay a greater emphasis on this issue than men. While there is support for reservation of seats for women in Parliament and State Legislatures, this support is much less among the men living in towns and cities as compared to those living in the villages.

## Nation and the World

There does not seem to be too high a level of awareness among the youth about the changes taking place in the contemporary world. A vast majority of them are not aware of globalisation. By and large, only the educated youth and those who live in cities know about globalisation. Consequently, it is the educated that tend to support globalisation more. The youth, showed a high level of awareness when it came to India's friends and foes. While a larger number of youth were aware of the United States they differed in their views on how India's relations with it should develop. There was interesting variance on how India should engage with the world.

## Anxieties and Aspirations

The anxieties and aspirations of the youth are clearly linked to three variables: their socio-economic status, educational level and whether they live in urban or rural areas. The aims and aspirations of the youth living in villages are often linked to the immediate world that they confront in their daily lives. Metropolitan India tends to present youth with a different set of anxieties and aspirations. Youth in small, emerging towns and cities seem to be at the threshold of the real change. Not yet fully cut off from their rural roots but significantly influenced by the scent of urbanisation and all its trappings, the high level of expectations as reflected both in their anxieties and aspirations underscore this point.

Overall, the study clearly indicates that the youth in India are on the cusp of change and represent an authentic multiplicity of aspirations, 'world views' and interest truly mirroring the rich tapestry of diversity that India is.

PROVE YOUR
IDENTITY PLEASE

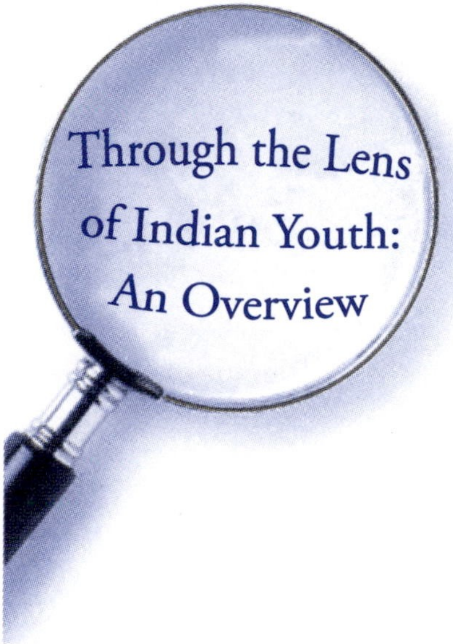

# Through the Lens of Indian Youth: An Overview

Two words, multiple and challenging, can be used to pithily describe India. To say that there are multiple religions, languages, cuisines, ethnicities, dress styles, ecosystems, markets, political organisations, customs, sports, film traditions, music preferences, etc is to state the obvious and yet one cannot avoid beginning any discussion of India by stating this truism if only to dissuade the enthusiast who wants to offer an essentialist view of India. Trying to present any one of these worlds is hence a big challenge since the sweep of easy generalisation is unavailable and yet we have to offer some less easy generalisations if only to explain the causal processes involved.

What is true for the larger canvas is also true for the world of Indian youth, a fascinating section of the population that is existentially located across different regions, social groups, economic segments, educational levels, and even sartorial choices. There are multiple worlds in which youth reside. These worlds socialize them in different ways. The worlds are not static since they too have been impacted by the processes of modernity and the forces of globalisation. The challenge that we confront is, therefore, to map the dynamics of this change, to see how the processes that are producing transformation are being refracted through the lens of Indian youth. After recognizing that there are multiple life-worlds, and multiple responses to the encounter with modernity and globalisation, we have, here, set about exploring the world of Indian youth. This report is the first product of that exploration.

## Background to the study

This study had its genesis when the Konrad Adenauer Stiftung (KAS) initiated and commissioned, in 2007, Lokniti programme of the Centre for the Study of Developing Societies to investigate the attitudes and perspectives of Indian Youth. The mandate that the

KAS gave was broad because they too saw this as a great opportunity to understand India's youth especially since India is seen as the new happening place by the global media. The changes taking place in the world of Indian youth will, it is believed, have a global impact in areas that range from economy to security, from culture to politics. Exploring the attitudes of Indian youth is therefore valuable to understand the present and also to prepare for the future. It would also help us compare youth in India with youth in other regions of the world, most specifically in Germany where the Shell Youth study has been one of the iconic studies on youth that has periodically, now for nearly six decades, produced snapshots of German youth. KAS thought it would be a good idea to step outside Germany and support a similar study in another region of the world. India offered itself as an ideal location because it is currently on the threshold of a significant 'demographic dividend', a historical chance for the society and polity to convert an unharnessed resource into a major societal asset.

In recent times studies have established a positive association between what is termed the age structure transition (specifically, a rising share of working age people in a population) and economic growth in India and China. Indeed, demographers and economists have predicted higher growth prospects for India compared to China over the next thirty years, since, as they put it, the effect of the fertility decline and the bulge of population age cohort in the working age group will sharpen in India in the coming decades. According to current estimates, India is—and will remain for some time—one of the youngest countries in the world. The following population figures from the World Bank gives a clear picture of the potential of India's demographic dividend. In 2000 India, Brazil and China had nearly 34% of their population as youth as compared to less than 28% in Germany and the USA. In 2020 India alone will have 34% of youth in its population while all

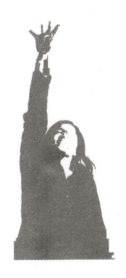

the other large countries will have dropped below 31% including China which will be 28.5% (see Appendix). In 2020, it is estimated, the average Indian will be only 29 years old, compared with the average age of 37 years in China and the US, 45 in west Europe and Japan. This demographic process entails a massive and growing labour force which, it is held, will deliver profound benefits in terms of growth and prosperity. The changed age structure of India's population also means an overall younger population as something more than simply a statistical fact since it has political and social consequences for India and the world. Exploring the attitudes and perspectives of India's young population, therefore, becomes as much an exercise of historical curiosity as it is a political necessity.

There are, therefore, several reasons for this study: comparative, in that it helps us see how Indian youth share or diverge from the attitudes and perspectives of youth elsewhere; policy planning, in that we need to create policies and to provide for new institutions that will take advantage of the promised demographic dividend; and academic, in that we can contribute to the interesting and rich debate on whether there is a single or whether there are multiple routes to entering, encountering, and engaging with modernity. But more on this later.

**Some preliminary concerns:**

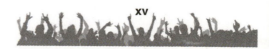

The study began with trying to sort out a big definitional issue. Who would be considered as youth? Would age be the sole criteria, or personal and social responsibility, or autonomy from family, or marital status, or individuality of personality, or preferences with respect to lifestyle, etc. We found ourselves in the middle of a complex cultural conundrum and finally, after several meetings of the advisory group that had been constituted to steer the project (see acknowledgements), we decided to limit our definition of youth to only the age cohort. Here too we had a problem since youth in India, as officially recognised by the Government of India, is all those in the age group 15–35. This was at variance with the youth cohort in most countries of the global north where it is 14–25—now the lower end is 12 years because of the early onset of puberty—since that is seen as a distinct segment of the population which has distinct attributes. In India, in contrast, and also interestingly in many other countries of the global south, the age group considered youth is the same as that of India, which is 15–34. Does this tell us something about the different cultural contexts of the youth, of their different life chances? Does it tell us something about the link between economic prosperity and the constitution of cultural selves?

To delve into the world of youth in India we decided to do both an attitudinal survey of youth across the country (see the appendices for the sampled locations, the methodology, and the questionnaire administered) and also commission several case studies. (see Appendix for the list of case studies). This dual strategy of entering this new brave, brazen, and bewitching world, we expected, would give us both quantitative and qualitative insights. The report as it is presented here has data from both approaches, the survey data which makes up the main body of the text together with the statistical appendix, while the case studies provide the embellishments and have been inserted periodically into the commentary to give a sense of the multiple layers of reality involved and also little glimpses into other aspects of the universe of youth in addition to that of attitudes and perspectives. These are small vignettes which are presented, alongside the commentary on attitudinal data, with the expressed intention of producing exclamations of surprise at the sites frequented by youth, smiles at the subtlety of the experiences, empathy at the challenges faced, and wonder at the fortitude of youth in India. Vignettes have also been extracted from newspapers which also tell their own story.

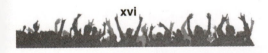

The study as it progressed repeatedly brought home to us the fact that not only are there new dimensions that we were unprepared for, but also how fast the world (worlds?) of youth is changing, with respect to values, perception, language, sartorial sense, aesthetics, etc. While the experience of being young is universal it takes different forms, partly cultural and political, partly personal and biographical. Indeed, with particular reference to the latter, it is important to recognize that people everywhere negotiate culture (or rather cultural processes) in terms of the cognitive and material resources available to them, and also that they are both products and producers of these cultural processes. When these cultural processes involve young people, even within the extended frame of reference lent by our survey—and indeed precisely because of this—we are dealing with distinctive attitudes and perceptions that need to be taken seriously in any negotiation of the space of modern India. There is a new world rising and we appear ill equipped to understand it.

Indeed, since the late 1990s, there has been some recognition of the idea that the visions and ideals informing the young in India possess a crucial significance in the contemporary context of liberalisation and globalisation. The study centres on the idea that the youth/adulthood distinction does not hold in the Indian context, because far too often in this context the young come to take on (or are not free from) adult responsibilities. To be sure, we realize that much writing on youth in terms of socialisation, education or human development depicts youth as objects of adult activity, and in breaking with this emphasis the present report seeks to come to terms with the world of the young from their own point of view. There is above all a consistent and systematic concern to show how Indian youth, across locales and different contexts, are active agents—in different ways and with varying force—in the construction of the meanings and forms that make up their worlds.

## The structure of the report:

The nexus of agency and meaning-making, in the context of India's young, is thus at the heart of this study. We have tried to account for it in the course of seven chapters mapping the 'personal/experiential' and the 'political/historical' context of India's youth. These are interesting axes along which to locate our findings since they, in a sense, suggest the two frames that will help us understand the multiplicity of attitudes that we need to recover. By identifying the distinct chapters as we have done—trust and circles of belonging, family and social networks, leisure and lifestyle, politics and democracy, governance and development, nation and the world, and anxiety and aspiration—we have captured the rubrics that are significant for the story we want to tell. They traverse, respectively, the immediate social circles that youth relate to, how socially and materially endowed they are (implicit in which is an account of constraints and opportunities), the family and social networks they interact with, (again signalling some aspects of constraints and opportunity), their lifestyle pattern, and their anxieties and aspirations. Alternatively, the report also maps the political values and orientations of the youth, including their attitudes to governance and development and to issues of globalisation and of India's role in a transforming world. In reporting this data we have also used the strategy of constructing indices, by combining responses to several questions into one index to indicate a trend, besides presenting the marginals themselves. For those who wish to probe further and deeper we have also given the basic survey data in an appendix.

To add to the value of the story we have used pictures to accompany the narrative. So it is a picture of a poster from a university campus stating 'what is your identity' for the overview chapter, since negotiating identity is one of the big themes that define youth, and for the chapter on 'governance and development', a picture of a young man throwing old flowers and garlands from a

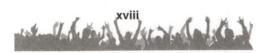

collection basket into a river while in the background can be seen a swanky multi-story building, a poignant visual of the cohabitation of the informal and the formal sectors of the economy reminding one of the rigours of earning a livelihood that some have to endure in contrast with the embarrassment of riches which others are privileged to enjoy. And for the chapter on 'anxiety and aspiration' we have used a picture of a painting done by one of our own scholars, Rajiv Kshetri, depicting a young man walking up a garden path, head somewhat bent, looking downwards in the anxiety of perhaps unsuccessful aspiration. There are 10 pictures that have been used and all are suggestive. If a picture is equivalent to a thousand words we may have saved some twelve thousand words of space.

## The first insights

The uncertainty about how to report the findings began with the selection of the cover design. A strong candidate for visually representing the new world of youth in India was the idea of a pair of jeans: blue jeans, black jeans, studded jeans, jeans with patch pockets, jeans with messages, jeans, jeans, jeans. They have become a ubiquitous symbol of youth in India, from the large village, to the small town, to the big city; from the designer, to the fake designer, to the locally crafted; from the student at college, to the youth in the informal sector of the economy; from the student's wing of the Congress to the student wing of the Communists (no petty bourgeois attire this), from the troubled regions of India's North East to the conservative temple towns of India's South, a pair of jeans has become the new symbol of having arrived in modernity. Jeans constitute a style statement announcing who you are, your identity. They suggest connection with the global and also perhaps, because of an abundance of local brands and local designs, and the local cultural contexts in which they are situated, that such a connection should not be overstated. Jeans and their place in the symbolic world of Indian youth lend themselves to an interesting cultural deconstruction. An enduring image that is not atypical is of a mother and her daughter walking down M.G. road in a small town, one dressed in a pair of jeans the other in a sari, one unembarrassed at the idea that the shape of her body is noticeable because of the jeans, the other making every effort to conceal hers, one walking with a self confident stride, the other more matter of fact. And yet in this contrast of images there is a connection since the daughter's arm is around her mother who can think of no other body language but this. Is this continuity with change? Is it expressive of a generation gap? Is it a statement on modernity and tradition? Much decoding is called for and our study will only offer some preliminary clues.

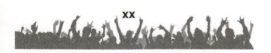

Similar insights, which are unavailable from quantitative data, can be selected from our several case studies. From the 15 we chose, of the 50 plus we were offered from across the country, we have cases that can be classified into at least four clusters: (i) those that describe sites at which economic and cultural modernity is negotiated, (ii) those that show how youth are responding to cultural and economic modernity, (iii) those that present different youth perspectives on issues, and (iv) those that display political resistance to new directions to Indian democracy. The case studies show that the number of sites are increasing where youth are negotiating with modernity, from the cyber cafe, to the mall, to the Business Process Outsourcing (BPO) centre, to the beauty and fitness parlour, and of course to the college campus where challenges to tradition are being fought. Identifying these sites is important for us to complete our mapping exercise of the world of youth for it is here where youth face and negotiate between the pulls of tradition and modernity. For example the mall is an interesting site, as the study shows, where conservative families do not mind sending their children since it is safer there than on the street. In the mall they buy little but consume a lot, consume leisure as the case study writer suggested. And the mall is culturally like the 0800 number since it could be anywhere and displays no distinctive cultural location. The same is the case of the many ways in which youth respond to modernity, particularly transgressing dress codes, what the case study referred to as 'sexy' dressing where orthodoxy is being resisted. Such resistance can also be seen in the politics of marginal and oppressed groups who are challenging both traditional authorities from within their own social group as well as hegemonies of the mind and of social practice within the wider society. The nine boxes on the case studies in the report briefly recount the findings of the various case studies.

## Seven rubrics

The findings from the survey data can be discussed at two levels; in terms of the specific findings in each rubric and in terms of the general significance of these findings for the larger ongoing debates. Let us begin with the specific findings. If one were to identify at least one interesting finding, from each of the seven rubrics, one would have at least seven issues on which to reflect.

The data on the first rubric on **Trust and Circles of Belonging** indicates that the social spaces in which youth are located constitute cultural islands with few bridges since the youth, by and large, count among their friends persons of the same religion, caste and gender. This is interesting since it suggests that social borders are still quite strong and border crossings are discouraged and that is why 27% had no friend from the other gender, religion or another caste. Another 21% crossed the border very occasionally. This is an important finding since it tells us that in spite of the big changes that have occurred in polity and economy, in the domain of the social world the changes are more slow. Is this finding a function of the already existing social geography of India where people can be seen to reside in social ghettos i.e., where the opportunity and the need to mix outside one's social group, defined in terms of same gender, caste and religion, is absent,

or is it reflective of prevailing cultural taboos where interaction across one's social group is discouraged if not prohibited. If this marks the world of youth, who are generally more rebellious, how much more forceful must it be in the world of adults. However, border crossings become more frequent when we disaggregate the data along the rural-urban axes or in terms of levels of education.

One can, within one perspective, read this as the prevalence of conservative mores within youth, but could, within another perspective, see it as illustrative of a lack of opportunity for interaction in a situation of greater opportunity, both spatial and material, conservative mores would not hold young people back from making friends across traditional borders. One could read the data to suggest that making friendships across social groups is not a matter of choice but of constraint, and when such constraints are removed by education and plural settings, then people are willing to dismantle the border. This has implications for social trust. The survey shows that people trust their friends more than members of their own caste but since their friends are from their own social group it should not be read as a secular trend. Interpersonal trust, so necessary for the impersonal functioning of institutions, is hence quite thin and this perhaps explains why nepotism occurs. Institutions in India are infected with group loyalties and the basis of this is set in the world of friends that the youth have.

The data on the second rubric, **Family and Social Networks**, yields an interesting finding about the institution of the family. As expected, there seems to be no clear disjuncture between youth and their parents with varying levels of acceptance of parental authority in areas as diverse as career and marriage. A majority of youth canvassed, as much as 60%, accepted that the final decision on marriage should be taken by parents. This would be unthinkable in most western societies. From it one can see that parental authority has considerable leverage in the life of most Indian

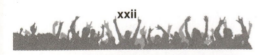

youth and even though variations are a function of education and socio economic status (SES), with small changes towards more autonomy of decision making as a result of higher SES, it is not enough to undermine the observation that no generation gap exists in India. Youth prefer to remain within the cultural codes of their family and social networks.

One could perhaps read more into this data and hypothesise that the strident individuality of Western youth is not present among Indian youth who are more embedded, and content to be, within the institution of the family. The fact that parental authority is not seen in adversarial but in benign terms can be gauged by the number of respondents (55%) who felt that they would like to bring up their children in more or less the same way as they were brought up. The family remains a key institution in the life-world of Indian youth. One could perhaps argue that even in a situation of expanded choice, youth in India, in contrast to the situation described in rubric one where conservative mores were regarded as a function of limited opportunity, would freely adopt conservative mores with respect to parental authority. Even though inter-religious and inter-caste marriage runs the risk of social violence, as the news report from Bhopal illustrates, one could hazard a view that youth buy in to these cultural mores and do not think that an assertion of individuality means that parents must not have a say in the making of decisions concerning marriage and careers. The Swedish saying that 'if the Stone Age children had obeyed their parents we would still be living in the Stone Age', does not appear to hold in India. Or does it?

The third rubric **Leisure and Life Style** yields this gem of data that dressing up in the latest styles is an important facet of self-expression and that this was a view strongly held by the younger segment of the youth. If on marriage youth seem to be different from their counterparts elsewhere here they seem to be no different. The power of the media, especially the electronic media, seems considerable with a majority of youth watching films and serials on television. Some message seems to be getting through and with youth icons from sport and the film industry becoming the models for youth. Jeans, metaphorically, seems to have captured the imagination of Indian youth. Although, in the world of dressing and fashion, youth seem to want to express their individuality and appear to be unconstrained by cultural mores, a point illustrated in greater detail by a case study. Our data tells us that 60% felt that consumption of alcohol was unacceptable. This is a statistic difficult to decipher. Is it an indicator of conservativeness or of progressiveness? Does the image of consumption of alcohol as a marker of modernity carry a cultural baggage? Does it suggest an alternative route to modernity? In what way does the consumption of alcohol relate to the transition from youth into adulthood?

The data on the fourth rubric **Politics and Democracy** presents a picture of politically engaged Indian youth and hence the concern among the trilateral countries of a declining interest in politics among youth in those countries is not a concern in India where youth exhibit several interesting attitudes: high participation in politics, high trust in democracy, high continuity and engagement in politics across generations, especially where there is a family tradition and—like the general population—a high trust in the army as an institution in contrast to the lowest trust in the police and political parties. The fact that the youth have a robust interest in politics and democracy is a good sign for the future of Indian democracy. India is an intensely political place with sites of democratic practice increasing in the polity as can be seen most vigorously in the university system where student politics is fairly competitive and intense, and currently undergoing reform as per the recommendations of the Lyngdoh report. Their participation is also supported by their political opinions where a large majority of youth believe in the values of democracy such as the importance of the political opposition, the importance

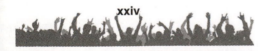

of freedom of expression, and the abjuring of violence to settle disputes etc. It is fair to say that democracy is becoming the commonsense of youth in India and hence arguing for it or defending its value appear to be redundant tasks. The acceptance by youth of the values of democracy indicates that in the political realm, at least, the journey to modernity has been quite straightforward. While there are differences between Indian and Western youth in their dispositions towards politics these may be more a difference of stages between the modern and the post-modern worlds of politics. In India most youth are still in the modern world of endorsing the state and its authority.

From the fifth rubric concerning **Governance and Development** the big story that is emerging is that of unemployment and poverty. An equal number of 27%, in both cases, listed these two as their biggest concerns. While this, in itself, is not unexpected, it is worth noting that the concerns are highest among those who are non-literate, of low socio-economic status, from rural areas and among marginal groups of dalits and adivasis. This is a cause for alarm since this concern of the lower social strata, that has fewer life chance opportunities, may turn into discontent and this in turn may undermine the commitment to the values of democracy that currently seem to be widely shared by the youth. The increasing violence in rural India, especially in the naxalite affected regions, and among dalit youth protesting against their life situations, something akin to the violence in the urban areas in France, needs to be borne in mind. This finding suggests, more than anything else, that we run the risk of squandering our demographic dividend.

From the sixth rubric **Nation and the World** the one issue that we could perhaps reflect on is the divided opinion of youth on the advantages and disadvantages of globalisation. The number of those who see it as advantages from among the lower socio economic group was about the same as those who saw it as disadvantageous, and those who saw it as disadvantageous dropped with higher income. There seems to be an increasing perception that globalisation is the only way to enter the future and that the older strategies of self-reliance and autarkic development are strategies of the past. And hence, even though there are concerns about the disadvantages, among a large section, these would need to be addressed and would fit into the aspiration to benefit from the demographic dividend. Since the challenge is to convert what is inevitable into an asset we need to democratise development, which is what many of the social movements are asking, in other words to make development more inclusive. For a more just order the policy goal should be both a recognition of the aspiration of a large proportion of youth for the benefits of globalisation and also a series of policy steps to address the concerns of the sizeable number who see it as disadvantageous.

The seventh rubric **Anxiety and Aspiration** shows that Indian youth have both very high levels of anxiety and high levels of aspiration. Further, on the specific question of how they saw their future and their children's future more than two-thirds saw the future as bright in both instances. Interestingly Indian youth appear to exhibit high levels of anxiety, high aspiration and high optimism about the future. This trend is somewhat puzzling since one would expect anxiety to be inversely related to optimism. Perhaps the only way to make sense of it is to go below the aggregate data and read it through the lens of how different social groups view the present and future. The plurality of worlds in which youth are located would help us account for the variations in these trends. We have not here delved at any length into how the different genders, or social groups such as minorities, dalits, adivasis, or differently abled youth, or even those in different localities, respond to these issues.

Since this will be done in the individual chapters, and since we have also given the marginals in the appendix, let us now move to a discussion of how the data allows us to join the larger discussion about societal change.

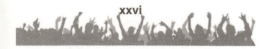

## The big picture

There are three big aspects, with respects to the ongoing debate on routes to modernity (alternative or common), that this attitudinal data on youth allows us to participate in. The first is to peer at youth attitudes and perspectives through the lens of education. From the data from the seven rubrics we find that those with higher educational levels begin to diverge from the general trend, for example having friends from across genders, caste, and religious groups, willing to assert their own views on marriage and career choices especially if they are different from the parental view, having clearer views on the values of democracy, are more aware of globalisation, and have higher aspirations for the future.

The conclusion is that education counts. Those who are better educated seem more willing to cross borders of social mores and to be more willing to assert their individual preferences. Which makes us ask the hypothetical question: Will the even spread of education at the higher levels, across region and socio economic groups, mean that much of what we regard as the cultural inflexion in youth attitudes and perspectives is in fact only a function of the availability of opportunity and the absence of material constraint. If youth with less advantage and opportunity were to be able to overcome these constraints, through the benefits of higher levels of education, would they then begin to have views similar to those that are currently expressed by those from higher socio economic status (SES). In other words is the thesis of alternative route to modernity somewhat overstated in the context of youth? It may be valid in other domains but is perhaps less so in the world of youth who display attitudes and perspectives similar to youth in other regions of the world.

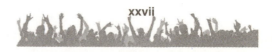

The second aspect of the big story is the sites at which youth stage their tryst with modernity. This is a peculiar turn of phrase since this involves entering, encountering, aspiring, engaging and perhaps even consuming modernity, and since these lend themselves to different logics, to use the telegraphic form of tryst to encapsulate the various experiences may be somewhat illegitimate. The case studies showed the emergence and increasing presence of new sites where this tryst takes place, such as the beauty parlour, gym, cyber cafe, mall, college campus, Business Process Outsourcing (BPO) centre, etc. The site that is the big revelation of the survey data is the small town. Youth in small towns appear to have the highest level of aspiration even compared to metropolitan areas. Because these spaces are perhaps the fastest growing, demographically and economically, and because they can be seen somewhat as half-way houses in terms of opportunity and constraint, as compared to the village and the big city, the small town is perhaps seen as the place where one has broken free from the frustrations of the village and is en-route to the freedom of the city. The other advantage of the small town for most of India's youth is its proximity, both geographical and personal, since there is a likelihood that one would be able here to connect to social networks more easily. The small town is one of the big sites for harnessing the energy of youth in India today.

The third aspect of the big story is the relationship of youth to modernity. If youth, in the West, are generally regarded as the flag-bearers of modernity, in India too they seem to have evolved a bi-cultural identity having elements of both local identity and global identity. The quantitative study of attitudes and perspectives seems to point to the conclusion that Indian youth are not following an alternative route to modernity. The differences in attitude appear to be more a function of material and cognitive opportunity, than of choice, and hence when opportunity is available youth are brought back in step with global trends. This is most evident in the domain of dressing where youth from all social groups and all locations aspire for dress styles that are no different than those in Durban, Sao Paulo or Beijing. Fab India may look local but it is global and to mistake it for local distinctiveness is to miss the point about the

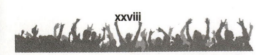

plurality of the global. An interesting point here is to distinguish between practice and tradition, i.e., where the former changes more easily because it is superficial while the latter changes more slowly because it is deeper. Is the form of dressing, practice or tradition? Is it superficial or is it the expression of something deeper that is changing? The study offers us a rich data set from which to explore this issue. In the world of youth in India we are therefore required to grapple with the thesis of alternative routes or multiple routes to modernity. A form and substance debate awaits us here.

But like all things Indian one must end with a puzzle that invites interpretation. Let me describe an ordinary morning, on a working day, at one of the new commuter stations, hi-tech city at Vidya Nagar in Hyderabad. This is a locality inhabited mostly by conservative upper caste Hindus, and the hi-tech city station is one from where persons, who are basically techies, travel to work at the many new IT companies on the outskirts of Hyderabad. The station is new, built specially for serving the hi tech city. The platform is largely populated by young people of both sexes. In the morning one can see them wearing holy marks on their forehead (a marker of tradition) or akshintalu (grains coated with turmeric) on their head, a sign that they performed puja. Many of these young persons are, however, engrossed in listening to music on their i-pods, which is the best of modern technology. Perhaps they are listening to hindi film music, which is as hybrid as you can get. And yet they are standing in clusters that are largely of the same sex. There seems to be no libido pressure here. When the commuter train comes, however, the women and men get into different compartments with the women largely into compartments reserved for women. Is this because of libidinal anxiety or just a concern of safety or just standard all India railway practice? Incredible India!

# CHAPTER 1: TRUST AND CIRCLES OF BELONGING

- The 'friends circle' mostly consists of those from the same gender, caste and religion. If one does have friends from outside this 'circle' it would primarily be those belonging to other castes, followed by those of the opposite sex and finally those from a different religion. The probability of having persons from the opposite gender, other caste or religion in one's core peer group is highest amongst the urban youth, those with a higher Socio Economic Status (SES) and higher education levels.
- The intensity of social trust that youth demonstrate is very stark within their immediate social circle of belonging. This is indicative of the nature of social interaction that youth in India are exposed to.
- Limited discrimination was experienced by the youth. The most apparent form of discrimination reported is linked to SES. While the experience of caste based discrimination is not very pronounced for most communities, it continues to be reported by Dalit youth.

A study of the attitudes, preferences and perspectives of the youth would necessarily involve a detailed study of the immediate social circle that they relate to. In this chapter we explore the 'circles of belonging' of modern Indian youth. The questions explored include whether or not the youth experience a sense of belonging in their primary social group and whom they consider as their close friends? We also present a snapshot of the level and intensity of trust that the youth have amongst those they interact with.

## Circle of Friends

To measure how broad based the primary peer group of the modern Indian youth is, a short battery of questions was posed. These questions attempted an analysis of whether the friend circle (top five friends) included those from the opposite gender, from other castes and other religions. This was essentially done to find out whether there was close interaction between young members of communities that were traditionally not known to interact with each other. It also aimed to determine patterns of inclusivity amongst various sections of the youth and if at all this trend was particularly visible amongst specific groups.

A Composite Index[1], combining data reported on friends from all three categories (opposite gender, other castes and other religions) was created. The index showed that on an average the friend circles do not include too many members from these categories. One out of every four young people has no one from the stated groups in their immediate friend circle. Further, 21 per cent have low interaction with people from these groups while the remaining report moderate (41 per cent) or high interaction (11 per cent) with those from these three groups *(Figure 1.1)*.

**Figure 1.1**

**Frequency of youth interaction levels with opposite gender, other caste and religion**

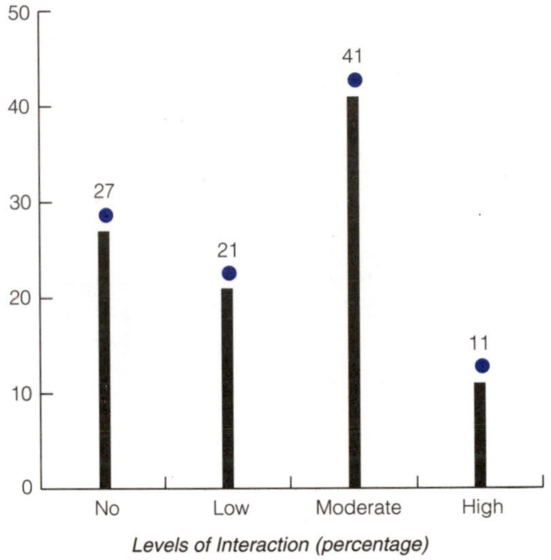


*Note: No, low, moderate and high are levels of interaction with opposite gender, caste and religious communities other than the respondent's. For details, see endnotes.*

Is the composition of friend circles amongst urban youth different from their counterparts in a rural setting?

To answer this question, responses from the national sample were compared with responses from urban respondents.

**Figure 1.2**

**Composition of friend circles: A comparison of all Indian youth with urban Indian youth**

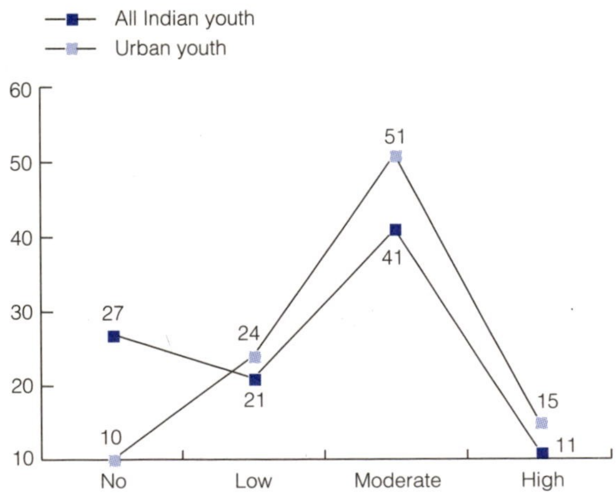

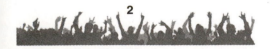

The analysis revealed that urban youth are more likely to interact with friends from the opposite gender, other castes and other religions *(Figure 1.2)*. The difference is important when one compares the figures for no interaction. If only one out of every ten urban youth (10 per cent) reports having no interaction with those from the opposite gender and other castes/religions, in the case of the national sample more than one-fourth report no interaction. The difference in urban-rural peer group composition is least pronounced between persons who state a moderate to high level of inter-category (the three stated categories) interaction. Majority of the urban youth reported moderate (51 per cent) or high interaction (15 per cent) with friends from these three categories while these figures for the national sample come slightly down at 41 per cent for moderate interaction and 11 per cent for high interaction *(Figure 1.2)*.

**Figure 1.3**

**Frequency of interaction of youth by education**

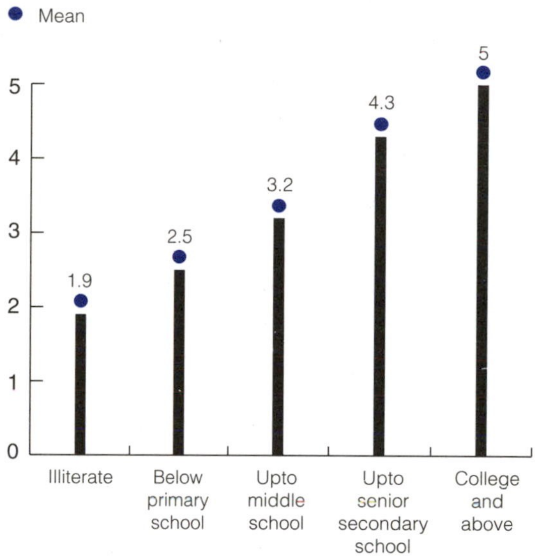


Another trend that is observed is that greater the exposure to formal education, greater is the likelihood of the youth having a more broad based circle of friends. The mean score steadily increases with the rise in the level of education *(Figure 1.3)*. The benefits of education exposes young people to greater opportunities for social interaction and this is evident in trends with regard to friend circles *(Figure 1.3)*.

Are there major differences in the friend circle of young men and women? Here too, the differences are more skewed at the lower end of the spectrum of interaction with a much higher percentage of young women (30 per cent) reporting no interaction with men and persons of other castes/religions, as compared to young men *(Figure 1.4)*.

**Figure 1.4**

**Levels of interaction with opposite gender**

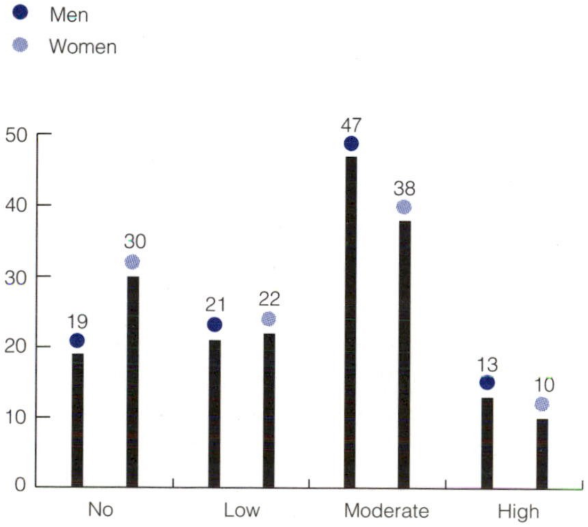

If locality is factored into the analysis, a few interesting trends emerge. The differences in the extended friend circles of young men and women appear to be more pronounced in rural areas as compared to urban areas. In rural areas, if a majority of the young men have moderate interaction with those from other castes or religions (54 per cent) and those from the opposite gender (46 per cent), in the case of young women a significant majority have no or limited interaction with a larger friend circle *(Figure 1.5)*. It is also noticed that while there is a marginal difference in the extended friend circle among rural and metropolitan male youth, the variation is more pronounced when it comes to young women living in rural and urban areas. Further, it is noticed that there is a relatively milder difference in the nature of the extended friend circle among young men and women in metropolitan areas *(Figure 1.5)*.

If six out of every ten young women (60 per cent) living in a village have no or low interaction with men and those from other castes/religions, this equation is the opposite in urban areas *(Figure 1.6)*.

**Figure 1.5**

**Levels of interaction by gender and locality**

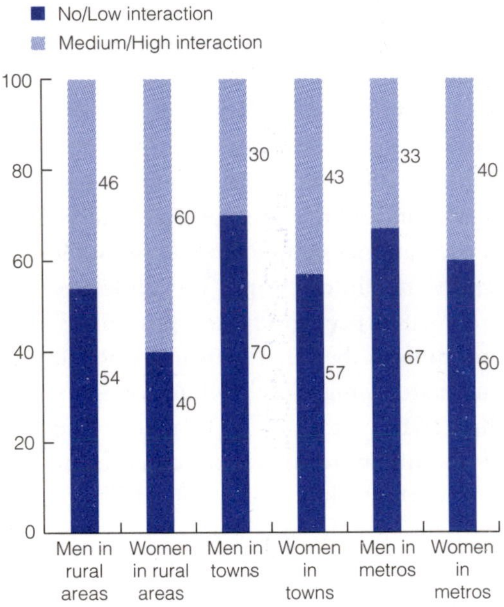


**Figure 1.6**

**Levels of interaction of young women with men by locality**

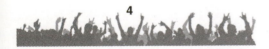

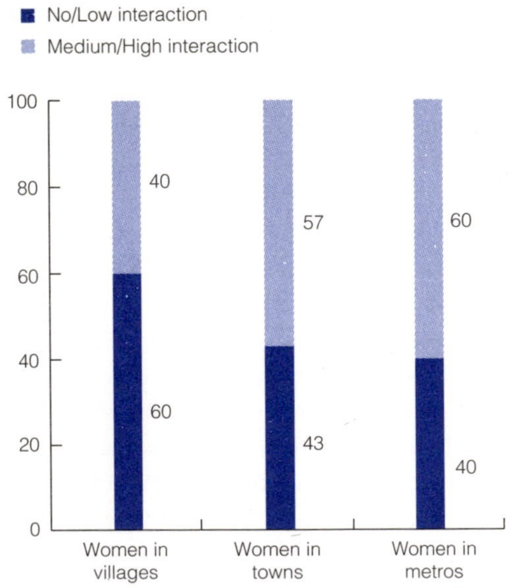


Towns present an interesting scenario. Young men in towns tend to have persons from the opposite gender and other castes/religions as part of their extended friend circle in larger numbers as compared to metropolitan areas/state capitals. In the case of young women the difference is marginal with a higher percentage of women in metropolitan areas having high interaction.

Does education have an impact on the friend circle of young women? It was found that greater the exposure of women to education the wider their friend circle. This study shows that education has positive relationship with the formulation of friend circles among the

Indian youth. However, in the no education upto high school education catagory, men have more friends than the women. This difference, however, disappears when we compare young men and women who have had the benefit of college education *(Figure 1.7)* .

Young women respondents were further classified into students, employed and homemakers. From this categorisation, it is seen that students are the most likely to have friends from among those belonging to communities/categories other than their own. Homemakers are the least likely to have friends from among the three specified categories. The trend is the same for young urban women and their counterparts across the country. The mean scores increase significantly when young women in urban areas alone are taken into account *(Figure 1.8)*.

**Figure 1.7**

**Circle of friends among young men and women from opposite gender and opposite caste**

**Mean score (Maximum 5)**

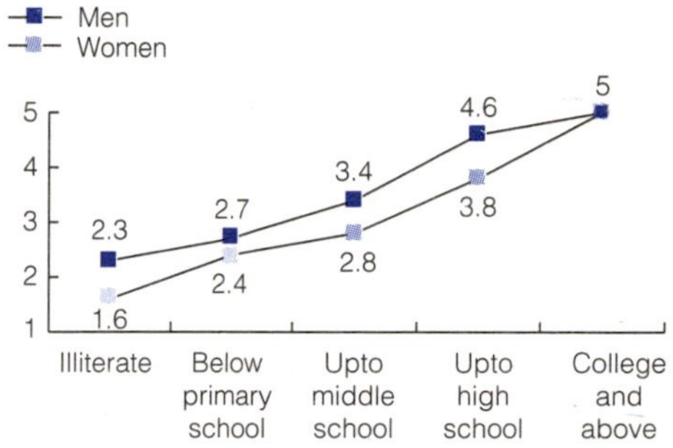


**Figure 1.8**

**Circle of friends among young women from opposite caste, gender and class**

**Mean score (Maximum 5)**

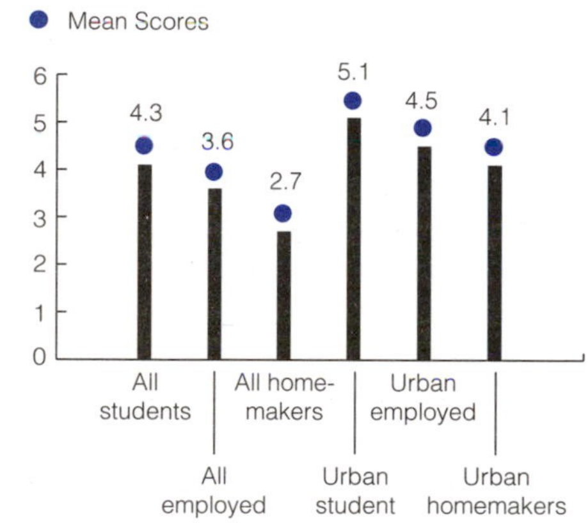


Does age of the youth influence the composition of their circle of friends? The younger the person, the more likely he/she is to have friends who belong to the opposite gender and other castes/religions. There is a clear difference in the responses of youth above 25 years of age and those below 25 years *(Figure 1.9)*.

In the three specified categories, the friend circle is most likely to have those belonging to another caste—nearly one-fourth of the respondents have high interaction with those belonging to other castes *(Figure 1.10)*. Four out of every ten have moderate interaction while the remaining have low or no interaction.

**Figure 1.9**

**Lower the age of youth, greater the level of interaction**

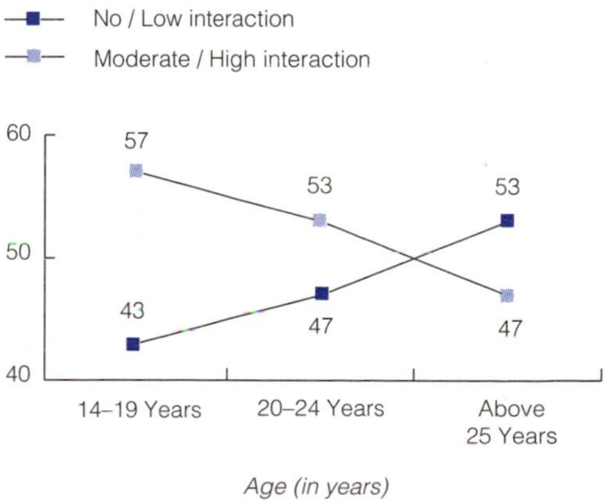

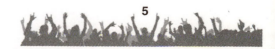

**We need no bans**

The students term the decision to ban boy-girl touch in two Mumbai schools as 'insane' and 'bizarre'.

June 2007: Two Mumbai schools specifically forbid boys and girls from touching or hugging members of the opposite sex in the school premises.

May 2007: Gujarat, Maharashtra, Madhya Pradesh, Chhattisgarh and Karnataka ban sex education in schools to 'preserve culture'.

November 2005: Bangalore colleges ban male and female students from sitting with each other in the classrooms.

**Opinion of some of the students:**

A student of Class XII is amazed at the school authorities. 'How bizarre is this one! After you have Bangalore colleges asking male-female students to sit separately and Mumbai asking for a ban on sex education session, now they have gone ahead and banned handshakes! If one was to accidentally brush against a student of the opposite sex, would he be penalized for that as we ll? This is our age to learn and that should translate into pure and unfettered freedom.'

Another student of Class XII says, 'I agree that sometimes people our age do get carried away, but is banning physical touch the solution to all this? It is as insane as it can ever get. The schools are not the only places where we meet people of the opposite sex. If someone were to indulge in something unacceptable, it would happen anywhere. I hope the school authorities have given it a proper thought before going ahead with the ban.

A Class XI student thinks these bans will never be fruitful. She asks 'Why go to co-eds then? If they want a segregation to exist, they should go ahead and have unisex schools. Why go to co-educational schools in the first place? The basic idea is to have a healthy interaction between opposite sexes.'

Nikhila Pant, *Times of India*, Delhi, June 19, 2007.

**Figure 1.10**

**Levels of interaction among youth with opposite gender, other caste and other religion**

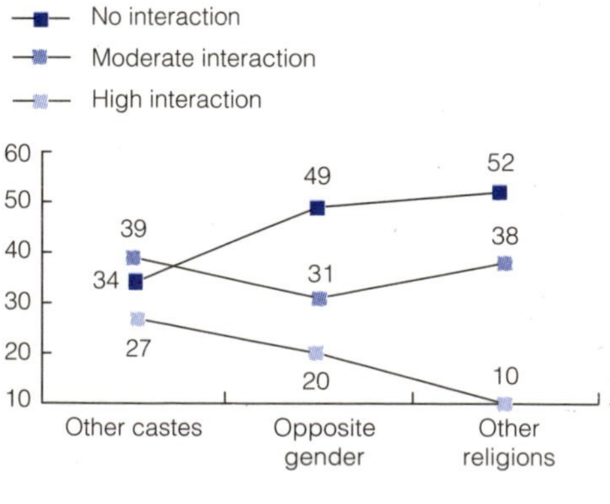


Having friends of the opposite gender is an option for only half of the youth. Nearly half do not have any interaction or have limited interaction (49 per cent) with those from the opposite sex. Only one out of every ten youth (10 per cent) had high interaction with those from the opposite sex.

It is noticed that more than half the youth do not have friends from other religions in their friends circle. Only one out of every ten young people had high interaction with persons from a religion different from their own *(Figure 1.10)*.

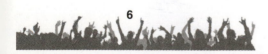

Having someone of another caste, religion or opposite sex among the close circle of friends is limited to a small percentage of the youth. They would invariably be from high SES, beneficiaries of higher education and those living in towns and cities and would be more likely to be men.

The social interaction of women in urban areas is similar to that of their male counterparts. There is not much difference between the sexes in urban areas in terms of the composition of their friends circle. However, a caveat needs to be added here—the question sought to tap the responses of the youth to those listed among their top five friends. It is possible that those from the opposite gender and other castes/religions were a part of the friend circle but not listed in the top five. This is linked to the 'world' within which a typical youth would interact. The fact that those in the 'top five' circle of friends may not include those from the opposite gender and other castes/religions in large numbers. This may be linked to their socialisation and the environment in which social interactions occur. Even in the case of the wider Indian population, studies have found that the close friend circle is often limited to those from the social group that an individual comes from (World Values Survey 2001, 2007).

**Figure 1.11**

**Levels of social trust among youth**

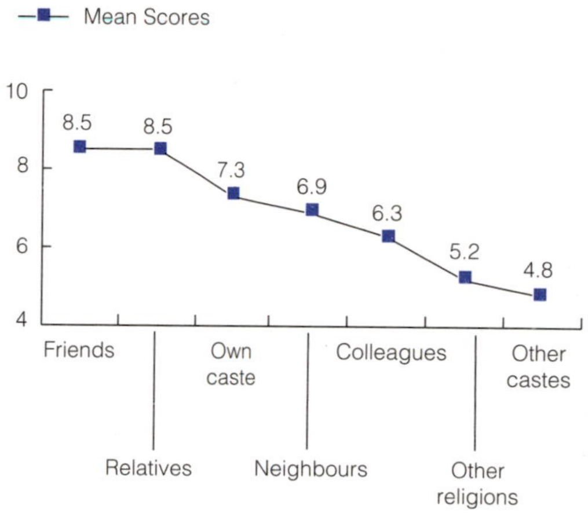


*Note: A score between 1 to 3 indicates 'low trust', 4 to 6 indicates 'moderate trust', while 7 and above indicates 'high trust'.*

## Social Trust

To measure the level of trust that the youth demonstrated towards those they interacted with in their life, a Social Trust Index was created.[2] The index tapped the trust that the youth reposed in their friends, relatives, colleagues at work, neighbours, people of their own caste, those from other castes and those from other religions. While computing the Index of Trust, three broad categories were created based on the responses to a selected set of questions—high level of trust, moderate degree of trust and low level of trust. It was found that an overwhelmingly high percentage of the youth expressed a 'moderate' level of trust in those they interact with. One out of every ten youth demonstrates a high level of trust in those they interact with while less than half report a low level of trust in those they interact with.

Youth demonstrate very different levels of trust in different groups of people. The highest is in friends and relatives followed by those from their own caste and neighbours. Hence, friends, relatives and those from one's own caste were at the top of the trust ladder, with neighbours and

**Figure 1.12**

**Primary and secondary circles of trust**

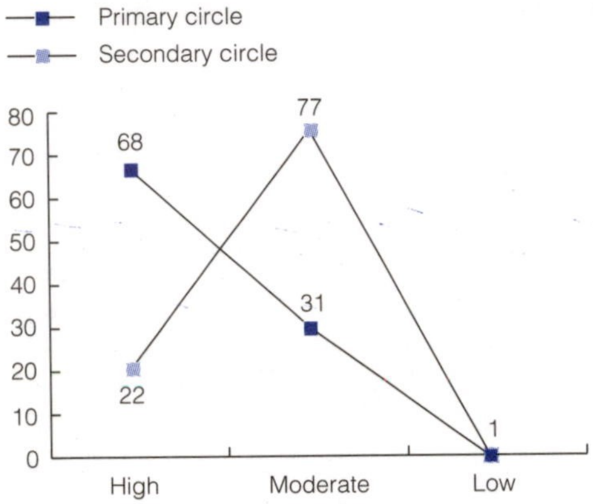


*Note: Primary circle includes relatives, neighbours and those from one's own caste while the secondary circle includes friends, colleagues and those of other castes/religions (all figures are in percentages)*

colleagues occupying the mid-space and those from other castes and religions being at the lowest level.

An attempt was made to distinguish between an individual's primary circle of contacts—own caste, relatives and neighbours as against his/her secondary circle of contacts, which included friends, colleagues and those from other religions and other castes. It was found that more than two-third of the youth have a high level of trust in those belonging to the primary circle of contacts. Close to one-third demonstrate moderate trust in those in the primary circle with very few expressing low trust *(Figure 1.12)*.

When it comes to the secondary circle of contacts more than three-fourth of the youth have moderate trust in its members. Around 20 per cent have high trust in those belonging to the secondary circle with a very small number expressing low trust. As the numbers are not substantially distributed among the different categories (high trust for the primary circle and moderate trust for the secondary circle) no trends on gender, caste, educational level and place of stay are evident.

There are no major differences in the level of trust expressed in those from one's caste group across different caste groups *(Figure 1.13)*. However trust in persons of other castes is minimal. The youth generally tend to trust those from their own caste as compared to those from other castes. It is important to record that this trend does not vary significantly across caste groups or with youth from different socio-economic backgrounds. Such a trend is also seen in other studies which have tried to assess social attitudes of the wider Indian population (World Values Survey 2001, 2007).

Nearly half the youth expressed moderate trust in those belonging to other religious groups. Over one-third of the respondents

**Figure 1.13**

**Levels of trust in own and other caste**

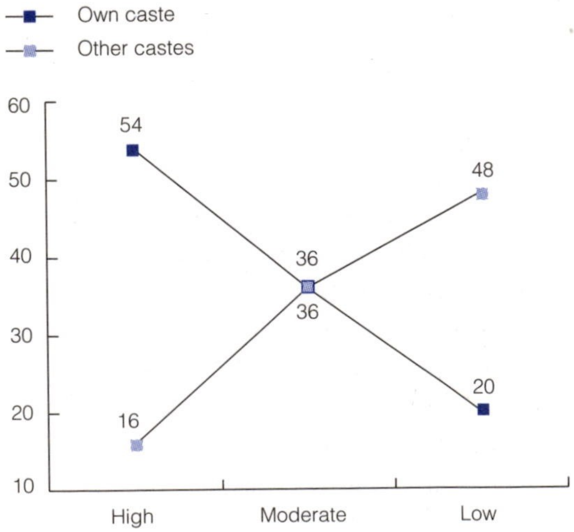

**Figure 1.14**

**Levels of trust in persons of own and other religion**

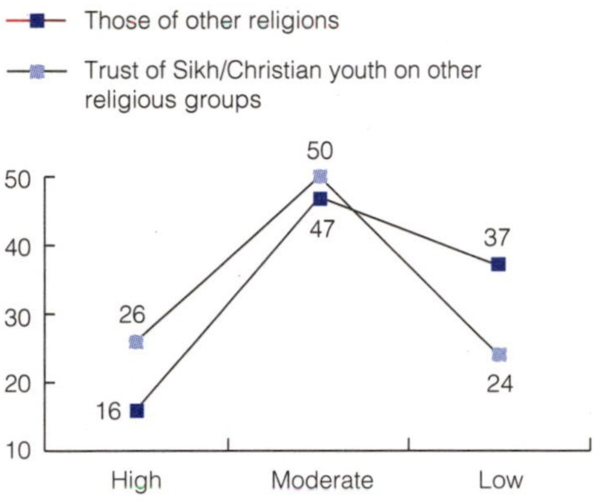


expressed a low level of trust in those from other religious persuasions. One relevant trend that needs to be stressed here is the attitudinal pattern among Hindu and Muslim youth. There was very little difference in their level of trust in those from other religions. In the case of Christians and Sikhs there was a greater demonstration of trust in those who belonged to other religions *(Figure 1.14)*.

There were no major differences in the level of trust expressed by those living in rural and urban areas. Those living in small towns and metropolitan areas articulated the same level of trust among those they interacted with as the youth in the rest of the country do.

It is important to note that the Index of Social Trust is indicative of the nature of interaction that a typical youth in India is exposed to. It is evident that for most youth, the 'inner circle of trust' consists largely of those who are one's friends, relatives, neighbours and those from one's own caste. This invariably implies that this is the circle that the youth are mostly exposed to in their day-to-day social interactions. If youth do not consider those of other castes and religions within this 'inner circle of trust' this may not be due to a lack of trust per se in either these castes/religious groups but may be a reflection of the absence of opportunities to interact frequently with these groups.

**Figure 1.15**

**Grounds of discrimination**

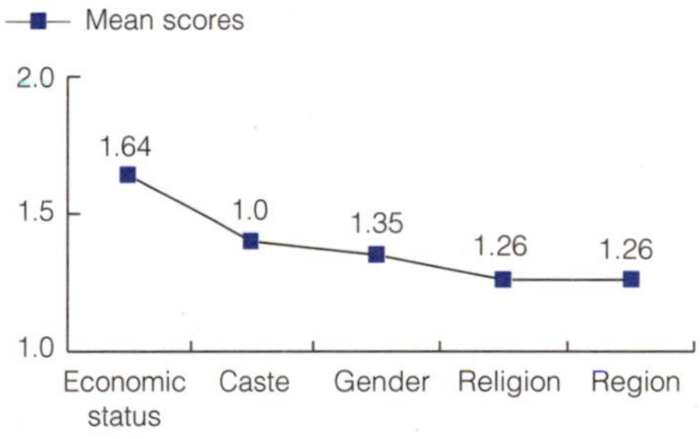


*Note: A mean score of 1 would indicate 'never faced discrimination', 2 would indicate sometimes faced discrimination' and 3 would indicate 'frequently experienced discrimination'*

## Sense of Belonging/Discrimination

Responses to whether the youth felt discriminated against were sought on five parameters—discrimination on the basis of their economic status, caste, gender, religion and region. A comprehensive Discrimination Index[3] was created combining the responses of the youth to questions linked to these parameters. The mean score shows that the youth does not experience a significant sense of discrimination. The lowest level of discrimination is associated with region and religion while the highest is linked to economic status.

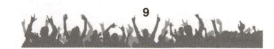

Case Study 1

***Youth and the Entertainment Mall: A Study of 'Prasads Imax' in Hyderabad***

by C. Ramachandraiah

## Sites at which economic and cultural modernity is negotiated

Many people go through the mall, window-shopping popular brands but very few people shop in the Imax. Most of the young customers' spending goes to the food court, the multiplexes, and the games and other attractions. Beyond effective consumption, the Imax is a place for strolling and hanging around where a large number of visitors cannot exactly be considered as consumers because they don't buy anything. But they are contsuming an experience. Many find it a 'great place to hang out with friends'. They are in the mall to access and enjoy the ambient mood of pleasure, freedom and safety. Both boys and girls hang out in uproarious, laughing groups, doing nothing else. Watching and enjoying the crowd is another attraction. The mass and multitude, in the closed context of the mall, make them feel invisible to the world. Therefore, they can behave as they wish and feel cosy. Anonymity leads to transgressions of ordinary norms that are manifested in different forms. Groups of fashionably dressed girls and boys don't really mix but gaze at one another. We can notice only a few people dating. At the same time they feel invisible to the outside world. Teenagers may be more visible to each other in the mall, 'showing off' by casual pose or trendy clothing.

Youngsters enjoy Imax as a place of recreation, where social control is loosened and where feminine presence is normalised. It is also a place of ostentation and freedom. Safety and slack social control are very important to feel comfortable in the mall, especially for young women. They can come on their own in the mall without the need of any masculine presence to protect them. They can dress as they want, without being disturbed by eve-teasers or frowned upon. Safety, especially for women, gives an extra-territorial dimension to the Imax mall. The space of the mall allows, and is probably built for, the transgression of norms and codes valid in traditional public spaces (couples dating, girls wearing 'modern' and skimpy clothes…though this number is still small). The ambience in Imax creates social links: groups don't really meet here, but being in the same place and enjoying it even if they are from different social and spatial backgrounds, makes them feel like a community. That may be a reason why many state that they 'like the crowd'. The Imax for them appears to be an oasis, a shelter from the commotion and social pressure of the city outside. The spacious and air-conditioned interiors, an attraction in itself in tropical weather, is also an advantage with the Imax.

For both producers and users, modernity is an important element of the mall, which is then considered as an airlock and bridge between the local and the global. The concept of modernity is a blend of loosening social control, mixed company, conviviality, emancipation from traditional mores, social display, new formats of consumption, access to communication etc. Somehow the mall may be considered as a westernised place, which can stir up both fascination and apprehension. However, the Imax is definitely not an uprooted place: the music, the meals, the films, even the people in their behaviour are a perpetual reference to an Indian way of life. It's a presence of a large gathering from the urban middle class.

As a business proposition, the Imax is designed to attract and make people, especially the growing middle class, spend on films, eating and shopping. In that sense, it is not a place for relaxation such as a public park with lots of greenery and walkways. For the youth, however, the Imax provides a space for enjoying a consumption experience, both real and imaginary: a sense of feeling free, shedding inhibitions, being in a world of their own, free from the social mores and gaze of the elders – along with some entertainment of watching films that have captured the imagination of the youth in Hyderabad. It has become possible due to, among others, the controlled and monitored nature of this space by the physical presence of the security personnel and the CCTVs with the management not tolerating any objectionable behaviour whatsoever producing a sense of security in the minds of teenage youth in the stressful, polluted and noisy atmosphere in Hyderabad city. This, in itself, has been a remarkable achievement of the Imax management. In a way these management practices were inevitable from the business point of view. All these factors have made the 'Prasads Imax' the most popular place for the youth and, as a modern entertainment mall, has allowed the construction of a new urban identity for Hyderabad.

The comprehensive Discrimination Index added the scores on all the five indicators (on grounds of their caste, economic status, gender, region and religion). Based on the responses, three levels of experience of discrimination were created—no discrimination, low discrimination and high

**Figure 1.16**

**Experience of discrimination by youth**

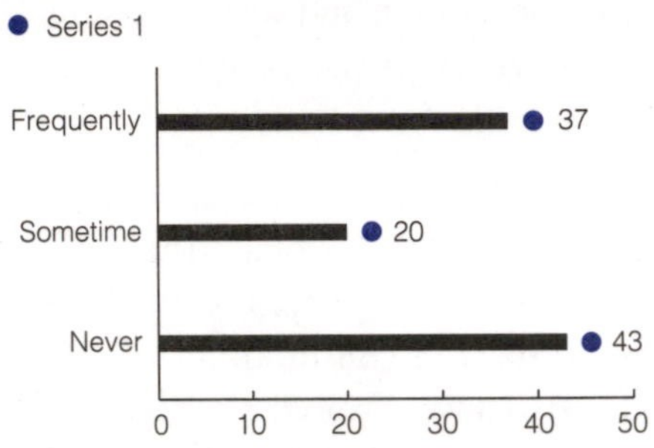


discrimination *(Figure 1.16)*. Nearly half the youth reported that they had never faced any discrimination. A little over one-third faced discrimination very frequently and two out of every ten respondents experienced discrimination sometimes.

As the highest mean score was for discrimination based on economic status, the response to this question was analysed keeping in mind the SES of the respondents. Close to six out of every ten respondents in the high SES category never face any discrimination based on their economic status. The percentage of those who never face discrimination based on their class status gradually, though steadily, reduces with the decline in the SES of the respondents. Over one-third of those who faced discrimination on grounds of economic status came from lower SES. As the SES rises, reports of discrimination on grounds of economic status decline *(Figure 1.17)*.

**Figure 1.17**

**Lower the SES of youth, higher the likelihood of facing discrimination**

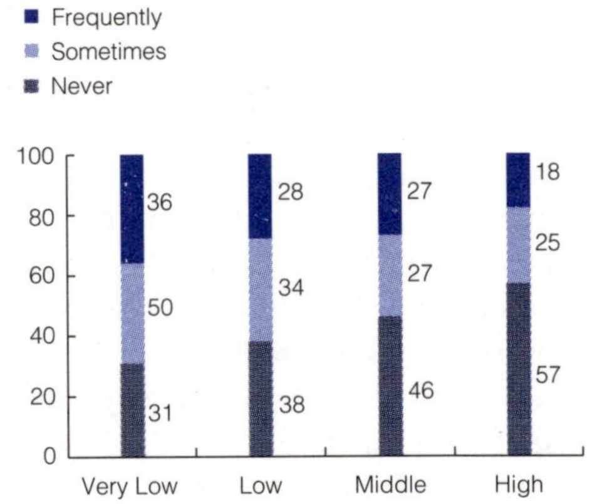


If we take into account the caste of the respondents, nearly 15 per cent of the Dalit respondents state that they frequently face discrimination on the grounds of their caste. In the case of Other Backward Castes (OBCs) and Forward Castes the percentage of those who report frequent discrimination on grounds of caste is significantly lower. In the case of OBCs, two-third reported never facing discrimination on the grounds of caste and nearly 80 per cent of the Others (including Forward Castes) reported never facing caste based discrimination *(Figure 1.18)*. Thus, the sense of discrimination encountered by Dalit youth is still very much a reality. It is also relevant to note that one out of ten tribal youth also feel that they are frequently discriminated against on grounds of caste. Over 60 per cent of the tribal youth never encounter discrimination on the basis of caste. This could be linked to the fact that tribal youth

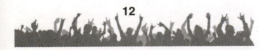

**Figure 1.18**

**Lower caste youth are more likely to face discrimination**

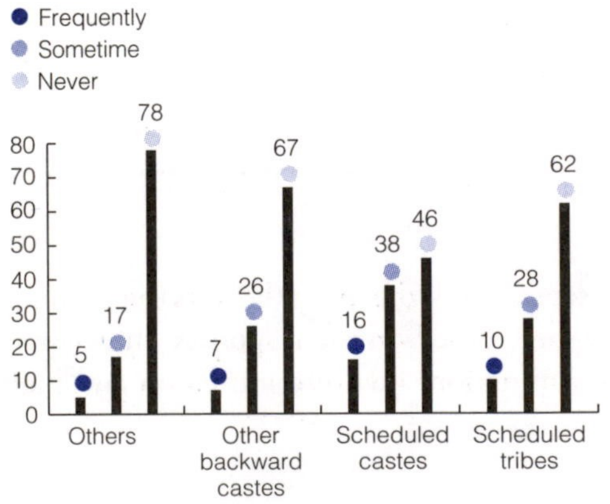

have had limited opportunities of interacting with those from outside their tribal groups and thus report a lower level of discrimination as compared to Dalit youth *(Figure1.18)*.

When it comes to discrimination on the grounds of religion, the religious group that reported the highest level of discrimination (frequently) was Muslim youth followed by Christians. Over 90 per cent of the Sikh youth have never faced discrimination on the grounds of their religion *(Figure 1.19)*.

**Figure 1.19**

**Muslim youth are more likely to face discrimination**

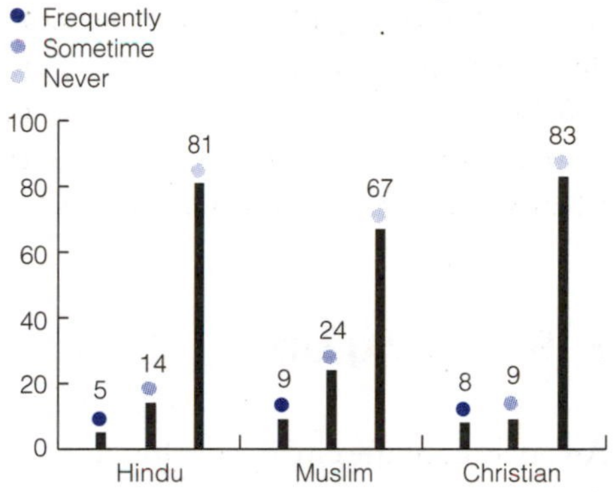


**Figure 1.20**

**Youth in metropolis are least likely to face discrimination**

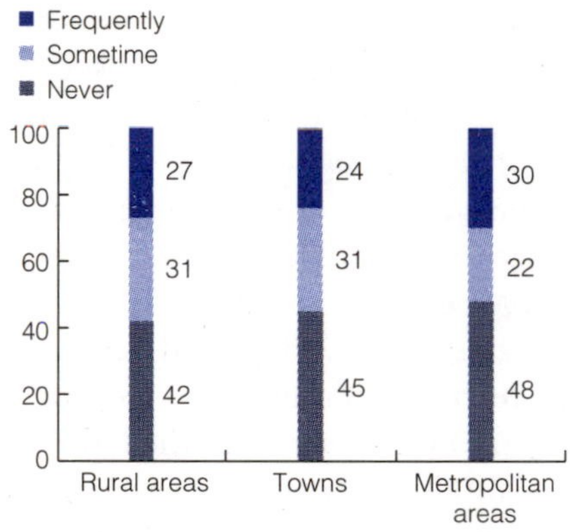


The Discrimination Index reveals that there is no major or perceptible difference between how the youth view and experience discrimination. Urban youth expressed more frequent discrimination than their counterparts in rural areas *(Figure 1.20)*. This possibly implies that urban areas are witness to diverse forms of social treatment. While the reporting of no discrimination is highest in urban areas, this space also witnesses the most frequent experience of high discrimination.

## White skin, brown soul

Born in India, but born white, these second generation immigrants suffer a unique identity crisis. 'Firangs' in India and plain 'weird' in the West. They are the Third Culture Kids (TCK). Much has been written about the NRI experience, their conflicts, their battles, their struggle to come to terms with their mixed identities. But the stories of reverse NRI' white on the outside and brown on the inside, has largely gone untold. 'Strangely, I relate more to NRI'. They, too, are mixed product' says Tara Chowdhry. Part American, part British, she is now married to an Indian (of Indian origin) in Chandigarh. These Indian of foreign origin suffer racism of a different kind. In a country where nationality is defined by narrow parameters of appearance, language and religion, white is not the colour of Indianness. For some, like Jamie Alter, the discrimination extends far into his personal life. 'I'll probably marry an 'Indian Indian' girl. But things did not work out with my previous girlfriend because her parents didn't accept me as Indian. I wanted to say, "You want to see my passport?" It says 'Indian", he recalls. Alter goes by the name Bunty and his Hindi is Bombaiyya, but that has made little difference to how the rest of India perceives him. Still, being TCK has its upsides- a worldview that is more accepting of different traditions. TCKs navigate easily between nationalities and customs, accepting all, judging none.

Riddhi Shah, *Sunday Hindustan Times,* New Delhi, April 29, 2007.

The discrimination that the youth experience is directly linked to their level of education. The more educated they are, the less likely they are to have felt discriminated against. Half the youth who were graduates or professionals never faced discrimination. This percentage gradually declines with reduced access to education. Among those who are illiterate, a little less than one-third report never facing discrimination.

It is noticed that the sense of discrimination is not connected to the nature of contact or friends circle that the individuals have.

## Summing Up

An analysis of the circles of belonging and trust among youth in India leads one to three important conclusions. First, in most cases the circle of close friends comprises of those who belong to the same gender, caste and religion. If the youth do have friends from outside these groups in their inner circle it is primarily those from other castes, followed by those from the opposite gender and finally those from other religions. Second, the youth demonstrate a moderate level of inter-personal trust in those they interact with. The intensity of trust is significantly higher among those who are part of their 'immediate social circle'. Both these trends are in consonance with the social environment in which most of them live and interact and this reflects the reality of social life and opportunities for interaction and not any conscious desire to avoid those from social groups that they do not come from. This trend is also reflective of the wider trend demonstrated by the Indian population in general. Finally, the youth reported limited experience of being discriminated against. However, those who are socio-economically disadvantaged did report facing discrimination for this specific reason. Dalit youth also reported facing some discrimination on grounds of caste as did youth from some minority religious groups on account of their religion.

Overall, the youth appeared to voice the flavour of changing times in terms of their levels of inter-personal social trust and circles of belonging even while reflecting the 'social environment' that shapes the reality and the times that they live in. The lack of a high degree of inter-personal trust among the youth towards certain groups is not a reflection of a lack of trust per se but is simply a manifestation of the limited nature of social interaction that they experience in their day-to-day lives. The same principle holds good when their close friends circle is assessed. Critical differences in trends are produced by three important variables—access to higher education, improved socio-economic status and exposure to urban life. These cause important and significant variations in the nature of social transactions that the Indian youth are exposed to and are a part of.

In social interactions that they nurture and nourish, Indian youth have pushed traditional boundaries. While the levels of inter-personal trust do not reflect any dramatic and significant changes from what was evidenced in the social attitudes of past generations, there are minor yet crucial differences. Even though friendships of the youth today in present times continue to be formed from among those traditionally considered the 'close circle', newer elements are becoming part of this circle. Most importantly, youth experience a sense of empowerment flowing both from the benefits of education and the increasing reality of social cohesiveness. At the same time, the markers of discrimination continue to be apparent, though in less significant ways.

---

## Endnotes

1) To measure how wide the friend circle was the following question was analysed:

   Question No. 31 which stated: 'Thinking of five close friends, tell me how many of them are (record number)

   a) Boys/girls (ask for opposite sex as applicable)
   b) From caste other than yours
   c) From religious community other than yours

   The answer categories were recoded with 0 friends implying no interaction, 1 or 2 friends signifying moderate interaction and 3 to 5 friends showing high interaction. All three questions were also integrated into a single index. The answers to all three questions were added resulting in a variance from 0 to 15. They were then categorised as 1–3 (low interaction), 4–7 (moderate interaction) and 8–15 (high interaction).

2) The Social Trust Index was created by combining the responses to seven linked questions. The composite Question 44 stated: 'Now I would ask you how much trust do you have in people from various groups? I will show you a ladder with 1 to 10 steps (Show Card). If you place at Step 1 those groups on whom you have a great deal of trust and at Step 10 those people on whom you have no trust, then where would you place

   a) Your friends
   b) Your relatives
   c) People from your own caste
   d) Your neighbours
   e) People from another religion
   f) Your colleagues at work
   g) People from castes other than yours

   While preparing the index the scores were reversed so if the respondent stated 10 for any group it was considered as 1 and placed as 'low trust', while an answer of 1 was reversed to 10 and placed as 'high trust'.

   An integrated Index of Social Trust was created using the above-mentioned questions. All the answers were summed up resulting in answer variance from 7 to 70. Values of 7 to 21 were categorised as 'low trust', 21 to 42 as 'moderate trust' and 42 and above as 'high trust'.

3) An Index of Discrimination was prepared bringing together five questions. The five questions were:

   Question 17: 'We often hear about people being discriminated against on various accounts in their day-to-day life. Please tell me how often have you felt discriminated about the following- frequently, sometimes and never,

   a) Economic status/condition
   b) Your caste
   c) Your gender
   d) Your religion
   e) Your region

   An integrated index was created dividing the variance into three categories—high discrimination, low discrimination, no discrimination.

# CHAPTER 2: FAMILY AND SOCIAL NETWORKS

- The nature of parental authority endorsed by modern youth provides sufficient proof of continuity with change.
- The middle class appears to be strongly anchored in strong parental authority. The attitude towards parental authority appears to be directly linked to the socio-economic status (SES) of the family, the locale they live in and the gender of the youth.
- Family values too are linked to SES, employment status, level of education, locale of residence and nature of parental authority.
- Parental authority is directly linked to the nature of family values.

This chapter primarily explores the linkages between the contemporary Indian youth and their family and social networks. Historically, the family is seen as an important institution for socialisation. This chapter attempts to assess the impact of family values and norms on the attitudes and preferences of youth. Some of the issues addressed in this chapter are:

- How do youth view parental authority and family values?
- How are their responses constructed?
- What is the nature of parental authority and the extent of its impact on their perspective and which factors impact their value system?

## Parental Authority

To measure the impact and implications of parental authority on the youth, a composite Index of Parental Authority (IPA) was created.[1] This index tracks both the experiences of how the youth were nurtured by their parents as well as their own perspectives on parenting. Based on this index, the variation in the nature of parental authority was mapped along four attitudinal categories—very strong parental authority, strong parental authority, moderate parental authority and limited parental authority. Overall, 20 per cent of the respondents believed in very strong parental authority. One-fourth of the respondents believed in strong parental authority. This implies that nearly half the youth endorsed strong or very strong parental authority. A little less than one-third of the respondents endorsed moderate parental authority. The remaining were in the limited parental authority zone *(Figure 2.1)*.

**Figure 2.1**

**Nature of parental authority experienced by youth**

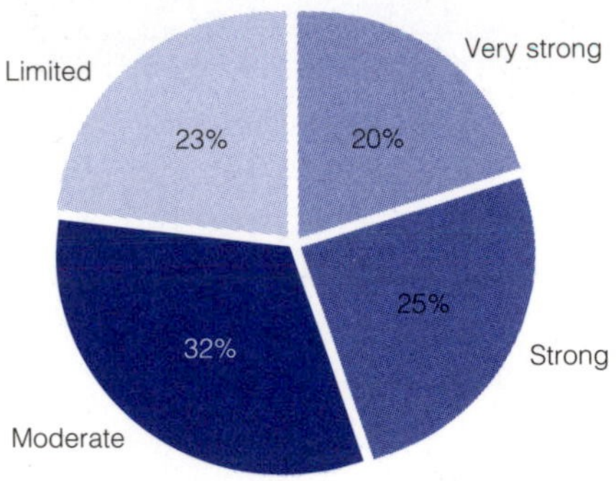


What are the socio-economic and cultural factors that propelled respondents into one of these categories? The critical factors appear to be the socio-economic status (SES) of the respondents, their gender and place of residence.

Families which could be termed as typically middle class were likely to witness lesser demonstration/expectation of limited parental authority compared to those of other SES. In the case of high SES, the reverse is witnessed with a higher percentage reporting limited parental authority *(Figure 2.2)*. In the case of the other SES groups and all other parameters, the level of parental authority experienced/endorsed is much closer to the national average.

It is noticed that the nature of parental authority experienced by a young person is linked to gender, albeit in a limited way. Women tend to report stronger parental authority as compared to men. The difference was, however, not very significant.

**Figure 2.2**

**Socio economic status of youth and nature of parental authority experienced by them**

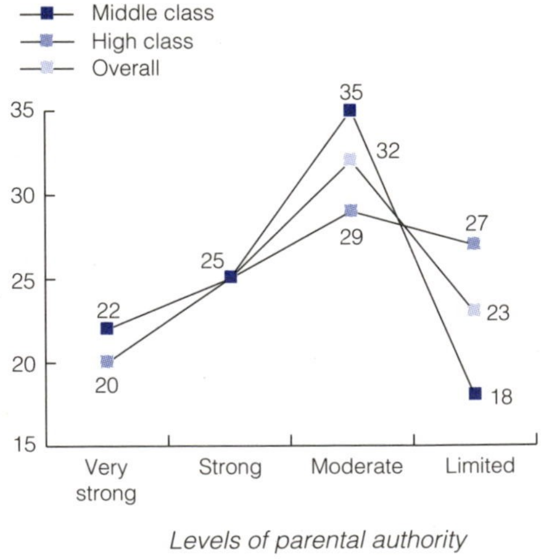

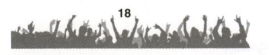

Further, while there is a difference in the attitude of young men in the metros and other locations towards parental authority, this difference is not as pronounced as in the case of women. In the metros, strong/very strong parental authority was reported less by young women *(Figure 2.3)*.

**Figure 2.3**

**Youth's experience of parental authority by gender and locality**

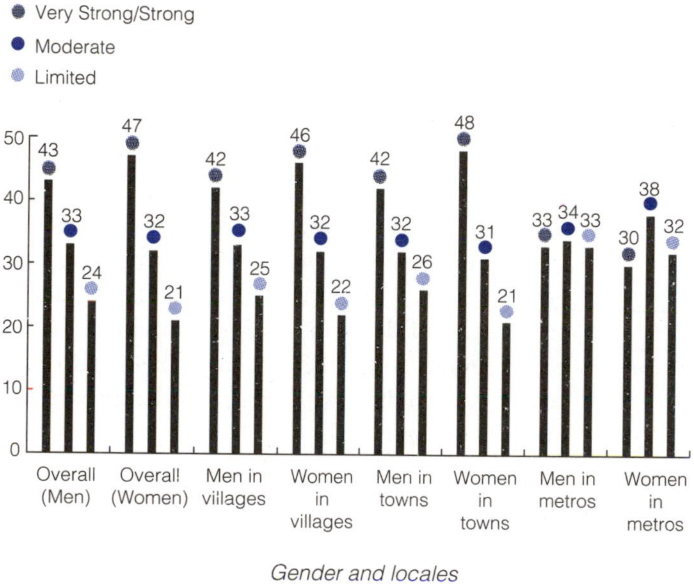


Most strikingly, the nature of parental authority is linked to young peoples' place of residence. In cities, the highest reporting of 'limited' and the lowest reporting of 'very strong' parental authority was recorded. In all the three locations i.e. villages, towns and metros, most of the youth reported moderate parental authority with this experience being most reported in the cities *(Figure 2.4)*. There were very marginal differences at all the four levels of authority in villages and towns. In cities, the number of people who reported strong parental authority was close to the national average.

### Dirty dancing: 14-yr-old files FIR against parents

A situation where a mother has been making a nautch girl out of her 14-year-old.

Ruma Sarkar and her husband Bapi have been battering their only child, Surbhi, to perform on dance floors at Raiganj and Bihar, till the girl lodged an FIR against her parents this week. This story would only corroborate the recent nation wide survey on rampant child abuse by parents and relatives. Surabhi, who secured 70% in her eight standard exams, told officials at Raiganj Thana that her parents even threatened to kill her if she refused. The cops, who got her complaint on Wednesday, called in the parents and made them submit an undertaking that they would stop exploiting the young teenager. The Sarkars made money at their daughter's expenses. The father is only a brick kiln worker and didn't earn much. Police found the Sarkars got in touch with some pimps who convinced them to take their daughter to various parts of Bihar for 'lagan' dance (household performances at the behest of village heads). Surbhi recalled one such session at Motihari, 'Hundreds of frenzied men, sporting guns, were asking me to dance. I had to perform all night with only 10-minute intervals.'

*The Sunday Times, The Times of India*, April 15, 2007.

**Figure 2.4**

**Youth's experience of parental authority by locality**

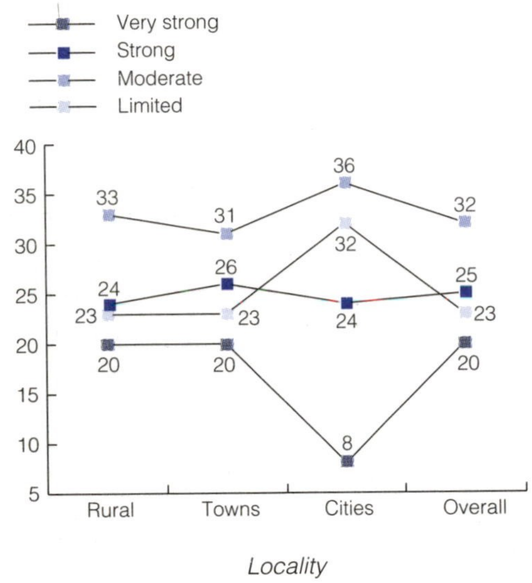


The nature of parental authority clearly expresses itself in the way the youth reflect on their decisions about academics and career choices. A majority of those who experience strong parental authority say that their parents take all decisions regarding their academics and career. A majority of those who are used to moderate parental authority believe that such decisions are made after discussions with parents. One-fourth of the youth who indicated that they had been subjected to limited parental authority felt that they enjoyed complete freedom about these decisions. A little over half of those who said that they were subjected to limited parental authority agreed that they took decisions in consultation with their parents, implying that consultations with parents is an inherent part of the process of decision making on matters linked to academics and career choices. This is also true with regard to those who report moderate parental authority *(Figure 2.5)*.

A review of how the youth perceive parental authority provides a glimpse of multi-track dimensions of both change and continuity. There is by and large an equal endorsement of very strong/ strong and moderate/limited parental authority. The divisions are clearly based on life experiences, social exposure and specific situations. The middle class is more conservative in its exercise of parental authority *(Figure 2.2)*. Women tended to be more supportive of strong parental authority in towns and villages as compared to men *(Figure 2.3)*. Youth, both male and female, in metropolitan areas tend to experience limited parental authority than those who belong to villages and towns *(Figure 2.3)*. Interestingly, those in towns thought more like those in the villages about the patterns of parental authority. The way youth look at parental authority is again linked to the experiences that they go through in their day-to-day lives. The variations in the responses are a reflection of this.

**Figure 2.5**

**Youth's experience of parental authority and pattern of decision making**

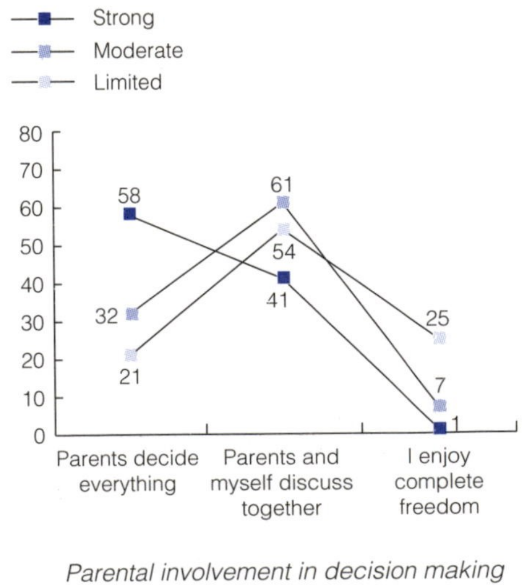

## Family Values

An Index of Family Values was constructed on the basis of responses to a set of questions linked to marriage and the role of the family in making that choice.[2] Based on the responses, the youth were divided into three categories—those who subscribed to conservative family values, those who were ambivalent and those who had a progressive value pattern. Close to 80 per cent of the youth were equally divided in the conservative and progressive family value moulds. The remaining were in the ambivalent zone. This is again reflective of the diversity prevalent in society that is articulated in the nature of parental authority *(Figure 2.6)*.

What factors contribute to a youth being in a conservative, ambivalent or progressive value mould? The study found that this was linked to five critical dimensions—gender, SES, age, the place of residence and the level of education of both the respondents and their parents.

**Figure 2.6**

**Family values of youth**

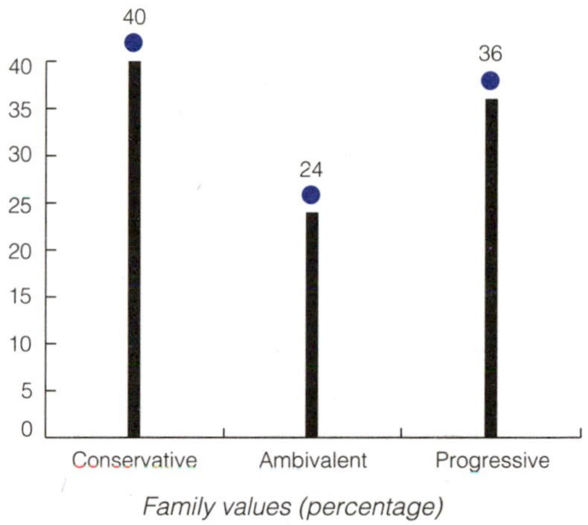


**In India, they say marriages are made in heaven: Views of an American student**

In a survey conducted by Lokniti-CSDS, two questions regarding the factors influencing a person's decision about marriage were asked. These were

1) In our society marriages must take place within one's own caste-community.
2) There is nothing wrong if boys and girls of different caste-community marry.

The results of this question shocked me. A total of 60.3 per cent agreed with the first statement that marriages should take place within one's own caste-community. In the U.S, it's not that uncommon for people of different classes/ethnicities/social backgrounds to marry. While there may have been protestation to those marriages in the past, today that generally is not the case. The results of this question make me think of social and economic mobility and how easy it is for people to move between classes and/economic levels, and also how willingly the Indian society accepts change. I realize that this question may speak to arranged marriages versus love marriages. If that is the case, I find the 60.3 per cent figure even more shocking. The concept of an arranged marriage would astound most American youth, I feel, to think that 60.3 per cent of polled youths still believe in it, is phenomenal. With the typical effects of democracy and globalisation in mind, India stands out as an exception, because liberalisation in the social realm seems to be lagging behind.

Laura Van Hyfte, An American student intern at Lokniti-CSDS, Delhi.

**Figure 2.7**

**Family values among youth by gender**

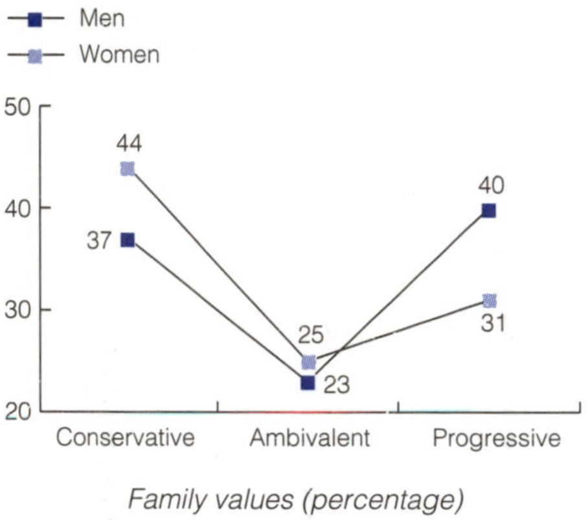


Women clearly appear to be more conservative compared to men. Nearly half the young women (44 per cent) adhere to conservative family values whereas only a little more than one-third of the men (37 per cent) do so. Four out of every ten men see themselves as having progressive values while only three out of every ten women fall in this bracket. In the zone of ambivalence there is only a marginal difference between men and women *(Figure 2.7)*.

Experience of conservatism in family values appears more prevalent among youth who have grown up in rural/village areas as compared to those who lived in towns and cities. Forty per cent of the youth who lived in villages reported a conservative value system. On the other hand, more than half of the youth (56 per cent) who lived in cities upheld progressive family values *(Figure 2.8)*. The percentage of ambivalence was uniform across locales. It is important to note that nearly one-third of the youth in villages espoused progressive family values *(Figure 2.8)*.

**Figure 2.8**

**Family values among youth by locality**

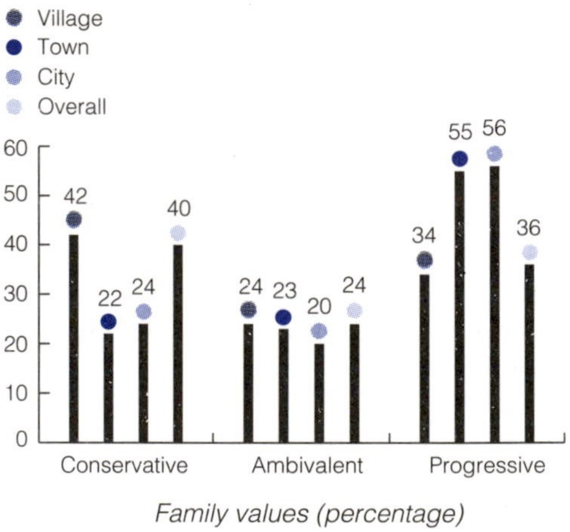


Interestingly, one out of every five young people in cities too fell in the conservative values slot. This implies that there is a trend in the specific direction of conservatism with important exceptions.

**Figure 2.9**

**Family values among youth by gender and locality**

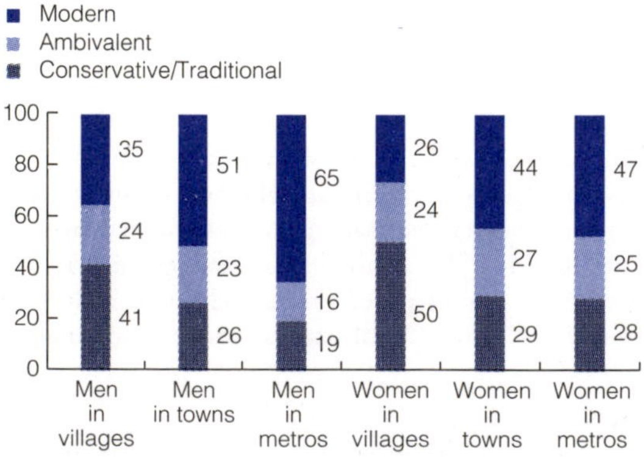


An attempt was made to assess whether young men and women in urban and rural locations differed in terms of their family values. The findings are similar for both young men and women—as one moves from the village to the city the level of conservatism declines and the youth appear to embrace a more modernistic perspective *(Figure 2.9)*.

## Kerala mixed marriages

These days an increasing trend among the Jat youth can be seen, that of journeying 3,000 km across the length of the country to find brides in Kerala. Haryanvi men are breaking culture, language and caste barriers to find suitable brides in Payyannur, a sleepy town in north Kerala's Kannur district. Popularly known as the 'Haryana kalyanam (marriage)' it has several explanations. Among sociologists it's got to do with female foeticide, while others who are not so well informed reason it by saying that 'women here are well educated and make loyal wives, good cooks.' According to local estimates, over 100 women from Payyannur town and nearby villages have been given in marriage to men in Haryana. While there is some explanation for Haryanvi men coming here, what about the women? They belong to the most literate state in the county and to accept a groom from a completely different culture and what some might call a retrograde one at that? Some explain it as a question of survival. Abject deprivation often forces local girls to traverse such great distances for a Haryanvi. According to locals, a single woman from an economically backward class, especially one who's past the 'marriageable age' is virtually an outcaste. Her own family either deserts her or she's seen as a burden. However such marriages are not without problems, the most common being language barrier. However the plus point of such marriages is that it comes without the hassles of a regular same culture marriage. No horoscope matching, no further enquiries about either the bride's or groom's antecedents. And most importantly, no dowry. Most single women from poor families prefer this uncomplicated, simple arrangement. The expenses for the marriage are borne by the groom. It all works out to no more than a few thousand rupees. By all accounts these are marriages of convenience. Haryanvi youth, many of them are farmers with only basic education to their credit, fail to find brides in their own state. So are such marriages bringing about any change in the lives of those involved? One opinion is that it is bringing about a change in the patriarchal attitudes of the Haryanvi men. This is reason enough to say three cheers to such cross-cultural connection, writes Mary John, the writer of this article.

*Outlook,* June 11, 2007.

The older among the youth are found to be more in tune with conservative family values. More than four out of every ten in those who were older than 25 years favour conservative values. Conversely, more than 40 per cent of those in the 14 to 17 years age group prefer modern family values.

A conservative family value system was found to be linked with the socio-economic status of the respondents. A progressive outlook was much more prevalent among those who were higher on the socio-economic ladder. More than half of those who had very low SES reported conservative values while more than half of those in the high SES reflected progressive values. However, 20 per cent in the low SES reported progressive social values while 20 per cent in the high SES reported conservative social values *(Figure 2.10)*.

**Figure 2.10**

**Family values among youth by socio economic status**

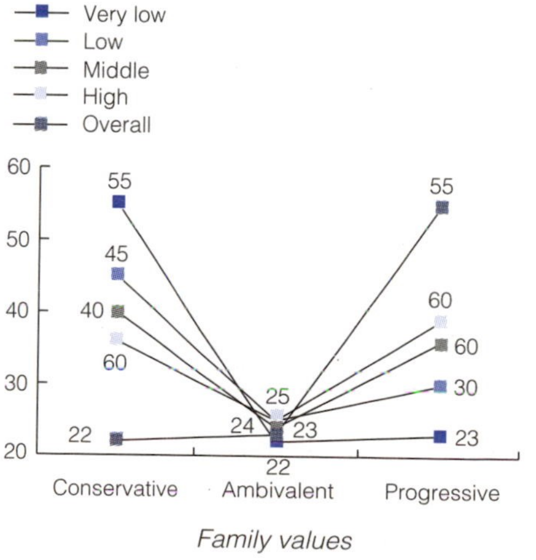

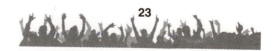

**Figure 2.11**

**Family values among youth by education**

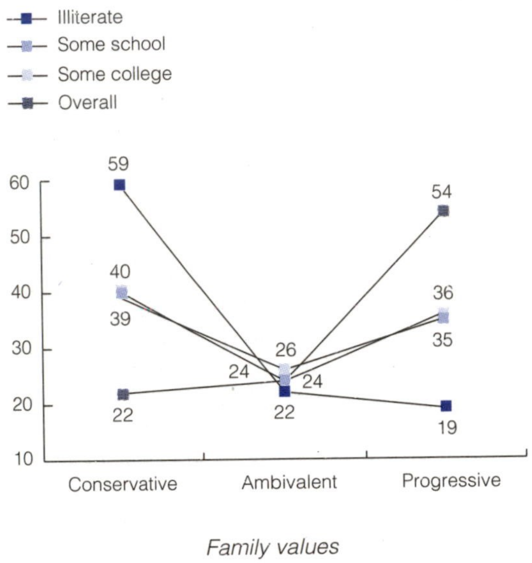


The more educated the respondent the more *(Figure 2.10)* likely he/she is to have progressive values. More than half the illiterate respondents upheld conservative values while more than half the graduates swore by progressive values. Again, the percentage of those in the zone of ambivalence did not differ significantly across educational levels. The level of conservativeness declined with education and the level of progressiveness increased with greater access to education. Yet there is a 20 per cent band both among the illiterate (who appear to have progressive values) and graduates (who have conservative values) who resist the trend in their groups *(Figure 2.11)*.

An analysis of the groups where the highest levels of conservatism and modernity are

**Bhopal rocked by protests over Hindu-Muslim marriage**

An inter-religious marriage between a Muslim boy and a Hindu girl has become a source of trouble for the administration. Today, Hindu organisations blocked traffic at 40 places across the city in protest and warned of more trouble in the future. Umar, a student of the School of Social Sciences, and Priyanka Wadhwani, a final year commerce student, eloped to Mumbai when they realised that her family was against their union. They married in Mumbai but fear has kept them from returning to Bhopal. Umar embraced Hinduism and changed his name to Umesh for the sake of his love, but the move has not convinced Hindu organisations or the Sindhi community, to which Priyanka belongs. The Hindu organisations, after observing symbolic chakka jam in the afternoon, formed a Hindu Kanya Raksha Samiti in the evening and threatened to intensify their protests against similar marriages, which they alleged were a conspiracy against the community by Islamic forces. Though both Umar and Priyanka are adults, her family lodged a kidnapping complaint with the Kohefiza Police Station that led to the detention of Umar's brother, Shakil, by the police. The police were under pressure to act as Hindu organisations had given them only 24 hours to bring back the couple. The police continued its search for the couple in Mumbai even after Priyanka called them up and confirmed that she had married Umar. The couple said they did not have the courage to return to Bhopal because efforts would be made to separate them. Narendra Lokwani, a member of the newly formed Samiti said the Samiti might give a call for Bhopal Bandh if the girl did not return soon.

Milind Ghatwai, *The Indian Express*, April 12, 2007.

found was undertaken across variables. This showed a majority among the illiterate youth belonging to the lower SES and are homemakers were in the conservative zone in terms of family values. At the other end of the spectrum were students, those who have attended college, belong to the high SES and live in cities. A majority of them are in the 'modern' family values zone *(Figure 2.12)*.

**Figure 2.12**

**Illiterate and poor youth are more likely to be conservative**

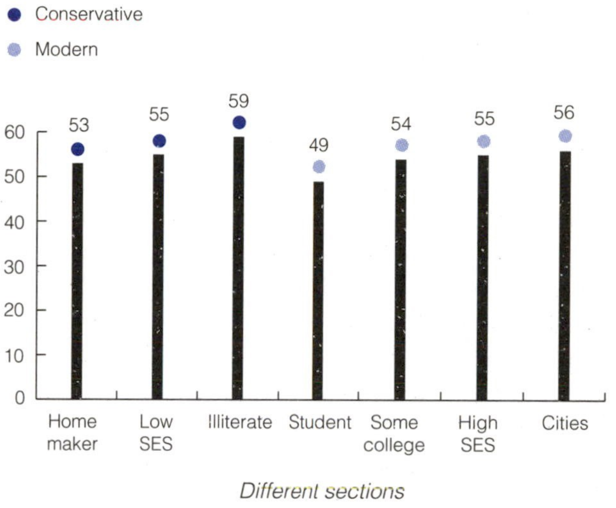


The attitude of the youth to critical issues related to the family was also analysed through a few other questions. The respondents were asked how they would view the earnings of their spouse. Did they feel that their spouse should earn more than them, less than them, the same as them or did it make no difference? The respondents also had the option of stating that the spouse should not work. More than four out of every ten young people felt that it was all right for the spouse to earn more than them. A quarter of the youth opined that it made no difference and just over 10 per cent felt that they should earn more than their spouse. Another 10 per cent felt that their spouse should not work.

**Figure 2.13**

**Opinion of the youth on earnings of spouse**

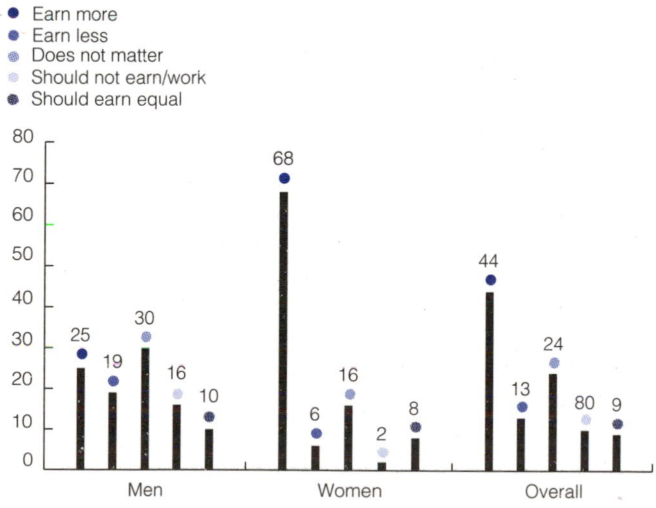


The better the education level of the respondents and the higher their SES, the more likely they were to say that the spouse earning more than them did not make a difference. Those in the towns and cities were more likely to support the 'did not make a difference' stand as compared to those in the villages.

The most significant difference in attitudes towards this question was between young men and women.

While only one-fourth of the men stated that they would be all right with the spouse earning more than them, more than two-third of the women endorsed this view. Two out of every ten men said that they should earn less than their spouse while very few women supported this stand. Thirty per cent of the men said that it did not make a difference if the spouse earned more while in the case of women only 15 per cent supported this attitude. Just 2 per cent of the women felt that the spouse should not earn or work while over one-sixth of the men felt that the spouse should not work/earn *(Figure 2.13)*.

There was a strong endorsement of the family as an important institution by the youth. Close to nine out of every ten youth felt that to be happy one needed a family. There was a marginal difference in this response across SES, caste groups, martial status, educational levels and gender. The only apparent difference was in the attitude of youth in metropolitan areas where 10 per cent endorsed the view that happiness was not dependent on whether one had a family or not *(Figure 2.14)*.

**Figure 2.14**

**Youth attach higher value to institution of family**

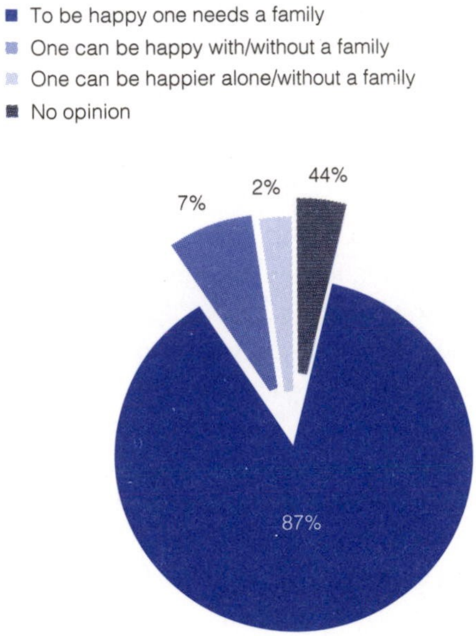


### Girls want to be boys

Disgusted by the discrimination they face, nearly half of Indian girls wish they were boys, says a study on child abuse in the country. Of the 5,981 girls interviewed for the National Study on Child Abuse, about 48.4% wanted to be boys. The study did not look into the specific reasons for the feeling but cited overall gender discrimination as a possible cause. 70% of girls do household work and 49% take care of siblings. This indicates that the girl child is deprived of developmental opportunities. Even in a state like Kerala, the figure for such girls is as high as 81%. The study pointed out that 70.57% girls reported neglect by their family members, leading to emotional abuse. About 85% of girls from Uttar Pradesh, 79% from Gujarat and 79% from Madhya Pradesh reported such emotional abuse by family members. Among girls who were young adults, the perception of emotional abuse was higher than among those from a lower age group. A majority of them also took umbrage at having to take care of their siblings at the cost of their education.

Chetan Chauhan, *Hindustan Times,* April 10, 2007.

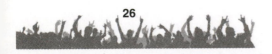

Case Study 2

## *Journeying Towards Equality: A Study of Muslim Girls at Undergraduate Level*

by **Suniti Nagpurkar**

### Responding to cultural and economic modernity

The choice of IDE data was also on the assumption that the Muslim community which is now emerging from being a late starter on the horizon of higher education to the stage where it registers the highest growth rate in female literacy, primary and secondary education, may still prefer distance education as a mode of receiving higher education for their girls rather than sending the girls to colleges. Therefore enrolment data from a distance education centre may provide a basis for capturing the emerging trend for this study. The data from Institute of Distance Education (IDE), University of Mumbai, was collected from the annual enrolment data maintained by the institute itself. However, the institute maintains the data classified on the basis of faculty and gender only. Therefore from the annual enrolment data the case study writer has separated the data on Muslim girls on the basis of names, surnames, father's name and mother's name. Thus from the annual enrolment data on female students, Muslim female was separated. From the data in the table it seems that Muslim girls show more preference for Arts than Commerce, though since 2000–01 there is an improvement in the absolute number of Muslim girls joining Commerce stream. In 1999-2000 there were only 75 Muslim girls who took admission in commerce at IDE, in 2004–05 the number increased to 232. Between 1995–96 to 1999–00 the enrollment of Muslim girls under Commerce stream at IDE increased only to 75 from 61. While in the next 5 years it increased from 75 to 232.

**Faculty wise Enrolment of Girls at Institute of Distance Education**

| Year | Enrolment of Girls in F.Y.BA | | Enrolment of Girls in F.Y. Bcom | |
|---|---|---|---|---|
| | Open category | Muslim girls | Open category | Muslim girls |
| 1995–96 | 758 | 67 (8.83%) | 1181 | 61 (5.165%) |
| 1996–97 | 1201 | 70 (5.825) | 1185 | 70 (5.90%) |
| 1997–98 | 1284 | 110 (8.56%) | 1329 | 63 (4.74%) |
| 1998–99 | 2021 | 204 (10.09%) | 1926 | 103 (5.34%) |
| 1999–00 | 1744 | 190 (10.89%) | 1445 | 75 (5.19%) |
| 2000–01 | 2413 | 250 (10.36%) | 2830 | 183 (6.46%) |
| 2001–02 | 2845 | 206 (7.24%) | 3883 | 111 (2.85%) |
| 2002–03 | 2339 | 301 (12.80%) | 2976 | 200 (6.72%) |
| 2003–04 | 2349 | 199 (8.47%) | 3091 | 241 (7.79%) |
| 2004–05 | 2945 | 272 (9.23%) | 3637 | 232 (6.37%) |

## Summing Up

The Index of Parental Authority and the Index of Family Values presented in this chapter provide a perspective on what influences the way youth think and act in their personal and social domains. The nature of parental authority is both a by-product of a set of value preferences and also something that shapes the world view that youth tend to develop on matters linked to family life and social relationships. The Family Value Index provides a snapshot of the values preferred by the youth. It is apparent that tradition and modernity play out in multiple ways in their lives. The nature of the social structure and the dynamics of social relationships that the youth are exposed to shape their family values in particular and their social values in general.

## Endnotes

1) Combining the responses of the respondents to a set of questions the Index of Parental Authority (IPA) was created. The questions included while preparing the index are: Question 5: 'If you recall your childhood days, how would you describe your upbringing—would you say that your upbringing was very strict, strict, not so strict or not at all strict?' Question 6: 'If you think of the way you would like to bring up your children, you would bring them up— exactly the same way your parents brought you up, more or less the same way, differently or very differently?' The answer categories were re-tabulated in order to permit an index to be created.

   The sub-categorisation into 'very strong' and 'strong' parental authority was done in view of the fact that a very large percentage of the respondents were in these two categories.

2) The Family Value Index was constructed by combining the responses of the youth to four questions. Question 19: 'Now I will read out two statements on various issues. Tell me whether you agree with statement (1) or statement (2)? a) Statement 1: In matters of marriage boys and girls may be consulted, however the final decision should be taken by parents; Statement 2: In matters of marriage though the parents may be consulted, the final decision should be left to the boys/girls themselves. b) Statement 1: In our society, meeting/dating of boys and girls before marriage should be restricted; Statement 2: There should be no restriction on meeting/dating of boys and girls before marriage. c) Statement 1: In our society marriages must take place within one's own caste/community; Statement 2: There is nothing wrong if boys and girls of different castes/community marry. d) Statement 1: Once married, a couple must stay together even if it requires certain compromises; Statement 2: If there are differences with one's partner, there is no harm in getting a divorce.' The recording of the index was based on the tabulation of responses in the following manner: 1. Agree with first. 2. No opinion. 3. Agree with the second. On this basis the index is classified into three categories—conservative, ambivalent and progressive.

# CHAPTER 3: LEISURE AND LIFESTYLE

- Youth across the country have different ways of looking at leisure. The formal and accepted forms of leisure appear to be patronised more by those from higher socio-economic status and those living in metropolitan areas.
- Television is a major source of entertainment and an important leisure activity for many. The sense of 'addiction' to it is linked to the age and the educational attainment of the youth.
- The use of the internet is limited to urban educated youth.
- Alcohol consumption is still seen as taboo among most youth though resistance to it among urban youth with higher educational levels seems to be on the decline.
- There is an increasing aspiration for what is termed 'fashionable' even though for many it does not translate into reality.

This chapter sketches the lifestyle patterns of the youth in India. The range of questions posed in the survey provides a glimpse of the emerging trends about the lifestyle pattern of the youth in contemporary times. The chapter also focuses on how the youth like to spend their free time. A set of questions sought to explore the interests and participation of youth in multi-track leisure activities to find out if any pattern exists with regard to the leisure preferences of the youth.

## Leisure

To explore the leisure preferences of Indian youth, a Leisure Index[1] was prepared on the basis of a series of questions that were asked in the survey. The leisure activities included listening to music, going out with friends, reading books and magazines, playing some sport and watching films and television. The responses were combined and then comprehensively divided into three categories—high, moderate and low. This division was done on the basis of the frequency/intensity with which the youth were involved in the leisure activity.

There is a more or less equal division between those who spent moderate time on leisure activities and those who spent a lot of time in leisure pursuits. A few people (about 14 per cent) spent very little time in leisure pursuits *(Figure 3.1)*.

Are there major variations in the leisure pattern of youth across critical variables? A detailed analysis of the Leisure Index found that there were significant differences across age groups, educational levels, gender and place of residence.

**Figure 3.1**

**Leisure time availed by youth**

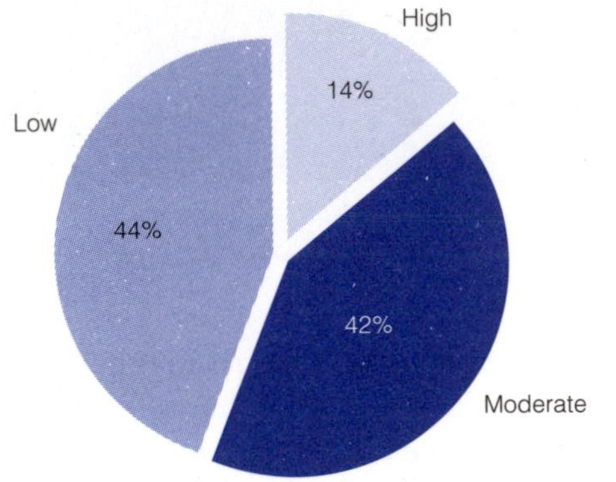


*Note: High, moderate and low are levels of leisure computed by creating a composite index of leisure activities. For details, see endnotes.*

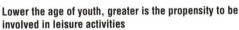

A clear pattern emerges across different age groups among the youth. The younger the person, the more likely he/she is to spend greater time on leisure activities. As they grow older the participation of the youth in leisure related activities also decreases *(Figure 3.2)*. Close to half the youth in each age category spend a moderate amount of time in leisure pursuits. While four out of every ten youth in the 19+ years age group devote very little time in leisure pursuits, the percentage of those who spend very little time on leisure activities is much less among those below 19 years of age.

**Figure 3.2**

**Lower the age of youth, greater is the propensity to be involved in leisure activities**

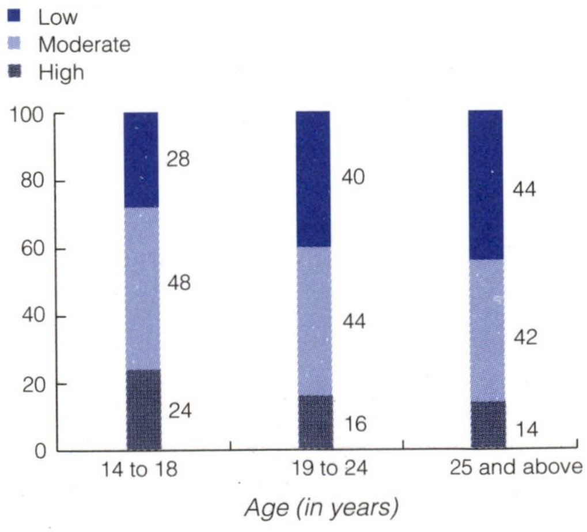

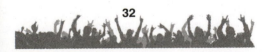

Among the youth who would be in the 'low' category in terms of time spent on leisure activities? The highest percentage is in the 25+ years age group—it accounts for a little less than half the youth in this age category. On the other hand, a little over one-fourth of the youth in the 14 to 18 years age band fall in the low category. There is very little difference across age groups when it comes to the moderate range. One-fourth of the youth in the 14 to 18 years age group have reported high participation in leisure activities. On the other hand, in the 19+ years age group around 15 per cent devote a great deal of time on leisure pursuits. It is clear that the younger the respondent, the more likely he/she is to have a schedule that leaves time for leisure pursuits. Hence, there is also a greater inclination to be involved in leisure activities. With increasing responsibility and focus on professional lives the time available for leisure pursuits steadily decreases.

**Figure 3.3**

**Higher the education of youth, greater is the propensity to be involved in leisure activities**

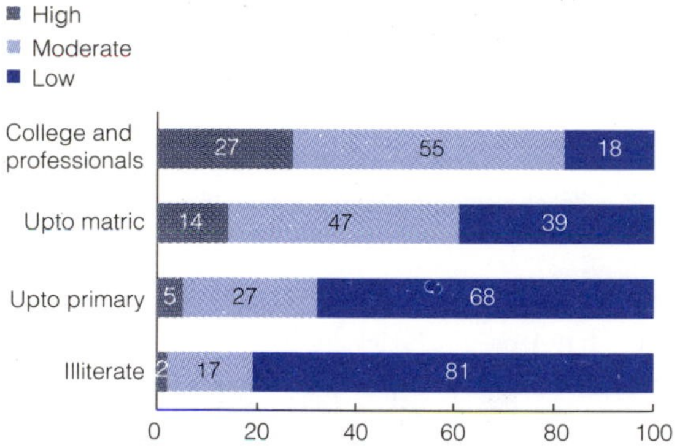


The quantum of time that the youth are able to devote to leisure activities is also linked to their educational attainment. More than 80 per cent among the illiterates reported low level of participation in leisure activities *(Figure 3.3)*. This percentage falls as the educational level of the respondents improves. Among the graduates only one of every ten belongs to this category. On the other hand, just over 2 per cent of those who are illiterate are in the high band for time spent on leisure activities while among the graduates more than one-fourth have reported that they spend a lot of time on leisure activities. The other question, which needs to be raised, is whether the Leisure Index taps only the formal parameters of leisure activities and does not capture the entire range of what could constitute leisure pursuits.

Youth in towns and cities appear to be able to devote more time to leisure activities as compared to those in the villages. More than half the youth in the villages devote very little time to leisure activities. In urban areas more than 20 per cent of the youth are in the low band. On the other hand, 11 per cent of the youth in rural areas are in the high category while in cities and towns this percentage is doubled *(Figure 3.4)*.

**Figure 3.4**

**Youth in metros are more likely to enjoy leisure time**

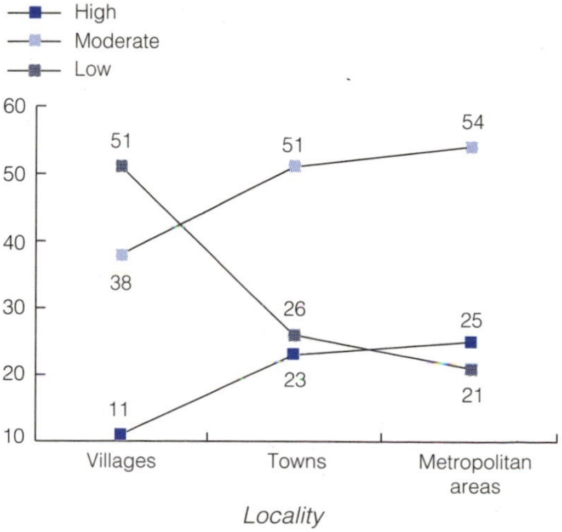

**Figure 3.5**

**Young women are less likely to enjoy leisure time**

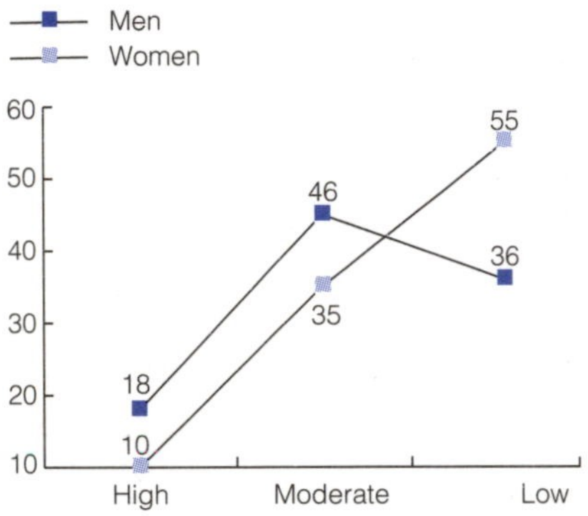


Women are able to spend less time on leisure activities as compared to men. The difference is especially skewed at the two ends of the range of low and high. More than half the young women fall in the low category in terms of time spent on leisure. In the case of men, over one-third are in this range. As many as 18 per cent of the men are in the high zone for time spent on leisure activities while just 10 per cent of the women are part of this categorisation *(Figure 3.5)*. However, a caveat needs to be added here: perhaps our index does not tap typical leisure activities that women are involved in, which leads to this difference in percentages among men and women.

Does the quantum of time spent on leisure by young men and women vary in different locations? The clear trend, which emerges is that young men and women living in cities and metros tend to have more time available for leisure as compared to those living in villages. Just 15 per cent of the young men in metros fall in the low bracket on the Leisure Index whereas in the villages this figure is three times higher at 45 per cent. In the case of women in metros, a little less than 30 per cent fall in the low bracket whereas in villages this figure is double *(Figure 3.6)*.

**Figure 3.6**

**Young women in village are more likely to enjoy leisure time**

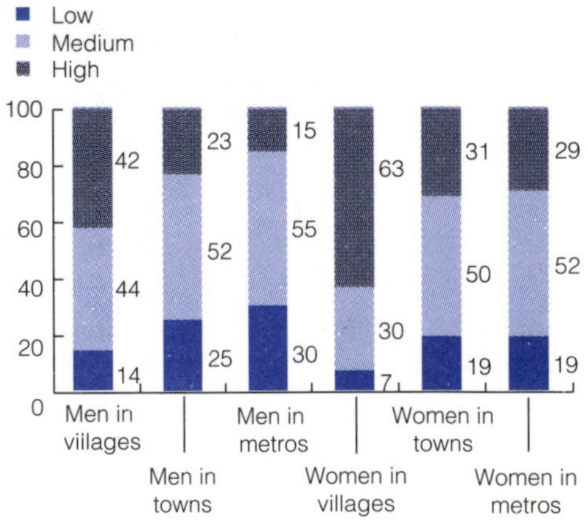


**Figure 3.7**

**Higher the socio economic status of youth, greater the intensity of leisure activities**

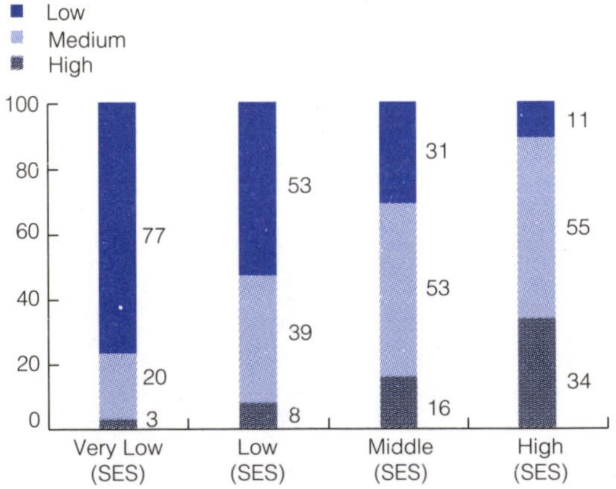


It was seen that the higher the socio-economic status (SES) of a youth the more likely he/she was to be involved in leisure activities. Over one-third of the youth in the high SES were actively involved in leisure activities while nearly eight of every ten youth from the very low SES rarely took part in leisure activities *(Figure 3.7)*.

It was also found that employed youth have more time for leisure as compared to those who do not work *(Figure 3.8)*.

**Figure 3.8**

**Employed youth are more likely to be involved in leisure activities**

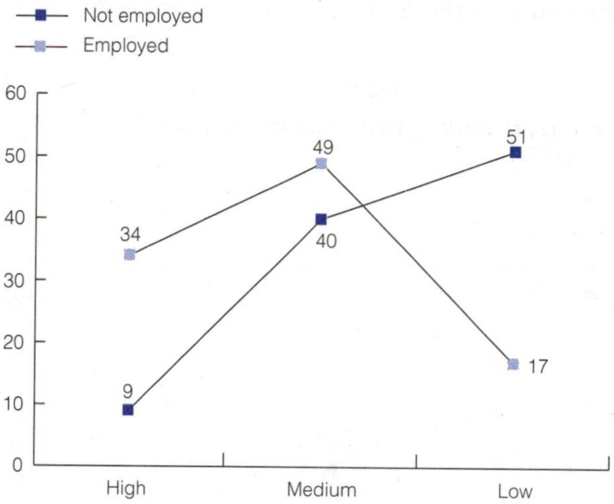


A regression analysis of the Leisure Index by determinants like gender, age, location, educational level, employment status, marital status and socio-economic status shows that the socio-economic status (SES) is the best predictor of time spent on leisure activities. This implies that youth from high SES spend more time on leisure. The next most critical factor is locality. Youth from metros clearly spend more time on leisure as compared to those living in villages.

Does the Leisure Index tap all categories of leisure activities that youth across the country may be involved in? Or does it cover only the formal forms of leisure available to those who are either educated or have a minimal level of economic status? Does this explain the skew in the responses when SES and place of residence are taken into account?

While analysing the time and interest that youth devote to leisure activities, an attempt was made to map their expenditure on important leisure related activities. This included expenditure on films and DVDs, clothes and footwear, music, I pods, mobiles and on eating out. The socio-economic status of the respondent was kept in mind while undertaking the analysis (those who could not say how much they spent were left out of the analysis).

Among those who are in the very low SES category, more than 80 per cent reported no expenditure on music and mobile phones. Close to half the respondents in this SES category reported no expenses on movies and eating out as well. Half the respondents in the very low SES category spend less than Rs. 100 a month on clothes and footwear.

In all the SES categories, 50 per cent of the respondents spend less than Rs. 100 a month on movies/DVDs. The same quantum of expenditure is reported by a majority of those in the very low, low and medium SES groups on eating out. Further, a majority of those in the low and medium SES ranges reported spending between Rs. 50 and Rs. 100 a month on clothes and footwear. Nearly half the respondents in the middle SES category spend over Rs. 100 a month on mobile phones.

Among those in the high SES category, more than half spend over Rs. 100 a month on eating out, more than Rs. 200 on clothes and footwear and more than Rs. 200 on mobile phones. One-third of those in the high SES category spend over Rs. 100 on movies/DVDs every month.

Watching television is an important leisure activity for the youth. Television viewing is linked to the age of the youth, their SES, educational level and place of residence. Nearly one-third of the youth in the 14 to 25 years age group reported that they watch television regularly during their free time. In the 30+ years age bracket, this figure drops to 10 per cent.

How important is television viewing as a leisure activity? Four out of every ten youth stated that they watched television regularly (by implication daily). Another four said that they watched television sometimes (once a week) and the rest never watched television. The time spent on watching television is found to be clearly linked to SES, education levels and place of residence of the youth. Those from higher SES tend to watch television more often. As the SES reduces television viewing also declines. Half the youth in the very low SES stated that they never watch television. In comparison only 4 per cent in the high SES said that they never watch television. Less than 20 per cent of those in the low SES reported watching television regularly *(Figure 3.9)*.

**Figure 3.9**

**Frequency of television viewing by socio economic status (SES)**

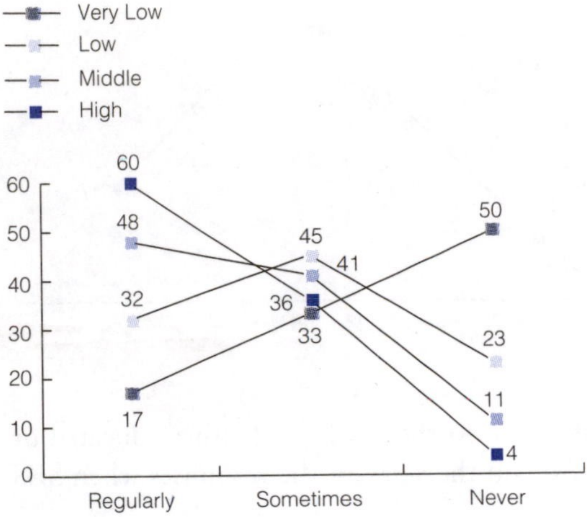


Among the youth who do not know how to read and write, more than half never watch television. The percentage of those who never watch television steadily declines with higher educational attainment. The more educated the youth, the more likelihood of them saying that they watch television frequently. More than half the graduates reported that they watch television regularly, while less than 20 per cent said so among the illiterate youth *(Figure 3.10)*.

While television viewing is an important pastime among urban youth, it is catching up among the

**Figure 3.10**

**Frequency of television viewing by education**

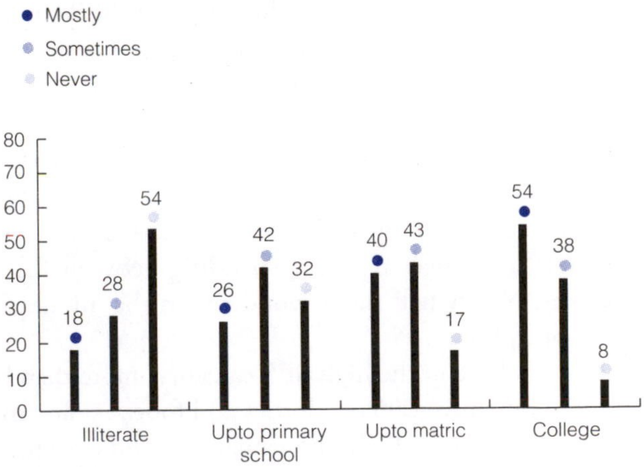

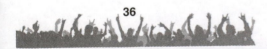

**Figure 3.11**

**Frequency of television viewing by locality**

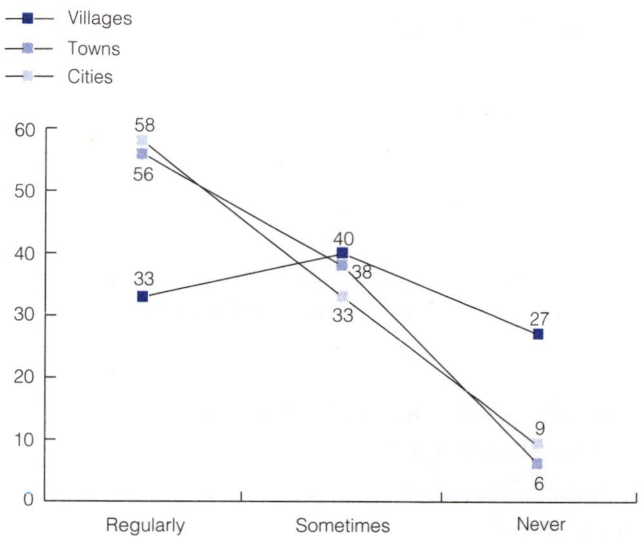


rural youth as well. More than half the youth in cities and towns reported watching television regularly during their leisure time; this response was marginally higher in towns than in cities. In villages, one-third of the youth said that they watched television regularly *(Figure 3.11)*. Less than 10 per cent of the youth in towns and cities stated that they never watched television while in the villages, more than one-fourth of the youth maintained that they never watched television. Town and city youth have very similar television viewing habits.

It is also interesting to note that nearly one-fourth of the youth watch films on television daily. Another 50 per cent watch movies on television more than once a week. The younger among the youth tend to watch films on television more often. Watching movies on television is more frequent among the youth with higher SES, more access to education and among those living in urban areas.

Television as a vehicle of entertainment appears to have captivated the younger age group among the youth who have access to education, come from affluent families and live in urban areas. A regression analysis was undertaken to identify the most significant variable that influences television viewing. It was found that age (those in the 14 to 18 years age bracket) was the most important factor followed by access to education.

## Lifestyle

Lifestyle preferences are an important hallmark of what is termed 'modern' youth. To map lifestyle patterns among the new generation of youngsters, a few important markers were chosen from among the survey questions.

An important dimension of the new lifestyle of the youth is the increasing use of information technology in their day-to-day lives. Among the questions dealing with this subject in the survey are: How prevalent is the use of the internet among the youth? Are the youth hooked on to the net? What do they use the internet for?

Case Study 3

***Modern Youth and Embodied Work: A Study of Kolkata***

by **Swati Ghosh**

## Responding to cultural and economic modernity

The research questions with which we started have been framed to bring out the various facets of body management and adaptability of the youth and to capture the nuances of the change regarding values, attitudes and outlook.

1. How has the concept of morality regarding body changed such that more and more youths are being drawn into jobs relating to the body?
2. What are the direct and indirect effects of the change on the youth due to
   a) possession of idealised body as a precondition of work
   b) providing bodily services to others?
3. How do the economic and the cultural determine each other with respect to the new job opportunities?

Today, the shape and beauty of the body is emerging as the marker of modernity for the youth in the metropolitan cultural milieu. Widespread concern with the body defying age, income group, or gender role across the society is creating new job opportunities. Different forms of indulging with the body find countenance in the services provided at the posh salons and subaltern beauty-parlours, in 'western' dance classes and mushrooming massage clinics, in the numerous grooming courses and informal care centres. Experience of the service providers reveal that social and economic recognition of their skill gives them satisfaction and makes them upwardly mobile. As they become proficient in handling the corporeality aspect of their job they not only cater to the demand for bodily service with perfect ease but soon become confident enough to tip their clients about what is to be done and how. A new sense of morality seems to be prevailing regarding dress code, beauty and fitness for both the teenagers and their parents which has outgrown the age-old societal tension of sticking to gender roles and is steadily pervading the city suburbs.

Body is viewed as an entity in the process of becoming and open to reconstruction which is linked to self-esteem and a sense of personal control over one's environment. The social body seeks to project the possession of a firm and slender body as an option available for individuals with promises of self-confidence and sense of security entangled with it. The real body is trained and disciplined through the representations of the idealised body. In contemporary society body becomes the primary site for operation of modern forms of power which is not repressive but subtle, productive, and self-initiating. The moral conditions ensuring monitoring of the self towards the idealised, disciplined body is one of the most powerful normalising strategies. The advice and guidance of the service provider results in subjugation of the self according to the normative standards and cultural ideals of the body. The regime of health beauty and self care is thus established in extension of markets into our lives, in conquering a deep sense of insecurity and in developing self-esteem as responsible citizens.

It was found that just over 10 per cent of the youth use the internet. While nearly one-third of the youth in cities use the internet, one-fifth of those in towns access the net. In villages less than 10 per cent of the youth use the internet.

Nearly one-third of all graduates among the youth access the net while among those who have not completed their matriculation, 5 per cent use the internet.

The most striking contrast in internet use is among different SES categories. Only 1 per cent from the very low SES category said that they used the net. Among the low SES category, less than 5 per cent use the internet. This figure is less than 10 per cent among the medium SES. However the figure jumps to 38 per cent among those from high SES category *(Figure 3.12)*.

**Figure 3.12**

**Frequency of internet usage among different sections of the youth**

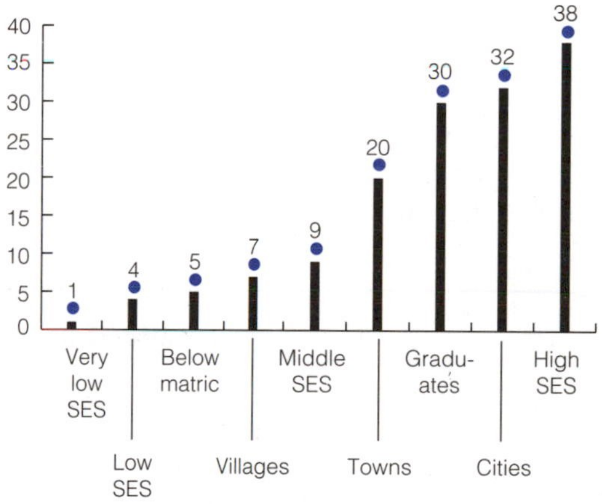


Youth in the younger age group (less than 19 years) tend to use the internet for a lesser amount of time as compared to those in the 20+ years category. In the 14 to 19 years age group the internet is used for emailing, chatting and downloading information in almost an equal proportion. Among the 20+ years age group, more than half the time on the net is used for downloading information with one-third of the time spent on emailing. Those in the cities tend to spend more time on the net. More than one-third of the youth in the cities who access the internet spend more than 15 hours per week on the net.

Previous studies in India have found that the use of the internet is largely an urban phenomenon (SONS 2006). This appears true in our study as well. Even among the urban youth, the internet is used more by the educated and more affluent. The younger among the youth use the internet more for transmitting information than for collecting it. The older among the youth appear to use the net for both information gathering as well as processing.

**Figure 3.13**

**Opinion of the youth on dressing up in latest styles**

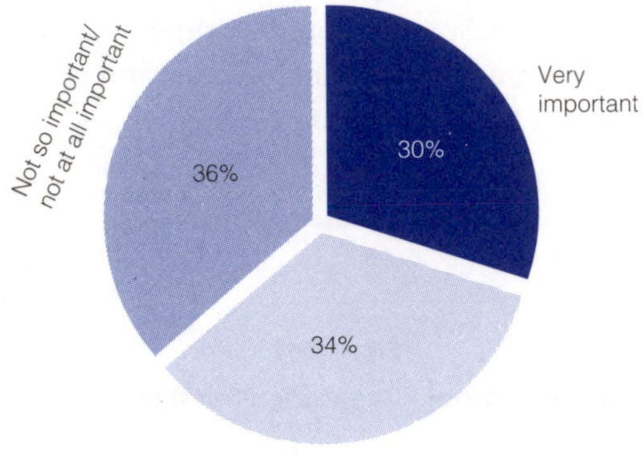


The survey asked youth how important it was to dress up in latest styles. The respondents were offered four answer categories—very important, somewhat important, not so important and not at all important. Overall there was a near equal three way split among those who said very important, somewhat important and not so important/not at all important *(Figure 3.13)*.

It was also found that giving greater importance to dressing up in latest styles is linked to age, SES, education, gender and place of residence.

The younger among the youth seem to be more focused on dressing up. Nearly 40 per cent of those in the 14 to 19 years age bracket feel that dressing up is very important. The percentage of those who said that dressing up in the latest styles is very important declines with age. One-third of the youth in all age groups feel that dressing up is somewhat important. If 40 per cent

**Imagined ugliness causes depression**

More and more youngsters these days are becoming increasingly obsessive about their looks. 'Imagined ugliness or body dysmorphic disorder (BDD), involves a preoccupation with a negative body image. Victims spend hours in front of the mirror, preoccupied with a minor or an imagined defect. They may try to camouflage it by donning a big hat, or wearing heavy makeup. Eventually they may become so obsessed with their appearance that they may not go to school or work,' says Dr. Y Matcheswalla, president of the Bombay Psychiatric Society. He adds that it is very common in teenagers and usually continues up to the age of 25, where youngsters put a lot emphasis on their looks. Self-consciousness and feeling of embarrassment, anxiety and fear that others will notice their flaws and judge them negatively leads to avoidance of usual activities, excessive checking and grooming as well as attempts at hiding, camouflaging or rectifying the imagined flaw through general medical, dental or surgical treatments. 'They may drop out of school, avoid job interviews, dating and intimacy and have few friends,' says Dr. PT Sundaram, psychologist at Mind Restore. Without doubt negative body image is associated with a great deal of emotional distress and life disruption. Talking about the repercussions of 'Imagined ugliness', Dr. Matcheswalla says that people usually become suicidal; stay aloof, brood, become depressed and neurotic.

Barnali Pal, *The Asian Age,* New Delhi, 26 April 2007.

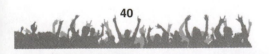

**Figure 3.14**

**Importance of dressing up for youth by age, SES and locality**

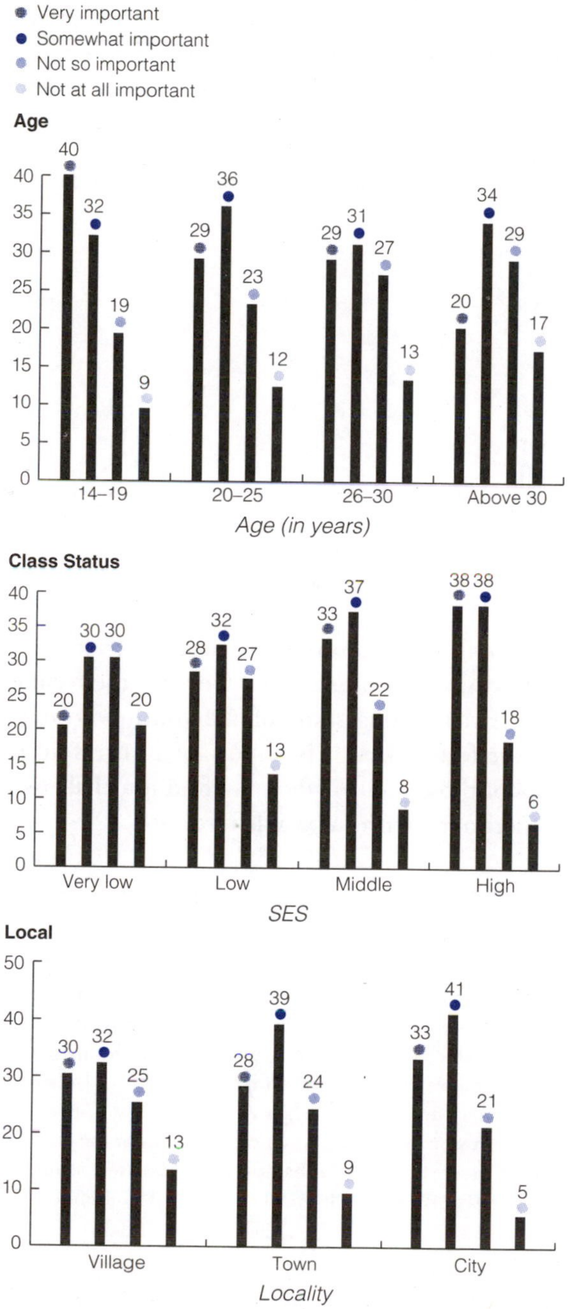


of the youth in the 25+ years age group said that dressing up in the latest styles is not at all important, only 12 per cent of those in the 20 to 25 years age bracket endorsed this stand as did just 9 per cent of those in the 14 to 19 years age group *(Figure 3.14)*. It is clear that among the youth, the younger one is the more likely it is that dressing up fashionably and being in 'sync' matters more. Peer pressure, entering the teen age and socialising within a 'new' friend circle may all be contributing to this trend.

Given the fact that dressing up in latest styles involves expenditure, it is not surprising that the socio-economic status of the youth defines whether they consider it to be important or not. A majority of those in the very low SES endorse the point that dressing up in latest styles is not so important/not at all important for them. Forty per cent of those in the low SES endorse this position. Among those in the middle SES, a little less than one-third support this stand, while among the high SES less than a quarter said that dressing up in latest styles is not so important/not at all important. It must also be stated that 20 per cent in the very low SES, and 28 per cent in the low SES, feel that dressing up in latest styles is very important. One-third of those in the middle SES also endorse the importance of dressing up fashionably *(Figure 3.14)*.

An overwhelmingly large number of youth across urban and rural areas felt that dressing up fashionably was somewhat important or very important. Though the endorsement was much higher in towns and cities it was quite significant in villages as well. Less than 10 per cent of the youth in urban areas said that dressing up in latest fashions was not at all important. Just 5 per cent of their city counterparts endorsed this point *(Figure 3.14)*.

The level of education also has an impact on the attitude of the youth towards fashion. A majority of those who had the benefit of some formal education endorse the point that fashionable dressing is important (somewhat or very). Even among the illiterate youth, there is a more or less equal division between those who feel that dressing up is important and those who feel that it is not. One out of five illiterate youth said that dressing up is very important. At the other end of the spectrum, once again one out of every five among the illiterate youth feels that this is not at all an important factor. Less than 10 per cent of the youth who are graduates took this stand.

**Figure 3.15**

**Opinion on dressing up in latest style by gender**

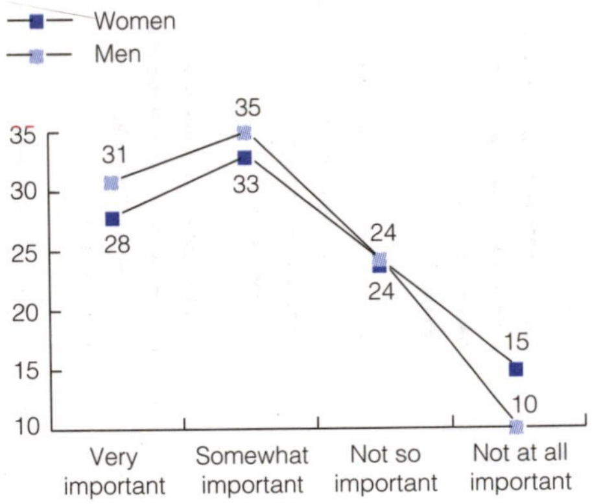


The most revealing aspect of the fashion preferences of the youth is that men seem to be more fashion conscious than women *(Figure 3.15)*. While this trend is in evidence consistently across all the answer categories it is especially skewed at the two extremes—very important and not at all important.

The aspiration to dress up in the latest fashion appears to have an influence upon a majority of the youth in the country. However, a distinction needs to be made between the actual capacity to dress up in fashionable clothes and the feeling that it is important to dress up in such a manner. Even among some of the youth who may not have the means to dress up in latest fashions, the feeling that it is important to dress up is distinctly prevalent. This is evident in the responses of those groups who may find it a challenge to actually dress up in latest fashions but who still harbour a wish to be able to do so.

**Save the sari from a sorry fate**

The salwar kameez, the trouser and even the western dress-suit have begun to supplant it (sari) everywhere. Youth clearly has something to do with it; very few of today's under-30 women seem to have the patience for draping a sari, and few of them seem to think it suitable for the speed with which they scurry through their lives. But there's also something less utilitarian about their rejection of the sari for daily wear. Today's younger generation of Indian women seem to associate the garment with an earlier era, a more traditional time when women did not compete on equal terms in a man's world. Putting on pants, or a Western woman's suit, or even desi leggings in the form of a salwar, strikes them as more modern. Freeing their legs to move more briskly than the sari permits, it seems, is a form of liberation; it removes a self-imposed handicap, releasing the wearer from all the cultural assumptions associated with the traditional attire.

Shashi Tharoor, *Sunday Times of India*, March 25, 2007.

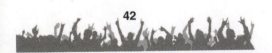

Case Study 4

***Whither Formalism, Fundamentalism or Feminism?***
***Sania Mirza, Sexy Dressing and the Politics of Youth Perception***

by **Surabhi Tiwari**

## Responding to cultural and economic modernity

In the case of the Sania Mirza debate, of course, these questions had to be rephrased, in terms of the problem of how to be individual or young with or without being sexy. There are grounds to believe that one can both be an individual and sexy since as the feminists argue that the body of the individual is owned by him/her, it is up to her/him to decide how the body will be arranged in encounters with the world. Here it is evident that this feminist position is in absolute agreement with a version of liberal possessive individualism. But whether this brave face can be sustained in the context of institutions that are not sexual is the question that is more important. In our FGD this problem got clearly located. While the discussants left the decision about dress to Sania herself, advocating personal freedom of choice when it came to choosing clothes for themselves, they were caught on the wrong foot when the issue of revealing clothes and the images of sex (sexy) could be endorsed and shared in schools as well. The discussants were nearly unanimous that for academic institutions (or institutions which we have been calling asexual) there is a necessity to forge uniformity and not encourage varieties of civil dressing: a dress code in short.

But while institutional codification may be urged in an attempt to distinguish places or institutions which can be eroticised from those which cannot, let us be clear in the Sania Mirza case that such a dress code does not exist. The International Tennis Federation (ITF) the world governing body of tennis in its Change to Dress Code declaration has provisions for arrangement of commercial logos on the dress but is meaningfully silent about the length of the skirt/shorts or whether cultural compatibility of the dress is allowed or not. An interesting point here is that it was Sania Mirza's father who had urged the tennis federation to frame certain rules so that the criticism, and the wrong attention that her revealing dress attracted, might be put to rest. Sania's father got criticised in turn for surrendering to the temptations of the fundamentalists and subsequently got dropped from accompanying Sania to the 2/3 tennis tours that she went following the uproar.

The solution then put forward by a group of formalists that asexual events ought not be eroticised but where there are civil spaces open to erotic taste such a distinction needs to be maintained. This is as it is clear a secular argument loaded with notions of institutional rationality. In the face of such incompatibility, one should desist from finding one correct answer to such problems. Recognizing this one allows disagreement in some form.

That the Sunni ulema who had passed a fatwa on Sania was opposed by the Muslim Personal Law Board of India is a case in point. In a drive to fashion Islamic women according to its norms (patriarchal as the norms are but right in their own terms) a division is borne among the advocates of Islam themselves. Now who is correct in terms of the scriptures? The debate is pending. And isn't the Law Board politically correct on this in 'secular' capitalist India? The answer is handy. It seems that the question of our title 'Whither feminism, fundamentalism or formalism?'—cannot be answered in the obviously singular way as it is expected to; they are all at once and none of them together. But it is still Sania Mirza who has helped the politics of 'dangerous' dressing by becoming a matter of symbolic dressing in today's India. It is the site of her identity- where such other identities (Islamic, formalist etc) are struggling to eke an identity of their own. The feminists are right to harbour a deep-seated anxiety over this.

**Figure 3.16**

**Opinion on consumption of alcohol**

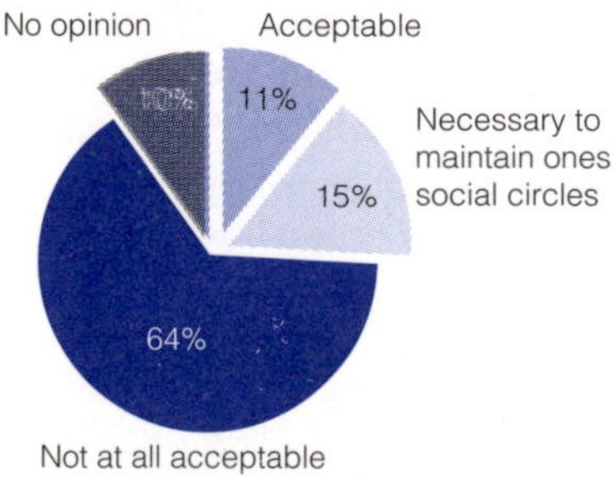


The survey also sought to tap the attitudes of the youth to drinking and alcohol consumption. As many as 64 per cent of the youth feel that alcohol consumption is not at all acceptable. One out of every ten youth said that it is acceptable and 15 per cent felt that it is necessary to maintain one's place in social circles. Another 10 per cent did not express any opinion on the matter *(Figure 3.16)*.

However, it is clear that alcohol consumption is by and large frowned upon by the youth. Gender, educational attainment and place of residence seem to have a great impact on the attitude of the youth towards drinking.

Women seemed to be clearly more opposed to alcohol consumption than young men. Nearly three-fourth of the women said that alcohol consumption is not acceptable to them while just over half the men felt the same way. Two out of every ten young men said that drinking is necessary to maintain one's standing in social circles while only one out of every ten women said the same. The differences between how young men and women viewed liquor consumption reduced significantly in metropolitan areas and among the educated.

Alcohol consumption appears to be more acceptable among the more educated. More than 20 per cent of professional degree holders said that it was acceptable. Further, those living in the cities are more likely to favour alcohol consumption. Nearly 20 per cent of the city youth feel that drinking is necessary to maintain one's status in society and one out of every six urban youth felt that it is acceptable.

The most significant marker in explaining the attitude of the youth to drinking is their educational background. Those with access to education are increasingly convinced that alcohol consumption is necessary to maintain one's status in social circles.

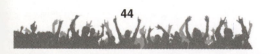

## Summing Up

The above analysis drives home the point that the leisure habits of the youth are linked to multiple factors. They are closely linked to SES, educational levels and place of stay. Television is a crucial source of entertainment and an important leisure activity for most youth, especially among those residing in urban areas and those who are educated. Internet use is largely limited to the cities and almost exclusively among those who have had the benefit of higher education. Wearing fashionable clothes is important for a large segment of the youth and this often reflects an aspiration rather than a fact of life.

There are clear patterns among the Indian youth with regard to their leisure pursuits and lifestyle choices. However, the critical question here is: Which youth is one talking to? On the issues that this study measured, the most crucial variables that delineated clear differences were gender and socio-economic status. Television has clearly become an important leisure activity for many, especially those who are in the younger age group, live in cities and have had the benefit of education. However, it must be stressed that identifying the group of youth that one is talking about helps in defining what constitutes leisure activities. What are considered as leisure activities and tapped in this study do not appear to be the favourite pastimes of many of those living in rural areas and those who have limited access to education and come from lower SES. They too would be pursuing leisure activities, which this survey did not map.

---

### Endnotes

The Leisure Index was prepared by combining the responses to a series of questions. The questions used for preparing the Leisure Index are:

Question No. 3: Now I am going to ask you about activities which people like you do in their spare time. How regularly do you do the following in your spare time—mostly, sometimes or never?

a) Listening to music
b) Going out with friends
c) Watching films
d) Watching television

Question No. 20: Do you use the internet – yes, no or no opinion?

The responses to the above mentioned questions were combined and three broad categories were created:

High: Those who reported engaging in many leisure activities and also reported 'yes' for internet usage were categorised as high.

Moderate: Those who reported sometimes engaging in some leisure activities and, may/may not be using the internet were categorised as moderate.

Low: Those who reported never engaging in leisure activities or engaged sometimes in very few leisure activities and reported as never using the internet were categorised low in the Leisure Index.

EMEMBER BHOP

# CHAPTER 4: POLITICS AND DEMOCRACY

- The level of trust in politics among the youth is reasonably high.
- There is no decline in trust in politics from one generation to the next.
- Youth whose parents are interested in politics show greater interest in politics and vice versa.
- Trust in democracy is reasonably high. This trust is higher among those who have a higher interest in politics.
- Participation in the direct form of politics, i.e. voting is reasonably high among the youth.
- Participation in non-institutional methods of politics (protests, rallies etc.) is also very high.
- Participation in politics (all forms) is higher among youth with higher levels of education.

The last three decades have witnessed immense changes in political, social and economic scenario of the country. In the present times, the youth have witnessed transitions—which include liberalisation, emergence of coalition politics and surfacing of competitive private media with multiple 24×7 news channels. Globally, the era is marked by the emergence of democracy as a pre dominant political form of governance. In such a transitional period, it is interesting to observe the nature of political values and orientation of the Indian youth.

According to the World Development Report 2007, youth interest in politics in the developed countries is on the decline but in countries like India, China and Nigeria; it may actually be on rise. Findings of the survey suggest that the Indian youth show moderate level of interest in politics.

## Interest in Politics

This chapter looks at the interest that the youth show in politics and political activities. In order to find out the level of interest in politics among the youth, an Index of Interest in Politics was formed.[1] This was based on three questions that the respondents were asked during the survey.

As per the findings, 13 per cent of the youth showed a high degree of interest in politics, while 24 per cent showed a moderate level of interest. If we combine both high and moderate interest we get about 37 per cent of the youth with a moderate interest in politics.

> In 2004, in a study titled 'State of Democracy in South Asia' respondents were asked how frequently they discussed politics with friends—a measure generally used globally to determine interest in politics. About 11% of respondents reported discussing politics with friends often and about 43% did so occasionally.

**Figure 4.1**

**Levels of interest in politics**

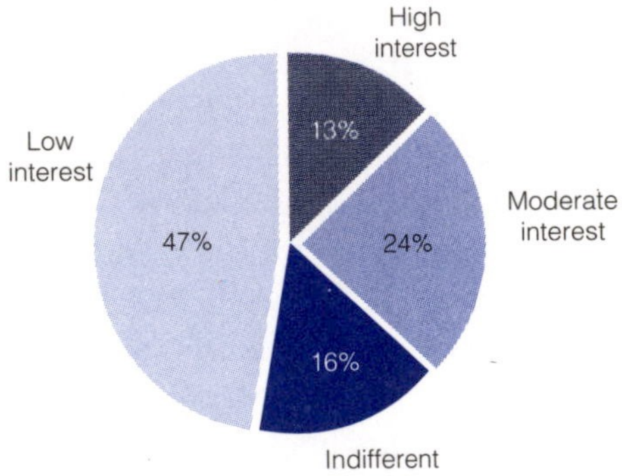


While youth in general show a moderate level of interest in politics, there seem to be some differences in the level of this interest among young men and women.

A majority among the women showed a low level of interest in politics, they are less interested in politics as compared to men. Also a sizeable number among the women showed indifference towards politics.

While there is some difference in the level of interest in politics among those living in rural and urban areas, the difference is not to the extent that may have been expected.

**Figure 4.2**

**Interest in politics by gender**

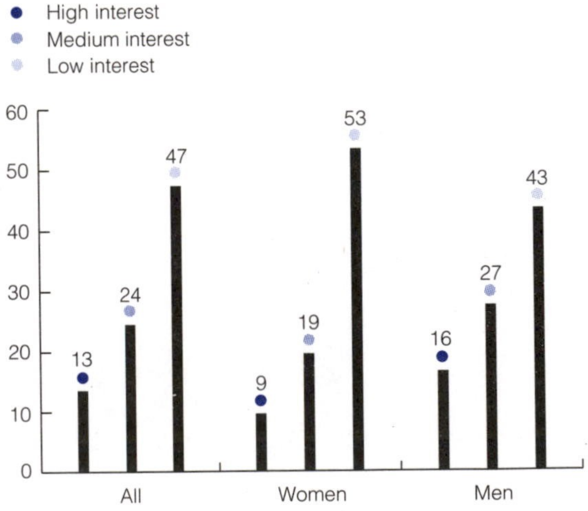


*Note: Rest indifferent.*

**Figure 4.3**

**Interest in politics by locality**

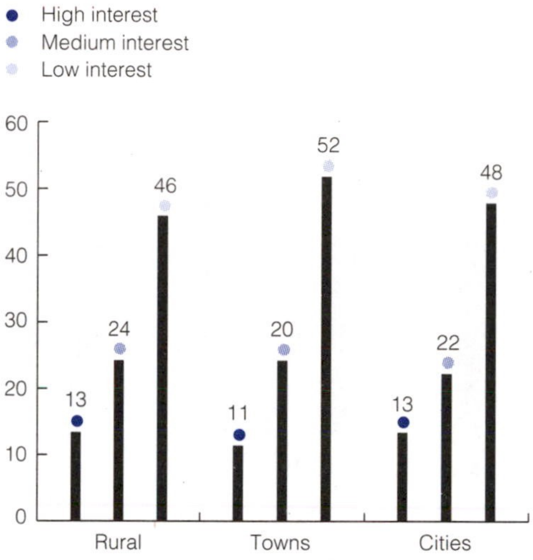


*Note: Rest indifferent.*

There is very little difference among the youth living in villages and in urban areas when it comes to a high level of interest in politics. However the proportion of youth who show a moderate level of interest in politics is higher in villages as compared to those living in urban areas. The youth living in towns and cities show a lower level of interest in politics as compared to those living in villages *(Figure 4.3).*

Education and interest in politics share a direct relationship. Education generates interest in politics and it also acts as what can be called an opinion influencer and greatly reduces indifference towards politics. College educated youth showed greater interest in politics compared to those who are either illiterate or who have not attained higher education. Among those who had completed their college education, 20 per cent showed greater interest in politics while among the illiterate, only

## Nehru Yuva Kendra Sangathans (NYKS)

The Nehru Yuva Kendras were launched in the year 1972 as part of the Silver Jubilee celebration of India's Independence with the objective of providing the non-student rural youth avenues to take part in nation building activities and also to provide opportunity for the development of their own personality and skills. In 1987, Nehru Yuva Kendra Sangathan (NYKS) became an autonomous organisation of the Department of Youth Affairs & Sports under the Ministry of Human Resource Development. Today, it functions under the Ministry of Youth Affairs & Sports. NYKS has a wide network of trained National Service Volunteers (NSVs) numbering about 5000. It has also 6.4 million rural youth volunteers enrolled through 1.81 lakh village level youth clubs.

**Objectives:**

- To form Youth Clubs and involve the youth in nation building activities.
- To develop their values & skills so that they may become responsible and productive citizens of India.
- To act as a catalytic agency in reaching the benefits of Central and State Government Schemes to the rural community in general and the youth in particular.
- To utilize NYKS' large network for development and promotion of programmes in priority sectors such as employment generation, literacy, family welfare, environment conservation, national integration, gender equality and women's empowerment.
- To inculcate in the rural youth the spirit of voluntarism and cooperation.

http://www.youth.nic.in/indexabout.html

7 per cent showed a high level of interest in politics *(Figure 4.4)*.

**Figure 4.4**

**Interest in politics by educational status**

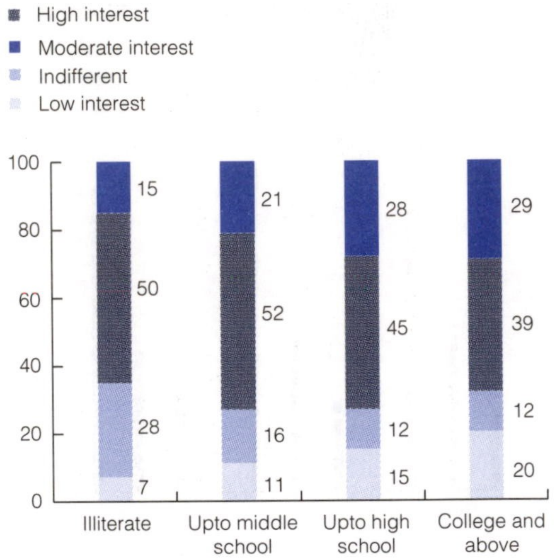


The findings of the survey also suggest that when it comes to interest in politics education has a greater impact on the youth living in villages. Hence, the difference in the level of interest shown by the educated and uneducated youth living in villages is more than the difference in the level of interest among similar categories of youth living in towns.

On the whole women show a lower interest in politics as compared to men. However, educated women showed a higher level of interest in politics as compared to uneducated ones. This applies to young men as well with educated men showing a higher level of interest in politics as compared to the uneducated ones.

The difference among men and women can be seen at the level of higher education as well. The college educated young men have shown a greater level of interest in politics as compared to college educated women. This shows that the difference between men and women when it comes to an interest in politics is maintained across different levels of educational attainment.

## Inter-generational Difference in Interest

During the survey the respondents were asked to assess how interested they thought their parents were in politics. Their responses suggest that about 40 per cent of the youth, in varying degrees, feel that their parents are interested in politics. While 12 per cent believe that they are very interested, about 28 per cent feel that they are somewhat interested in politics and nearly one-third of the respondents feel that their parents are not at all interested in politics *(Figure 4.5)*. If we compare the youth who were themselves interested in politics with those who mentioned that their parents took an interest in politics there is hardly any difference in the proportion. From these findings it can be said that there is hardly any decline in interest in politics among the younger generation.

But there seems to be some differences in this pattern. While the interest that youth show in politics does not vary much across locations, their parents' interest in politics varies across localities. The youth in towns and cities see their parents as more interested in politics as compared

**Figure 4.5**

**Perceptions of youth regarding their parents' interest in politics**

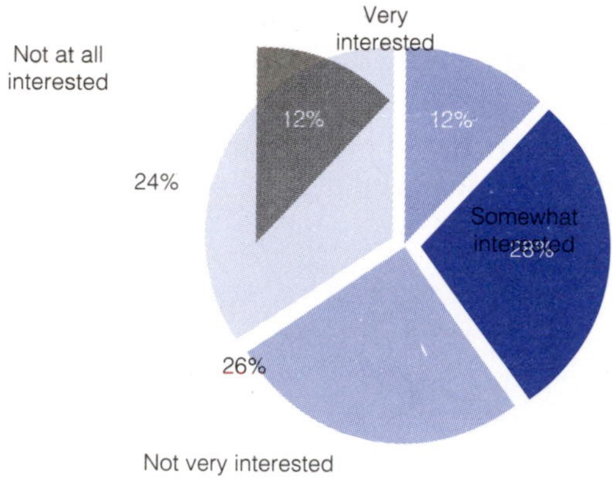


to those living in rural areas *(Figure 4.6)*. While about 37 per cent of the youth in villages feel that their parents are interested in politics, about 48 per cent of those living in cities feel the same. Since personal interest in politics remains constant across localities it may also lead us to say that the transmission of interest from one generation to the next is slightly higher in rural areas than it is in the towns and metros.

**Figure 4.6**

**Parents' interest in politics by locality**

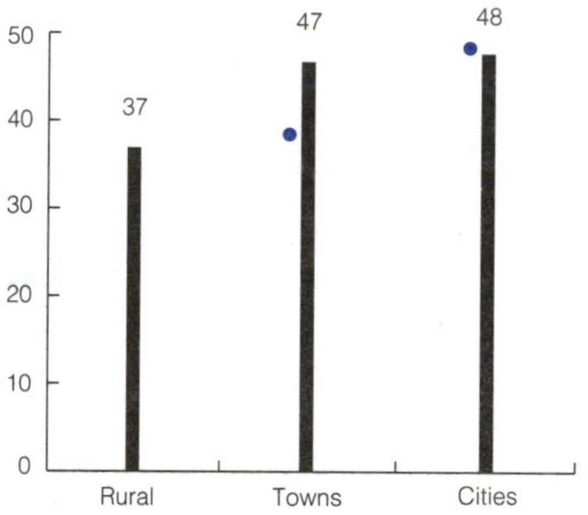


*Note: Parents' interest is the summation of percentage in categories 'very interested' and 'somewhat interested'*

The findings of the survey, however, suggest one difference between the interest that the youth and their parents have in politics. The proportion of parents taking an interest in politics is much higher among those families where the youth too are interested in politics. Conversely, the proportion of parents who are less interested in politics are also those families where the youth either showed an indifferent attitude or were not interested in politics.

**Figure 4.7**

**Interest in politics and belief in democracy**

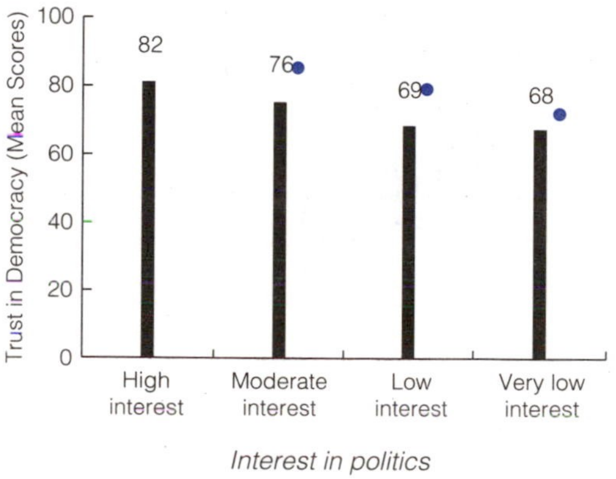


Hence, it can be said that there is a generational transmission of interest in politics. So 62 per cent of those youth whose parents are interested in politics are also found to be interested in politics. Furthermore, among those parents who were not interested in politics, 59 per cent of the youth did not find it interesting.

What these figures suggest is that the transmission of interest in politics from one generation to the next is higher compared to the passing down of lack of interest from one generation to the next. What these figures also indicate is that while interest in politics still remains low, there has been some increase in this interest over two generations as perceived by the youth.

Does interest in politics translate to stronger opinions and ideologies about the various forms of political governance? The answers of the youth suggest that there is a strong correlation between interest in politics and trust in democracy. Among those who have a great deal of interest in politics, the trust for democracy is very high. As levels of interest in politics go down, the trust in democracy also goes down. Interest in politics makes a substantial difference and impacts the support for democracy positively *(Figure 4.7)*.

## Belief in Democracy

India has seen a long journey of popularly elected democratic governments through regular elections ever since its independence. While the country has a record of uninterrupted rule by democratically elected governments, what cannot be said with certainty is that there is popular approval of this form of government as well. The non-fulfillment of promises by successive governments have led a large number of people to believe that democracy is not suitable for delivering goods to the people and that their needs and problems could be addressed better through other forms of government.

While this is what one may think, this is not what the common people of this country believe. This had been repeatedly found out from other surveys conducted by the Centre for the Study of Developing Societies (CSDS). It is true that there is low trust in political parties and elected representatives, but that hardly affects people's trust in the system of democracy. Over the years, people of India have shown a high degree of trust in democracy and rejection for other alternative forms of government whether it is military rule or any other form. With some variations this holds true even now.

The participants were asked a series of questions on the various aspects of democracy. Based on the responses an Index of Belief in Democracy was formed[2]. The index traced the responses from strong to weak belief in democracy.

**Figure 4.8**

**Youth's belief in democracy**

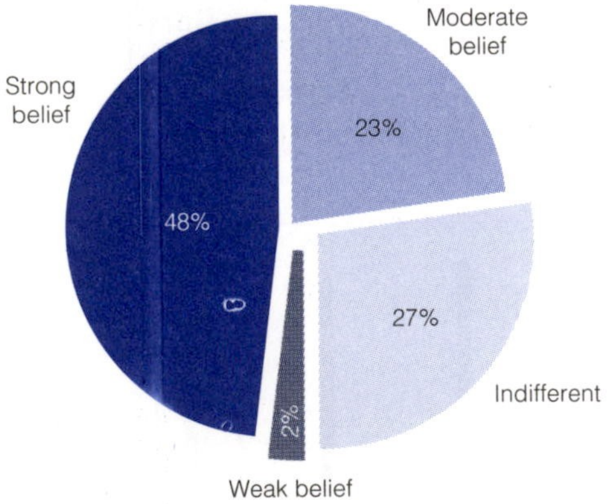

## Case Study 5

### *Regimes of Control: Hindi Films and Political Cultures of Youth in Manipur*

by **Yengkhom Jilangamba**

## Political resistances to new directions in Indian democracy

The development of distinct youth cultures in Manipur, in the course of the twentieth century, in terms of their clothing, hairstyle, taste of music was closely related with the politico-cultural scene of that period. The influence of Hindi as a medium through which many would watch films was directly linked with Manipur's cultural associations with Indic civilisation and its political relationship. The later part of the 1950s and 60s saw the ascendancy of youth into the political scenario of Manipur, at a time when dramatic changes were taking place in terms of reviving and revitalising the political and cultural medium through the deployment of Manipuri language in patriotic songs, Manipuri literature and so on. Within this politicised space, certain features are distinct in the youth of Manipur. They form a visible and forceful presence in the political and social activities and are seen as a formidable force both by the state as well as non-state forces. Within the contemporary militarised political situation in Manipur they are also more susceptible to suspicion and thus seen as a threat to political order. The ban on Hindi films, within the ensuing culture of diktats, and the new interest in Manipuri digital films is closely linked to an attempt by different forces to control and regulate this very youth culture, as well as a testimony to a youth culture of political engagements.

Thus, the transition from celluloid films to the new digital format, which has been fittingly described as the 'digital revolution' in film-making in Manipur has to be understood within the larger socio-politico-economic issues. It is not merely the influence of politics in films or its portrayal but rather it is the film itself and the very act of viewing that has become the terrain on which political spaces are fought for and negotiated.

The most important form of subversi on, by which the 'outside' forces of Hindi films seem to have crept back into Manipur, is however, through the Manipuri films that replaced Bollywood in the theatres in Manipur. The Bollywood influences are seeping into Manipuri digital films to such a large extent that one finds a Manipuri *Devdas* following the success of the Shah Rukh Khan starrer *Devdas*, turning the very logic of the ban on its head. The influences of Hindi films on Manipuri digital films extend to music, costumes, plots and often one has remakes closely mirroring or, if one would prefer, shabbily imitating the Hindi original. Most parties acknowledge that despite the ban on Hindi films, channels and music, a complete eradication of these films in Manipur is impossible. They serve as subversive activities in lieu of political protests, a form of social resistance in the everyday form, rather than outward political participation.

The youth culture of Manipur, on close observation, reveals itself to be simultaneously controlled and restrictive with dictatorial impulses on the one hand, and politically active and subversive on the other. A direct opinion on the question of the ban on Hindi films in Manipur has been difficult to needle out of the average youth on the street. As a fall out of a long experience of conflict, suspicion seeps into the consciousness of the people in everyday life. Looking for a direct perception, sentiment, or a political position on a specific issue is likely to be a non-starter in any 'serious' research-oriented conversation. A 'normal' conversation, however, is replete with anger, dissatisfaction and defiance.

But within the context of Manipur, it has as its backdrop, an increasing and omnipresent threat of violence in the conflict between the state and non-state armed groups. In such a situation, one witnessed a more assertive identity politics encompassing both the larger politics of Manipur and the cultural patterns of its everyday. This marked the period in which ban on Hindi films came about, and has to be thus seen within this context. Films are also seen to be a form of 'acquiring' modernity for the youth in Manipur. What they see in modernised cultures of the 'other', be it English, Korean or Bollywood add to the visual assurance of a young Manipur 'catching up' with the world of modernity. Acquiring consumer goods and new information become a means of entering modernity. The offshore location, in an obvious borrowing from Bollywood, is increasingly becoming a trend in Manipuri digital films. The addition of foreign locales, especially in song sequences within the film adds to the flavour of visually defined modernity, that Manipur is yet to reach. These are, perhaps, some of the reasons why young Manipuris are more receptive to 'outside' culture. The influx of Indian' culture and the increasing tendency of young Manipuris to travel outside the state for work or study have also created channels of mobility of culture.

From the composite index on belief in democracy, it can be seen that a little less than half (48 per cent) of the youth seem to have a strong belief in democracy. A little less than one-fourth (23 per cent) have a moderate degree of belief in democracy. Nearly 2 per cent have showed a weak belief in democracy while 27 per cent seem to be indifferent *(Figure 4.8)*.

**Figure 4.9**

**Belief in democracy by locality**

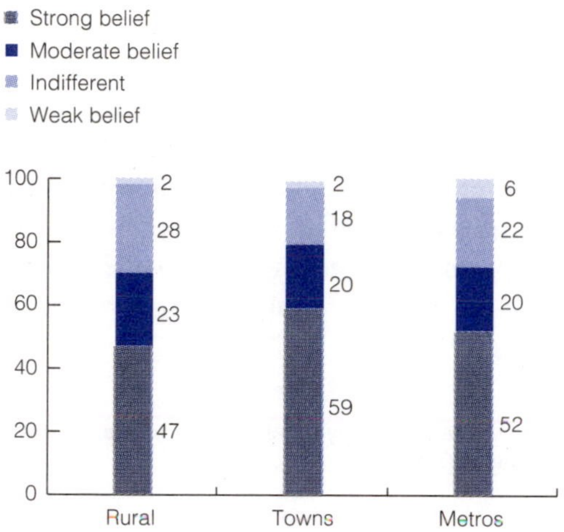


The findings of the survey suggest that the trust in democracy is higher among the youth living in small towns and cities compared to those living in villages. In the rural areas large proportions of youth showed indifference towards democracy *(Figure 4.9)*.

Gender and age do not seem to have any effect on the level of trust in democracy. Young men and women have shown a more or less equal trust in democracy, as do the youth from different age groups. However, this level of trust varies significantly across youth with different levels of educational attainment and media exposure. The higher the level of education, the greater is the trust in democracy.

A similar relationship exists between media exposure and belief in democracy. The greater the exposure to the media, the higher is the level of belief in democracy. Among those who figure high on media exposure, 83 per cent have shown trust in democracy while among those with low levels of media exposure, a little more than the majority (57 per cent) has expressed trust in democracy. Exposure to the media leads to support for democracy and along with education, it seems to act as a positive opinion generation tool for democracy *(Figure 4.10)*.

**Figure 4.10**

**Belief in democracy and media exposure**

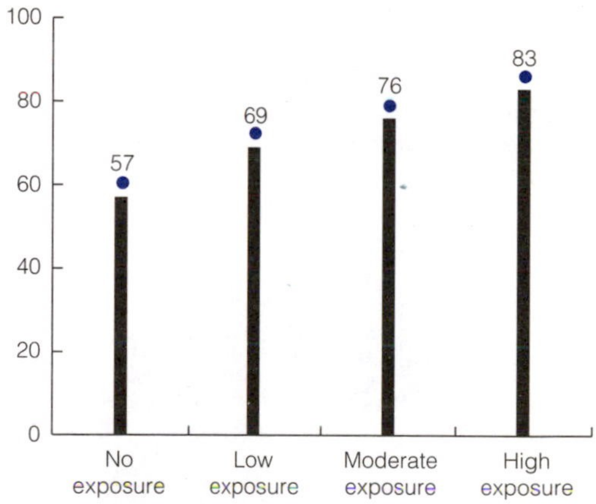


## Elements of Democracy

The youth have a strong belief in democracy mainly because they attach importance to the different elements of democracy. They attach a great deal of importance to political parties.

**Figure 4.11**

**Political parties are necessary in a democracy**

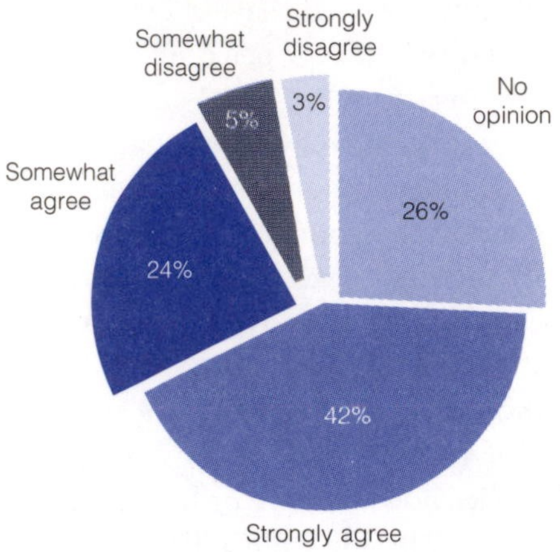


More than two-third of the youth in varying degrees agree that political parties are necessary for democracy against only 8 per cent holding a different opinion on the issue of importance of political parties for democracy. One-fourth of the youth did not express any opinion on this issue *(Figure 4.11)*.

The youth also attach importance to political opposition. On the question of the importance of political opposition for democracy, more than one-third of the youth have strongly reaffirmed this view while another one-fourth have also supported this view but somewhat moderately. The opposition to this view is found to be negligible. On the whole, 62 per cent of the youth recognise the importance of opposition for democracy with only 9 per cent being opposed to this view. Another 29 per cent did not express any opinion *(Figure 4.12)*.

While this opinion is shared by the youth across localities, opposition to this opinion is somewhat higher among urban youth as compared to those living in villages.

**Figure 4.12**

**A viable democracy is not possible without political opposition**

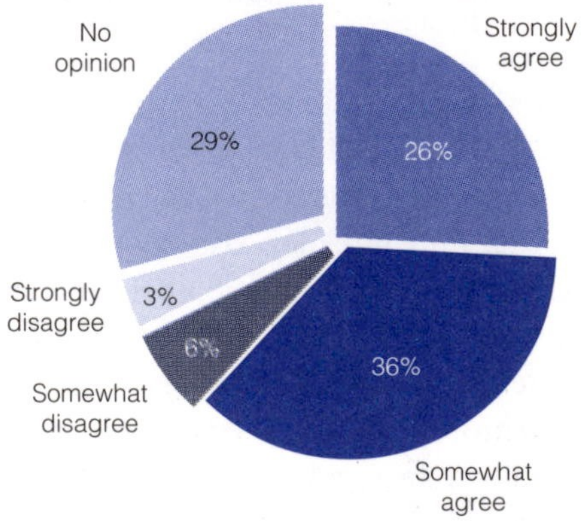


**Figure 4.13**

**Every one should have the right to express his/her opinion even though the majority have a different opinion**

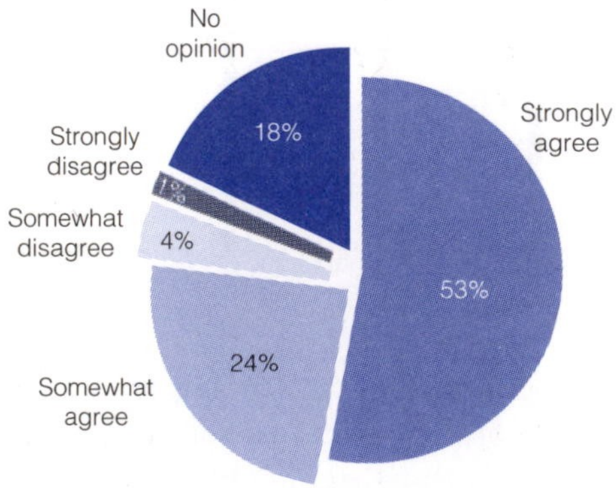


A majority of the youth strongly supports the view that everyone should have the right to express his/her views without fear while another one-fourth showed mild support for this view *(Figure 4.13)*. While there is not much difference in opinion on this issue among different religious groups, some slight differences surface when it comes to levels of educational attainment. The educated youth disagree with this view much more as compared to the uneducated youth. The higher the level of educational attainment, greater is the disagreement with this view.

A majority of the youth strongly believe that it is a citizen's duty to vote in every election. Only a small proportion (4 per cent) believes in the opposite while 10 per cent does not express any views on this issue *(Figure 4.14)*. Differences, however, come up when one considers the level of education, place of residence and SES. There are differences of opinion in terms of youth with different levels of educational attainment. More educated youth tend to believe that it is their duty to vote in every election as compared to those who are illiterate. Similarly, youth living in urban locations tend to agree more that it is citizen's duty to vote in every election as compared to those living in the rural areas. We find a similar pattern in youth belonging to different economic backgrounds. Youth from rich and middle class backgrounds tend to agree more with this view compared to those coming from families with low income.

**Figure 4.14**

**It is citizens' duty to vote during elections**

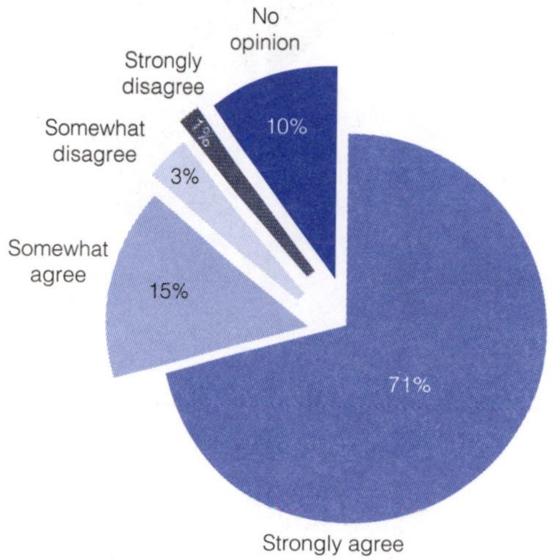


## Participation in Politics

The belief in democracy among the youth also translates into a moderately high number of them voting during elections. Among those eligible for voting, a little more than two-third said that they had either voted in all the elections or in most of the elections. There is also not much variation in the pattern of voting across different social brackets.

> As compared to the youth the general population attaches a greater importance to the act of voting. A survey conducted in 2004 for the SDSA Study showed that in India while 68% of the population had voted in every election and about 19% voted in most of the elections, only about 2% of the population are extremely irregular voters i.e. they had hardly ever voted.

The high interest in voting could be a result of an overwhelming sense of duty that the youth claim to feel about casting their votes. About 85 per cent of the youth agree that it is every citizen's duty to vote during elections. It is important to note that while 80 per cent of the youth who have completed college education strongly agree that it is a citizen's duty to vote about 55 per cent of the non-literates too agree with this thinking.

**Figure 4.15**

**Voting behaviour among the youth**

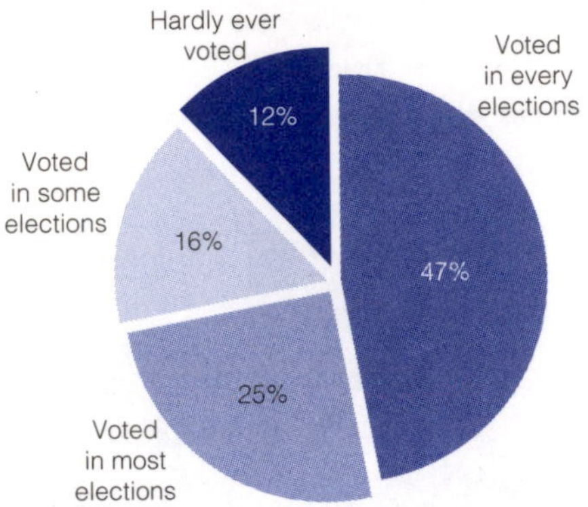


However this is not to say that the non-literates don't consider it to be their duty but they claim to hold no opinion on this matter. As far as the practice of voting is concerned there is no substantive difference among the youth having very varied levels of education on this matter. In fact the non-literates and lesser-educated are slightly better voters then college educated and above *(Figure 4.16)*.

**Figure 4.16**

**Voting behaviour by locality**

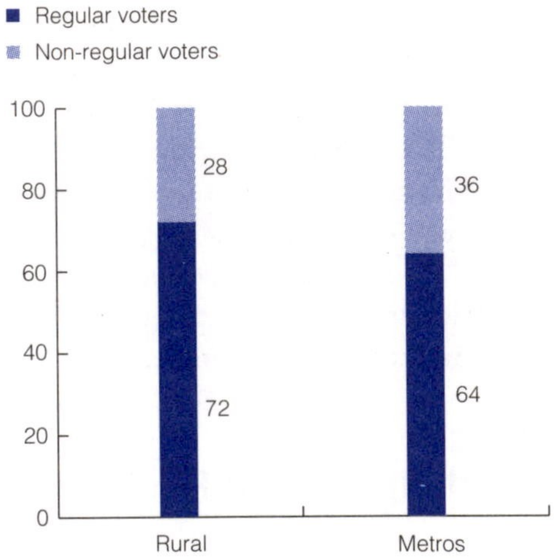


*Note: Regular voters are those who have voted in every election or those who have voted in most elections*

About 66 per cent of the youth feel that their vote makes a difference on how things are run in this country. However, voter turnout among the youth is slightly less than what is observed during the general population. This could be because of pessimism towards the system among the youth.

As per the findings of the survey, 53 per cent of those interested in politics said that they had voted in every election, while this figure was 44 per cent among those who said that they were not interested in politics. The percentage of those who have voted in every election is much lower among those youth who showed indifference towards politics. Further, the number of those who have hardly voted or never voted is higher among those who either have no interest in politics or who show indifference towards it *(Figure 4.17)*.

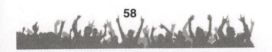

**Figure 4.17**

**Interest in politics and voting**

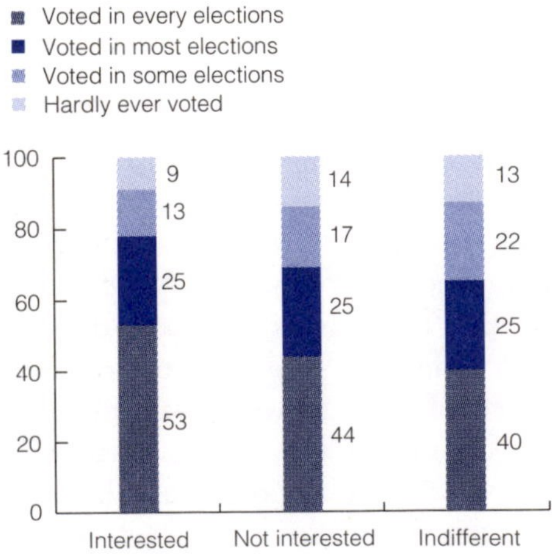

## Participation in Indirect Politics: Participation in Political Protest

The youth showed a high degree of participation in political protest with the findings of the survey suggesting that about one-fifth of the youth had participated in protests, rallies or demonstrations. But the pattern of participation in the non-formal political process doest not remain uniform across various SES groups.

There is a significant difference between how young men and women perceive participation in non-institutional forms of democracy/protests. Among the men, 30 per cent said that they had participated in protest rallies while this figure is just 12 per cent among the women.

> The general population of the country seems more optimistic about their vote making a difference in the governance of the country.
>
> In the National Election Study 2004, 17% of the population felt that their vote did not make any difference. This number has almost remained constant over the years. In 1971, in a similar study, about 16% of respondents felt that their vote did not make any difference. This number rose to 21% in 1998 and then stabilised at 17% in 1999 and 2004.
>
> However, there is a heightened sense of cynicism among the youth, in the present survey about 34% of the young generation feels that their vote does not make any difference in the way things are run in the country.

> As compared to the general population, the youth seem to be considerably more politically active. In the SDSA cross sectional study, about 13% of the population claimed to have participated in some protest, rally or demonstration as against 21% of respondents in this survey.

Education seems to have a positive effect on different forms of non-institutional participation among the youth. The higher the level of education, the greater is the participation in political protests. Hence, while only 11 per cent of the uneducated youth said that they had participated in political protests, 35 per cent among those who had completed college education said that they had participated in political protests. There is a gradual increase in the level of participation with increase in educational levels. This participation increases dramatically among those who have completed college education. Colleges and universities therefore seem to be emerging as catalysts for political participation among the youth *(Figure 4.18)*. The youth living in villages and urban areas exhibit different levels of participation in protest movements, but this

**Figure 4.18**

**Participation in political protest by education**

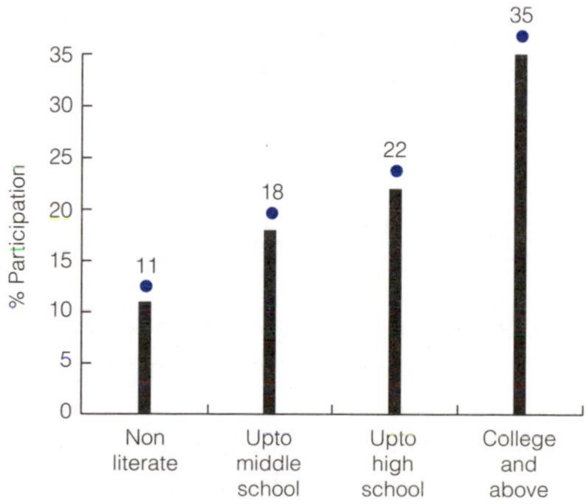

**Figure 4.19**

**Participation in politictal protest by locality**

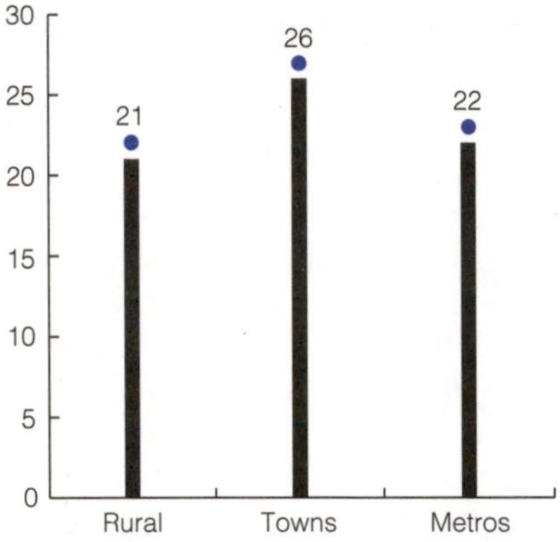


difference is not to the extent that may have been expected. Twenty-one per cent of the youth living in villages said that they had participated in political protests, while 26 per cent of those living in cities said that they had participated in political protests. Further, the percentage of those living in bigger cities was lower as compared to those living in small towns *(Figure 4.19).*

A strong correlation was found between participation in protest movements and interest in politics. Participation in non-formal methods of politics is higher among those who have a higher level of interest in politics while this participation is much lower among those who have a low level of interest in politics and those who are indifferent to the political process. Among those interested in politics, 56 per cent have stated that they had participated in political protests.

Media exposure too is seen to be directly linked to participation in protest movements. The higher the level of media exposure, the greater is the participation in protest movements. Among youth with low media exposure only 19 per cent said that they had participated in political protests. On the other hand, this figure is 31 per cent among those with higher levels of media exposure.

**Figure 4.20**

**Trust in institutions**

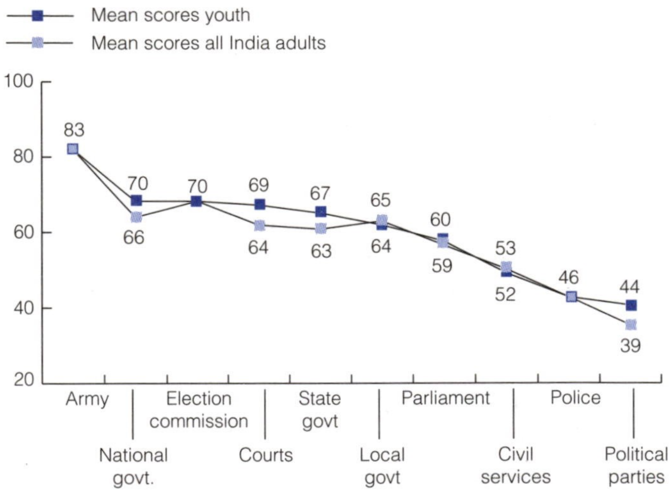


## Trust in Institutions

During the survey, the participants were also asked questions about the trust that they have in various institutions. The army emerged as the most trusted institution followed by the national government and the election commission with the judiciary just being marginally behind. The long drawn out judicial process does not seem to be adversely affecting the image of the judiciary in the eyes of the youth.

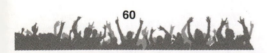

Case Study 6

***Spheres of Rage: Understanding Dalit Youth in Maharashtra***

by **Gopal Guru**

## Political resistances to new directions in Indian democracy

In contemporary times dalit youth, particularly from urban Maharashtra, seem to be articulating their rage primarily against the state. This is something, which is different from the Dalit Panther movement which expressed its rage primarily against the twice born civil society (TBCS). During the early 1970s, the state provided the Dalit Panther activist a potent patronage system that made him/her jump around the structures of patronage such as the social welfare ministry, directorate of social welfare, various SC/ST development corporations, created by the state government from time to time as part of their tokenism. This capacity of the state to keep dalit youth busy with such structures of patronage offered some space to dalit youth to take on the TBCS. The question today then is why are dalit youth against the state and not so much against civil society. It is because the state is losing its capacity to keep the youth from the fuzzy sphere built around the structures of patronage. The continuous withdrawal of the state from the sphere of welfare has made the opportunity structures less attractive as far as dalits are concerned. In fact this growing disenchantment with the state is reflected in the rage that is expressed by the youth from urban slums. Today it is the urban slum dwelling dalit youth who are active in expressing rage in a way that they do. This is because the sense of cultural injustice among the slum dwelling dalit is so deep that even the educated employed dalit youth sought to protest against the Khairlanji killing of dalits. Of course the Khairlanji tragedy (where a family of dalits was brutally killed) provided an immediate cause to the articulation of an accumulated anger of dalit youth from the slum. They seem to have contained within themselves a sizzling smoldering sense of rage which like hydraulic water gushed out and started overflowing in the context of the Khairlanji tragedy. This overflow of anger was basically directed against the state primarily because, dalit thought the state failed in providing the dalit youth any concrete assistance in overcoming everyday forms of embarrassment that necessarily result from the saturated life of slums. It is normally noticed that young dalit male and female share the same space for defecating. Ironically, the compression of space has led to 'democracy in defecation'! This is not to suggest that the state government is not doing anything but it is not doing enough. Of course Ratnakar Gaikwad has done something to overcome this embarrassment. The dalit youth from the slums in Pune, Mumbai and Nasik expressed their anger against this public embarrassment by trashing government property. It could be argued that the protest of dalit youth against the tragic events like Khairlanji, is the culmination of anger against everyday forms of embarrassment that dalit youth face in the urban slums. It is the subhuman conditions that force dalit youth to go for action and let loose their anger against the state. Historically speaking, the slums have been the source of dalit rage that was evident in the Warli riots of 1972, to Ramabai Nagar in 1997, to Khairlanji in 2007. The compounded forms of suppression—the emotional, psychological, social, cultural, and material leads to the outburst of anger. Youth for equality protest against the state on the ground that they find the state limiting their sphere of equality. Dalit youth from the slum on the contrary fight for minimum guarantee for decency not for themselves but for the entire dalit community.

The objective incapacity of the state to offer any concrete promises to dalits has led them to look for other avenues of engagement. It is interesting to note that these youth who are shut out from the opportunity structure find dalit political groups in the state no longer attractive in terms of eking out "meaning" for themselves. Today a common dalit does not require a dalit political platform or a conduit to connect to the patronage system controlled by the dominant castes. Now, a common dalit can straight a way bargain with mainstream parties and they do not require a middle man. The nature of electoral politics has pushed the dalit youth into a morally uncomfortable zone of instrumentalism. The dalit youth, which is now inclined to instrumentalism, forms the conceptual basis of the fuzzy sphere that we have been talking about. This kind of instrumentalism seems to have freed dalit youth from the ideological commitment to principled politics that kept them away from the Hindutva politics all these years. The compelling sense of instrumentalism among the dalit youth seems to indicate that the politics of discourse as visualised by Ambedkar is losing its hold. Conversely, discourse of real politics seems to have acquired a firm hold on the political imagination of dalit youth not only in Maharashtra but more recently in UP too.

Political parties and the police are the least trusted institutions *(Figure 4.20)*. Though a large number of the educated youth aspire to join the Indian civil services, it is surprising that the level of trust shown for the civil services is very low. The popular notion of civil servants being corrupt seems to reflect the low level of trust in the Indian civil service.

## Summing Up

On the basis of the findings of the survey it can be concluded that the youth in India defy the global trend of declining interest in politics. The Indian youth not only show a high level of interest in politics, but what is also important is that there is no decline in this interest across generations. There is a reasonably high level of participation in all forms of politics—direct, indirect, formal or non-formal—as well among the youth. The trust in democracy is also high.

The youth do no seem to be very different from the general population when it comes to expressing opinions about politics and democracy. The few variations that exist are more a result of the level of educational attainment among the youth. Education seems to be an instrument of building opinion at least among the youth, as educated youth show greater trust in democracy compared to those who do not have the benefits of education. Media exposure, which is also an offshoot of educational attainment, has also resulted in the crystallisation of opinions among the youth.

---

## Endnotes

1. Political Interest Index:
   The Index was created by combining a number of variables which are as follows:

   Q14b: Now I am going to read out few things, you tell me how important are they for you—
   Are they very important, somewhat important, somewhat unimportant, or not important at all?

   Q35: Now I am going to read out a few statements about peoples' opinion about politics. For each of them you tell me, whether you agree or disagree:

   d. I find understanding politics too complicated
   f. I find politics interesting

   Respondents who held No Opinion were placed into a middle category. The values of each of these questions were converted into standardised scores or Z Scores and the standardised values of each question were added up. The variance achieved was then divided by 4 to create categories:

   High Interest in Politics
   Moderate Interest in Politics
   Indifferent
   Low Interest in Politics

2. The Index of belief in democracy was created by combining the following variables:

   Q35: Now I am going to read out a few statements about peoples' opinion about politics. For each of them you tell me, whether you agree or disagree:
   a. Political parties are necessary in a democracy
   c. It is a citizens' duty to vote during elections

   Q51: I am going to read out a few statements. Tell me, whether you agree or disagree.
   A viable democracy is not possible without political opposition.

   a. Everyone should have the right to express their opinion, even if the majority is of a different opinion.
   b. Respondents who held 'No Opinion' were placed into a middle category.

   The values of each of these questions were converted into standardised scores or Z Scores and the standardised values of each question were added up. The variance achieved was then divided by 4 to create categories:

   High trust
   Moderate trust
   Indifferent
   Low trust

# CHAPTER 5: GOVERNANCE AND DEVELOPMENT

- The youth consider unemployment and poverty to be the biggest problems confronting the country.
- Youth in metropolitan cities are more likely to describe unemployment as the biggest problem than those living in villages.
- Illiterate youth and those belonging to Dalit and Tribal communities are more concerned about poverty than others.
- The youth have mixed opinions about the performance of the government when it comes to providing educational facilities.
- Among employment, health and education, the youth consider employment as the topmost priority of the government.
- Among health related problems, combating HIV/AIDS was the first priority for the youth.
- The youth overwhelmingly support reservation for women in Parliament and State Legislatures.

The major problems facing India are those found in most developing countries, like unemployment, poverty, illiteracy, high mortality rate and high growth rate of population. These are the problems that are generally perceived as being urgent and serious. Successive governments have underscored these as top priority. However despite various governments focussing on these problems, they continue to defy all the programmes and strategies aimed at alleviating them. India's continued low position in terms of human development, compared to a number of developing countries, which is largely due to the persistence of these problems, in a sense, signals the 'governance/ policy failure' of the Indian state. How do the youth, the segment of population worst hit by these problems, take on such issues? This chapter seeks to examine and address the following questions:

How do the youth view socio-economic problems on the 'importance scale'?
What according to them are the problems that the government should give top priority to?
How far do the youth support policies aimed at ensuring social equality and justice?

## Major Problems as Identified by the Youth

Unemployment and poverty are the two biggest problems identified by the youth. A majority of Indian youth (54 per cent) identified unemployment and poverty as the biggest problems facing the country. The least important problems as identified by the youth are corruption, illiteracy and terrorism *(Figure 5.1)*.

Youth living in the cities and in villages express different views when it comes to unemployment. About 25 per cent of the youth living in metros cited unemployment as a problem as compared to 29 per cent in rural areas.

**Figure 5.1**

**Major problems identified by the youth**

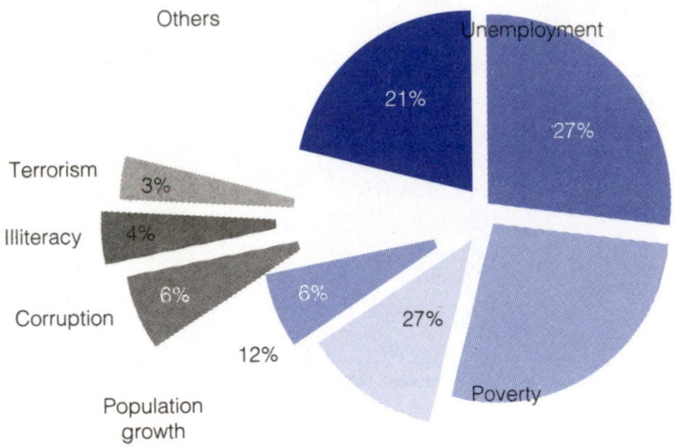


> According to National Human Development Report 2002, about 2.3 per cent of the labour force (population above 15 years) was unemployed during 1999-2000. The incidence of unemployment in urban India (4.8 per cent) was much higher than in rural areas (1.5 per cent). In 1991, the International Commission on Peace and Food in its report, stated that India needed to create 10 million jobs every year for the next 10 years to provide employment to all the job seekers.
>
> Based on an estimate, the unemployment rate among Indian youth (aged 15-24 years) was as high as 10.1 per cent in 2001 as against 9.2, 8.1 and 3.1 per cent for Japan, Germany and China respectively. [Source: United Nations Statistics Division]

It was seen that the educational background of the youth does not make a difference to the perceptions that they have about unemployment. This study clearly shows that the entire labour force, whether illiterate or well educated considers unemployment as a big problem facing the country.

Poverty was cited by most of the youth as another important problem facing the country. It is seen that irrespective of place of residence, the youth share a more or less equal perception of poverty as a major problem. Those living in towns and villages are categorical in identifying poverty as a major problem. In fact, the youth living in towns attach equal importance to poverty and unemployment. However, among those living in metros, unemployment seems to be a bigger concern as compared to poverty.

Rapidly increasing population was seen as a major problem by 12 per cent of the youth. There are differences in the level of importance attached to this problem among those living in cities and in villages. The youth living in metros consider population growth as a bigger problem as compared to those living in villages and small towns *(Figure 5.2)*.

While unemployment, poverty and population growth have emerged as the three biggest concerns amongst the youth, there are differences in the priority accorded to them in relation to the respondents' educational background. For the illiterate youth, poverty is a much bigger problem as compared to unemployment and for those who have some formal education or who have completed their college education, it is unemployment, which is seen as a bigger problem. About 39 per cent of the illiterate youth, as opposed to 16 per cent of those who have attained higher education said that poverty is the biggest national problem.

**Figure 5.2**

**Youth's perception of national problems by locality**

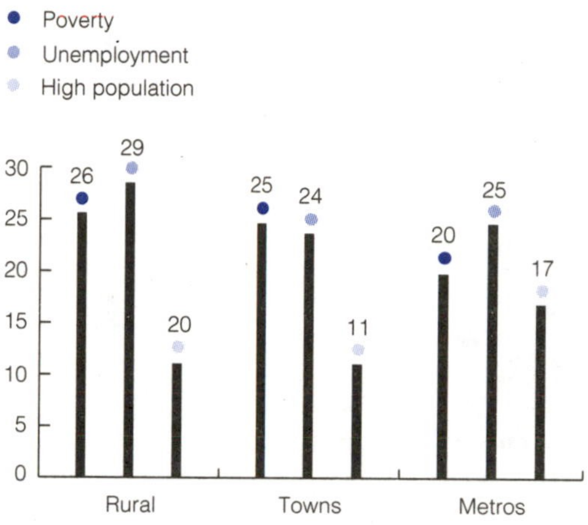


Further, though 12 per cent of the youth consider population growth as the biggest problem, the priority given to this also depends on educational attainment. Those who are educated are more likely to consider population growth as a big problem as compared to the uneducated *(Figure 5.3)*.

An interesting finding of the survey is that cumulative figures for illiteracy and lack of educational facilities find the weakest resonance among the youth who are not literate. The higher the level of educational attainment, the higher is the articulation of lack of education and illiteracy as national problem.

With such a prevailing scenario about unemployment, it is not surprising to note that 27 per cent of the youth considered unemployment as the biggest problem of this country.

**Figure 5.3**

**Educated and uneducated both identify poverty and employment as biggest problems of the nation**

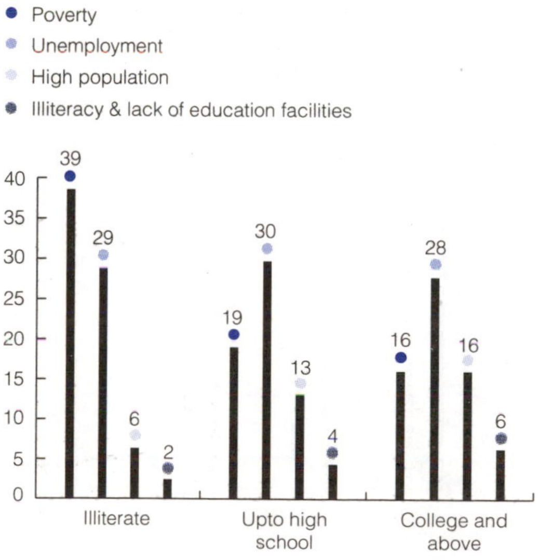

Sharp differences emerge when it comes to caste and the priority accorded to different problems facing the country. Findings from various other research and government data indicate that people from some communities, especially Dalits and Adivasis, experience poverty in a greater degree as compared to those from the upper castes.

The findings of this survey also suggest that more Dalit and Adivasi youth consider poverty as the biggest problem facing the country. Amongst the upper castes, only 21 per cent consider poverty as the biggest problem while this figure is 30 per cent among Dalit youth. Though there are shades of differences, the youth from all social communities seem equally concerned about the problem of unemployment.

According to National Human Development Report 2002, about 26 per cent of the population lived below the poverty line during 1999-2000. In the Global Hunger Index of the International Food Policy Research, India is placed in the bottom fourth of the world's nations, with a rank of 94 among 118 countries, which is far below China's 47 and even lower than Pakistan's 88.

Furthermore, poverty ratios vary a great deal by regions, socio-religious community and also by rural-urban backgrounds.

**Figure 5.4**

**Youth's perception of national problems by caste**

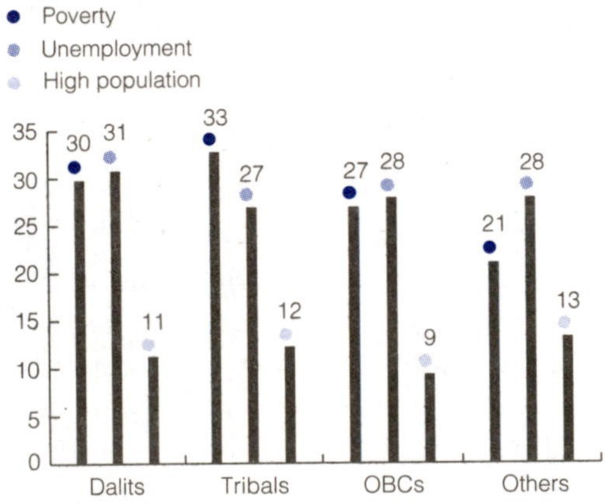


The perception of youth regarding how they prioritise various problems changes according to their SES. For those, who have a very low SES, poverty seems to be the biggest problem, but for those from high in come and high social status families, it is unemployment, which is the biggest problem.

Even the youth from middle SES families, consider unemployment as a bigger problem compared to poverty or high population. The youth from low SES families attach maximum importance to poverty as the most important problem facing this country. Youth from the middle and high SES families attach more importance to increasing population as compared to those from the lower or poor income families. Among the youth from high SES families, 14 per cent considered population growth as the biggest problem compared to only 7 per cent among those with very low SES *(Figure 5.5)*.

**Figure 5.5**

**Youth's perception of national problems by caste**

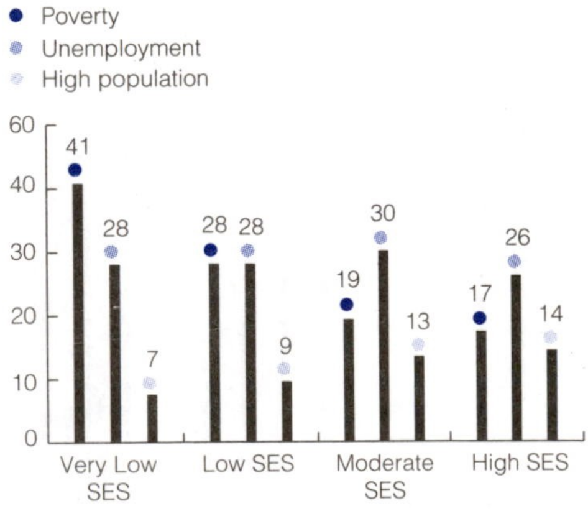

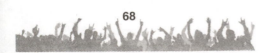

While there has been a growing realisation that corruption is eating into the delivery system of public goods and services and halting the progress of the country, only 6 per cent among the youth consider this to be the biggest problem.

What is even more surprising is that despite high levels of illiteracy and glaring lack of educational facilities, only a miniscule proportion of the youth (4 per cent) express concern about it. Similarly, despite considerable media focus on terrorism and the toll it is taking on human lives, only 3 per cent of the youth consider it as the biggest problem facing the country.

These responses offer two conclusions. Firstly, that corruption and incidents of terrorism are so commonplace that people have learnt to live with them, and secondly, that concerns about poverty and unemployment are so overwhelming that all other issues move to the background.

## Mixed Opinion on the Performance of the Government

Two problems were picked up to find out the views of the youth on the performance of the government: 1) the level of educational facilities available 2) what should be the priority of the government-education, employment or health.

On the first issue, a clear majority of the youth expressed their satisfaction with the available educational facilities.

**Figure 5.6**

**Satisfaction with existing educational facilities by locality**

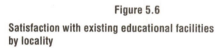

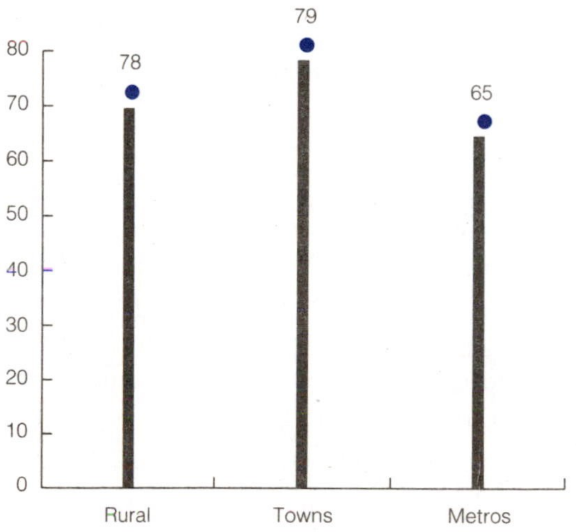


In response to the second question, a majority said that employment should be the first priority of the government, followed by education and finally health. Clearly, employment seems to be the biggest concern amongst the youth as compared to any other issue.

When it comes to satisfaction with the availability of educational facilities, an interesting finding of the survey is that there is a difference in the satisfaction levels between those living in rural areas and those living in urban areas. Even though the distribution of educational facilities and resources is skewed in favour of towns and cities, it is the youth in these two locations who are less satisfied. This can perhaps be explained by the fact that the expectations of the youth are comparatively higher in the urban areas and the existing facilities do not match these expectations.

On the other hand, the demand for education is quite low in the rural areas and therefore perhaps are the expectations of the youth living in these areas. Hence, they are content with whatever facilities are available *(Figure 5.6)*.

Though it is only a small percentage of the youth who consider terrorism to be the biggest problem facing the country, this does not mean that they are satisfied with the way terrorism is being handled by the government. About 35 per cent of the youth feel that the government has failed to curb terrorism, while about 40 per cent have expressed their satisfaction with whatever efforts the government is undertaking for handling this issue *(Figure 5.7)*. However, what is interesting to note is that about 54 per cent of the youth feel insecure about global terrorism.

**Figure 5.7**

**Opinion on government's handling of terrorism**

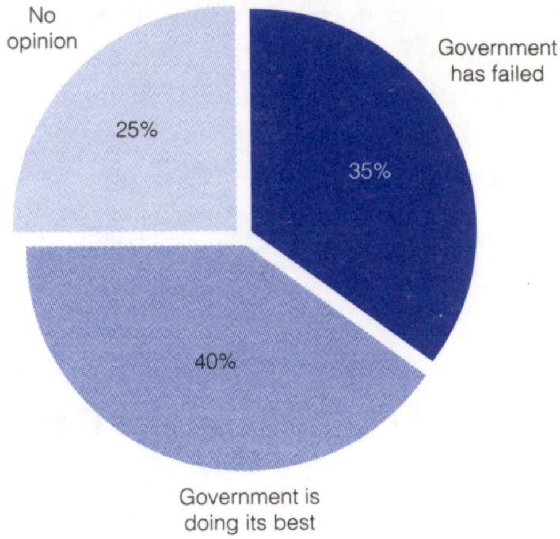


Since urban areas, especially big cities and towns, witness more terrorist activities, the youth living in these two areas express greater concern about terrorism and are more critical of the government's efforts to deal with the issue as compared to those living in the rural areas *(Figure 5.8)*.

**Figure 5.8**

**Opinion on handling of terrorism by locality**

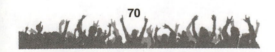

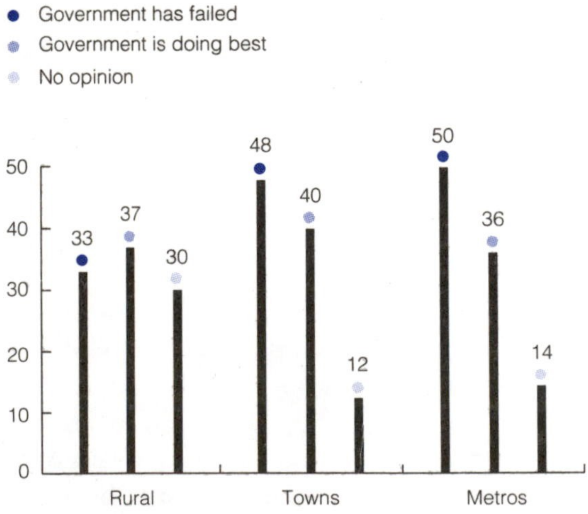


Though the opinion of the youth is divided about whether terrorism is the result of the failure of the government or not, the findings of the survey suggest that there is hardly any difference of opinion among the young followers of Hinduism and Islam. A little more than one third of the youth, both among the Hindus and Muslims, blame the government for terrorist activities in India. They share a common view that terrorism is the result of the failure of the government. A similar proportion of youth across communities (Hindu/Muslim) also believe that government is doing its best to control terrorism. *(Figure 5.9)*.

## Hierarchy of Priorities

Figure 5.9

**Opinion by religion on government's handling of terrorism**

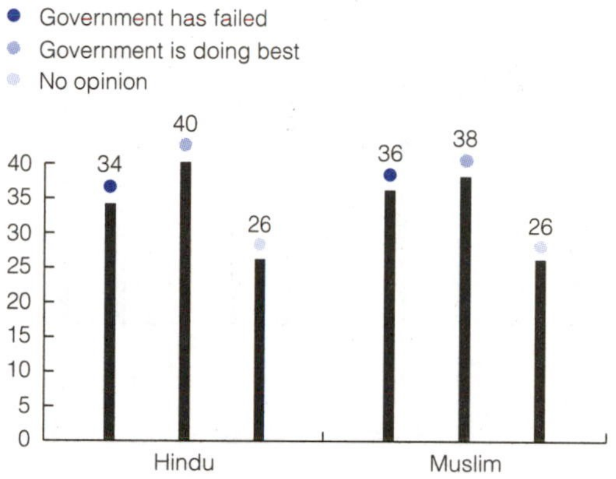


The survey also sought the opinion of the youth on how the government should prioritise a number of other important problems. Among these problems is the lack of educational facilities, the spread of HIV, poor maternal health and a considerably high child mortality rate. Given that the list of problems is large, they were divided into sets of three for the level of priority that the government should accord to these issues.

The first set related to employment, education and health, the second set included issues relating to tackling HIV/AIDS, improving maternal health and reducing child mortality and the third set dealt with greater gender equality, strengthening the defence system and maintaining a sustainable environment.

Unemployment rate among Indian youth is higher than the youth in many other countries. In 2001, the unemployment rate among the Indian youth was estimated to be around 10 per cent as against 3.1 per cent in China, 8.3 per cent in Germany and 9.2 per cent in Japan. (Source: United Nation Statistics Division:http://unstats.un.org/unsd/cdb/cdb_dict)

Overall, the youth prefer the generation and guarantee of employment as the first priority for the nation, followed by provision of good educational and health facilities *(Figure 5.10)*.

Some of the reasons for the youth marking employment as the country's first priority include, firstly by the time a person turns 15, he/she is more likely to discontinue education and hence become available for work, secondly many would like to settle down financially as early as possible and for that they need jobs. Statistics show that the unemployment rate is the highest among the youth. Therefore, the anxiety of getting employment dominates their minds.

After employment, the next most important priority according to the youth is provision of educational opportunities. This reflects an increasing demand for education and endorses the widely held view that better employment

Figure 5.10

**What should be the first priority of the government?**

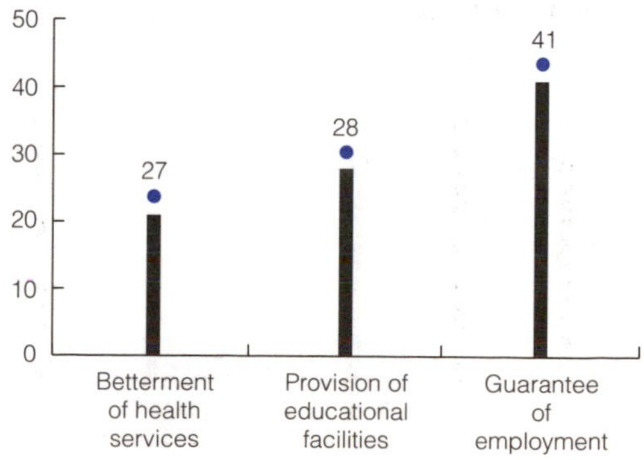

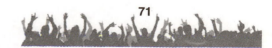

**Figure 5.11**

**Opinion on employment as top priority by location, education and SES**

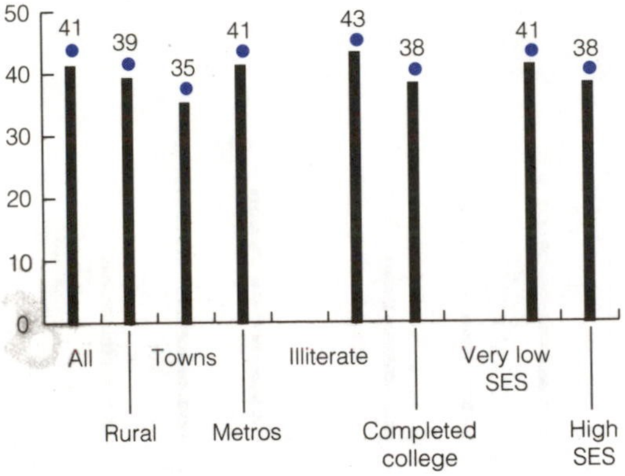


is linked to better education. Though there are some variations in the opinions expressed by the youth when it comes to SES and place of residence, in general employment continues to remain the top priority *(Figure 5.11)*.

Besides concerns about employment and education, the youth are also concerned about the spread of HIV, maternal health and child mortality. Of these three health related issues, the youth placed combating HIV as the top priority for the government. For about 48 per cent of the youth, tackling the spread of HIV should constitute the government's first priority among the various health related issues. About 33 per cent of the youth placed maternal health on the top slot while the problem of child mortality was ranked third in the priority list *(Figure 5.12)*.

The second set of problems that the youth were asked to prioritise for the government were those related to HIV/AIDS, improving maternal health and reducing child mortality.

The gravity of different health problems is seen by the youth in many different ways depending on their demographic, socio economic and residential backgrounds. While young men are more concerned about diseases like HIV/AIDS as compared to young women, those living in towns and cities too are more concerned about it than those living in the villages. Similarly, compared to the non-literates, those who are educated are more concerned about HIV/AIDS and give it top priority *(Figure 5.13)*.

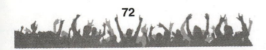

**Figure 5.12**

**Opinion of youth on priority health issues**

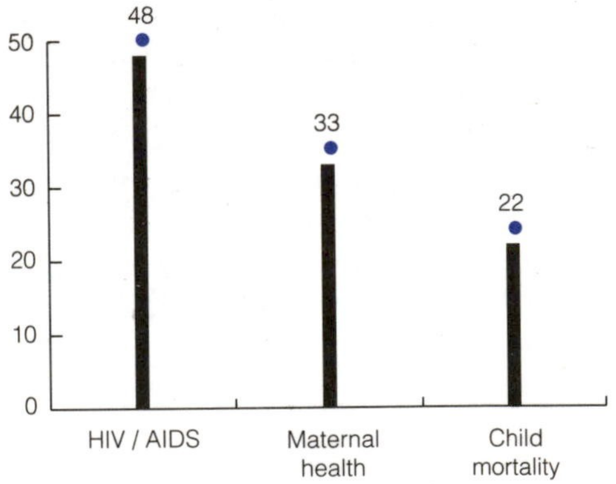


**Figure 5.13**

**Opinion of youth on HIV/AIDS as the priority health issue by locality and education**

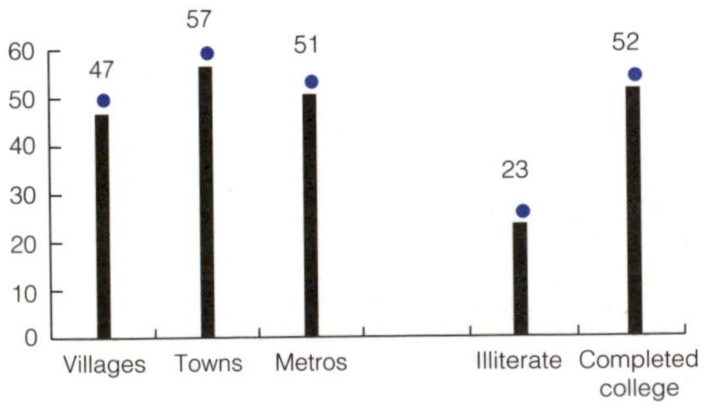

Case Study 7

***Youth Residing in Two Slum Areas of Mumbai***

by **Rohini Kashikar Sudhakar**

## Youth Perspectives

The life histories of youth, based on true incidents, as told by youth themselves or others involved with them:

## Rakhi: A case of recklessness

Rakhi is a seventeen year old girl, residing in Asha Nagar Slum. Ever since she lost her father, at the age of eight years, she was stopped from going to school. Instead, she was made to work as a maid servant in other people's houses. Her mother Nirmala remarried and soon gave birth to a baby boy. But soon Rakhi lost her step father too. Now she had to work harder as she had to earn not only for the house rent and upkeep of her mother but also for her brother and his school fees. The experiences matured her beyond her age. She was transformed from a shy girl to a bold 'chamiyaan' wearing gaudy and revealing outfits. She started having affairs with many men which resulted in unwanted pregnancies. She underwent abortions thrice. Eventually, Rakhi fell in love with a married man and forced him to divorce his wife. She then married him in a temple against her mother's wishes. Rahki's husband did not have a house and very reluctantly, Nirmala, her mother, agreed to give them shelter for a few weeks in her own house. But things didn't change for Rakhi. She continued working as a maid servant and her idle husband lived off her like a parasite. Soon she was pregnant. Nirmala realised that she would have to take care of her daughter's family and future too. This was unacceptable to her. Hence, she asked them to leave her house. Now Rakhi's husband is jobless and a drug addict. Her brother has left school and works as a newspaper boy. Rakhi works as a maid servant. She has rented a house in Asha Nagar. She deeply repents her actions and prays that no one should follow her footsteps and destroy one's life.

## Avinash: A newspaper boy

Avinash is a 17 year old boy. He appeared for S.S.C. Board examinations in March, this year. He had failed in 6th standard due to which he had lagged behind other boys of his age. He looks much younger than his age, wears a torn and rag like vest and filthy trousers. But the smile that he sports makes him look quite charming. Even during his three month long vacation after the exams, he had to get up at 4 o' clock in the morning to deliver newspapers to people's houses. His monthly earning is only Rs. 200. His parents have bought a new house in the same locality as their old house was about to collapse. They had to take a loan in order to buy the house which meant, all the members of the family had to work to repay the loan.

Avinash loves swimming and playing football but these days he gives these activities a miss because he has to take care of his house when his parents go to work. When asked about his problems, tears trickled down his cheeks. He said that he gets only two dresses which he has to use for two years. He washes all his clothes by himself. The family does not have the resources to own a personal tap, so, every day he has to get up and fill 4-5 drums of water. Many a times, he got involved in fights over water due to which he was even taken to police station. He hates the fact that his mother has to work as a maid-servant in other people's houses. He also hates sleeping on the bridge at night due to lack of space at home. He wishes to have some really good food but is not able to afford it and has to be satisfied with tea and bread. Avinash has big dreams. He wants to buy a huge house for his parents so that they don't have to work for building a house. Basically, he wants to escape from slum life … forever.

Placing HIV/AIDS on the top of the list of priorities is linked with the level of awareness about the disease. Since the educated youth are more aware of HIV/AIDS, they give it a higher priority as compared to those who are not educated.

Attaching importance to maternal health has a relationship with the place of residence of the youth. Those living in rural areas attach more importance to this issue. The lack of health facilities and lack of access to already available facilities are the reasons why those living in the villages are more concerned about maternal health *(Figure 5.14)*.

**Figure 5.14**

**Rural and poor youth attach higher importance to maternal health**

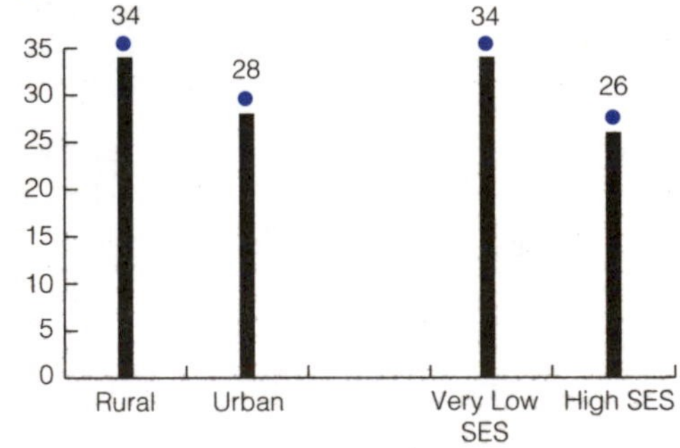


**Figure 5.15**

**Rural and poor young women attach higher importance to maternal health**

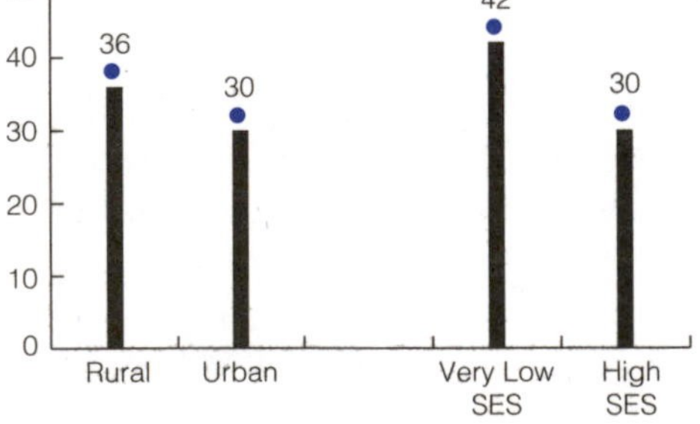


The survey tried to find out the opinion of women from different SES and different places of residence about the issue of maternal health. It came to light that those belonging to poor families and those living in the rural areas are more concerned about maternal health than the rest *(Figure 5.15)*.

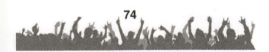

Only one-fifth of the youth surveyed wanted child mortality to be the government's first priority among health related problems *(Figure 5.16)*. This low priority is almost the same across different SES.

This opinion can be attributed to the significant reduction in child mortality rates in recent decades, even though child mortality is still higher in India as compared to the developed countries.

In 2006 UNAIDS estimated that there were 5.6 million people in India living with HIV, i.e. in absolute terms India had the highest population of people living with HIV. However, the grim reality also is that India accounts for 21 per cent of the global child mortality and 23 per cent of global maternal deaths. Despite this, it is HIV/AIDS that is given more importance. The most important reason for this is media exposure *(Figure 5.17)*.

**Figure 5.16**

**Opinion of youth on reducing child mortality as a priority health issue by locality and SES**

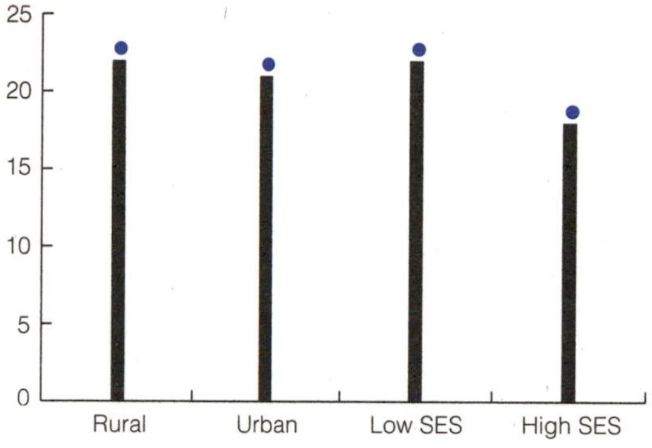


**Figure 5.17**

**Media exposure and priority for health related issues**

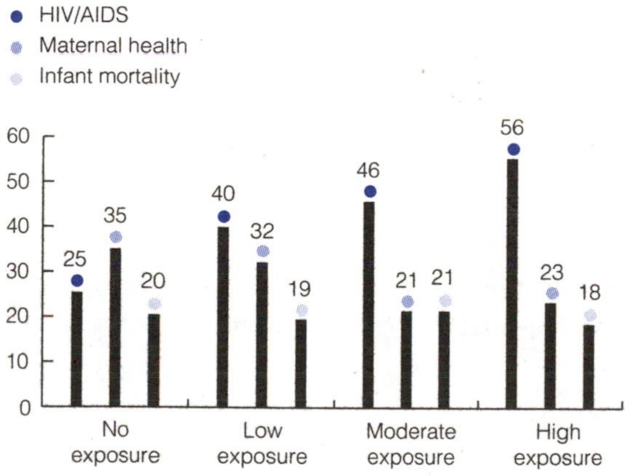


Another set of problems that the youth were asked to prioritise concerned gender equality, strengthening the defense system and maintaining environmental sustainability. The youth gave gender equality the first priority among these three problems.

In the survey, 40 per cent of the youth were of the opinion that promoting gender equality should be the topmost priority of the government. However, this is closely followed by strengthening the defence system (38 per cent) with only 26 per cent of the youth considering environmental sustainability as the topmost priority of the government *(Figure 5.18)*.

**Figure 5.18**

**Priority among youth for gender equality, strengthening defence system and environment sustainability**

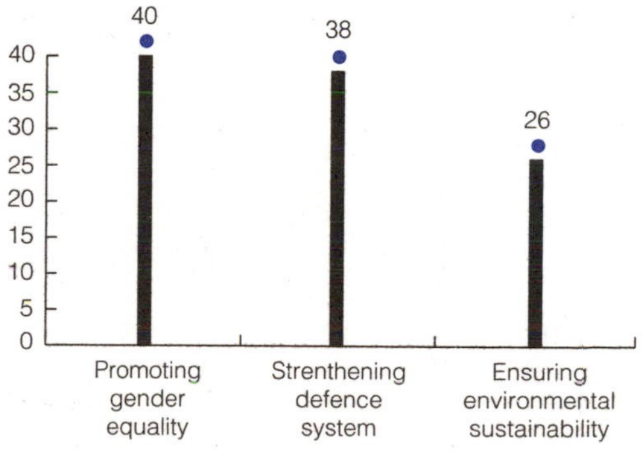

The Constitution of India in its various articles prohibits gender discrimination. Besides, the States are empowered to adopt measures of positive discrimination in favour of women through legislation. The Central government has also announced the National Policy for Empowerment of Women in 2001 in order to bring advancement, development and empowerment of women.

India has also ratified various international conventions and human rights forums to secure equal rights of women, such as ratification of Convention on Elimination of All Forms of Discrimination Against Women (CEDAW).

The divide between young men and women when it comes to gender equality is quite clear. It is mainly the women who are concerned about this issue. Only 31 per cent of the young men as compared to 52 per cent of the young women would like the government to give top priority to the issue of gender equality. What merits attention and what defies common sense is the lower priority attached to gender equality by those who have attained higher education *(Figure 5.19)*.

A further probe reveals that while the education level of young men does not influence the priority that they accord to gender equality, among the young women, the level of educational attainment and the desire for greater gender equality moves in opposite directions. It is the less educated women who attach much more importance to greater gender equality compared to those who are more educated. This could perhaps be because the educated women enjoy more or less equal status with men both within their families and also outside of their homes while the uneducated or less educated women remain on the margins and bear the brunt of patriarchy *(Figure 5.20)*.

**Figure 5.19**

**Opinion on gender equality as first priority by gender and education**

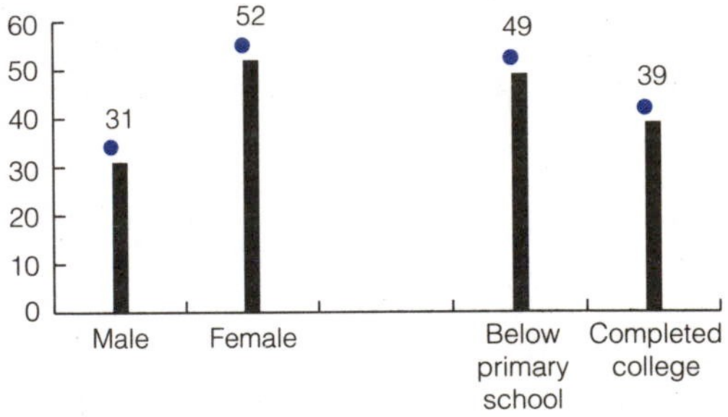


**Figure 5.20**

**Opinion on gender equality by SES**

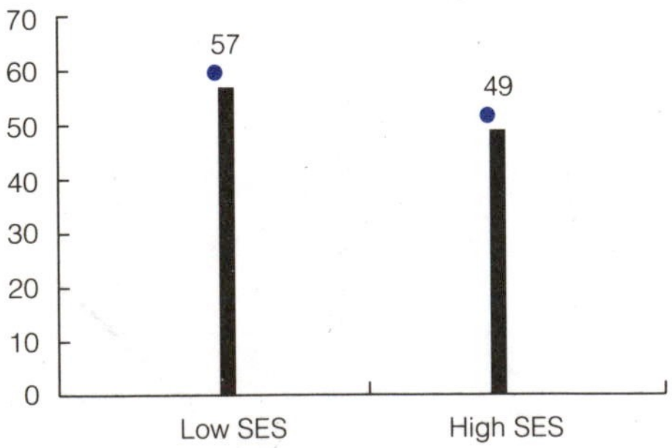

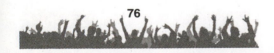

There is a popular perception that urban youth would be more supportive of gender equality as compared to those living in villages. But the findings of this survey suggest that contrary to the popular perception, it is young men from rural areas who are more supportive of greater gender equality as the first priority of the government. About 32 per cent of the young men living in rural areas are likely to give greater gender equality the topmost priority of the government as compared to 30 per cent and 28 per cent male youth living in towns and cities respectively. Amongst the male youth living in towns and cities, 42 per cent and 44 per cent respectively mentioned promoting greater gender equality as the third priority of the government *(Figure 5.21)*.

Strengthening the defence system is largely the concern of young men. Young women do not attach much importance to this issue. About 45 per cent of the young men would like the government to give top most priority to strengthening the defence system as compared to 31 per cent of young women. Among young men too, those who are least educated and belong to lower SES appear to be more concerned about the defence system of the country. It is difficult to say whether these youth are more nationalistic in a limited sense of the term or whether they have only a vague idea of the defence system of the country due to which they attach greater importance to strengthening it as compared to the others.

**Figure 5.21**

**Opinion of young men on gender equality by location**

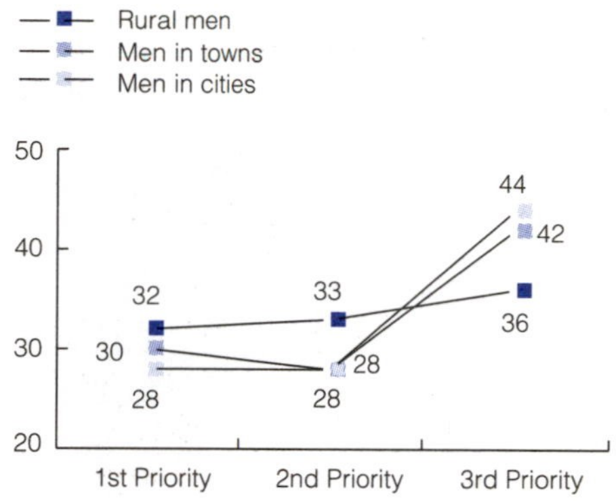


> **Window to the world, courtesy the Metro**
>
> The safety and comfort of Delhi Metro is helping Muslim women to venture out of their homes. Travelling and working in Connaught Place is becoming the norm for women who earlier had not been outside the walled city. Seclusion is inflicted by insecurity, points out Subhashini Ali, President of All-India Democratic Women's Association, a lack of safe and affordable public transport is a major reason for that insecurity. 'Just see the one small change that the Delhi metro has wrought the large numbers of happy, chattering Muslim women in burqas who throng Connaught Place and Janpath after being 'confined' to the walled city for most of their lives. That's the liberating effect that easy access to civic amenities can have,' she says. It's the liberation that 26-year-old Parveen who stays in Dariba Kalan, celebrates everyday when she takes the metro to go to her workplace in Connaught Place. 'Earlier, I had to work close by as my parents didn't want me to travel so far on a bus. Because of the metro, I now have a good job at a travel agency and earn double my earlier salary,' says Parveen, before hurrying off to board a train bound for New Delhi station. 'Now, I even run the odd errand for my parents so long as its on the metro route. Buses are so crowded and one gets pushed and shoved, says the diminutive Parveen, clad in jeans and a matching blue *nikaab*.
>
> Neelam Raaj, *Times of India*, March 25, 2007.

## Attitude Towards Social Equality and Justice

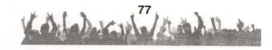

Of late, there has been rising criticism and opposition to affirmative action for the deprived and underprivileged sections of society (namely the Dalits and the Adivasis) and it is predominantly the youth that have risen in favour of or against the affirmative action. Hence, this survey sought to study: To what extent do the youth support affirmative action policies as a measure of ensuring social equality and justice? Who among the youth support or oppose these policies?

**Figure 5.22**

**Support for reservation in higher educational institutions**

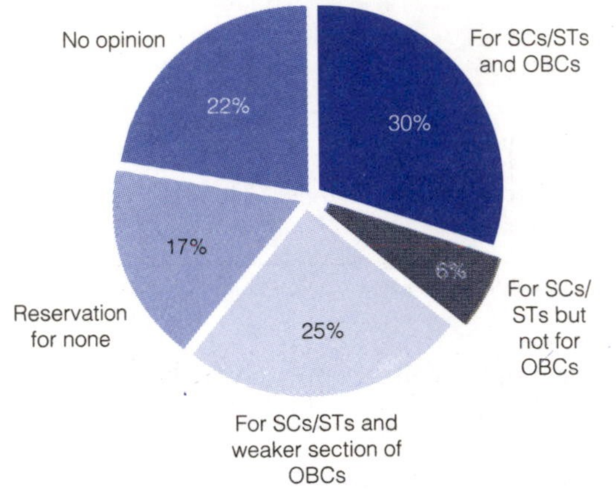


Over all, the youth appear to be sharply divided on the issue of reservation of seats for some communities in institutions of higher education. Over 60 per cent of the youth supported the policy of reservation in some form or the other, while 39 per cent of them did not support the policy of reservation (putting together those who are against reservation and also those who did not express any opinion on this issue). While 30 per cent of the youth agree with extending the provision of reservation in higher educational institutions for the Other Backward Castes (OBCs), 25 per cent would like this provision to be extended but only for those from the economically weaker sections amongst the OBC communities *(Figure 5.22)*.

It is important to note that those who favour extending unconditional reservation facilities in higher educational institutions for OBCs outnumber those who would like this facility to be extended only to the economically weaker sections amongst the OBCs. This indicates that it is the 'group' and not the 'individual' that is deeply rooted in the concept and meaning of affirmative action.

**Figure 5.23**

**Support for reservations for SC/ST and OBC by caste**

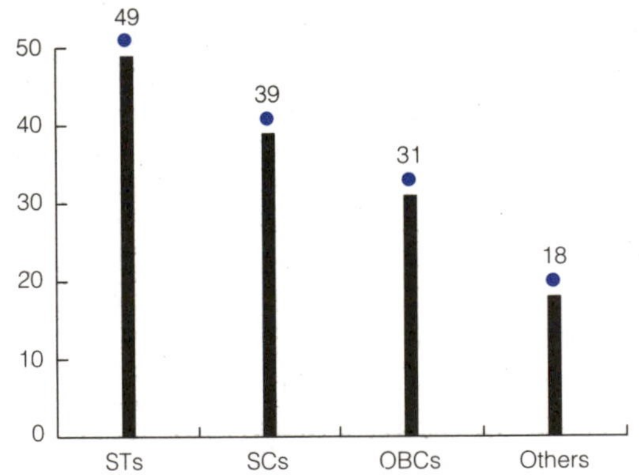


Reservations are based on caste. Since upper caste youth are outside the reservation policy and they are primarily opposed to it *(Figure 5.23)*. The reasons for their opposition stems from the belief that reservation of seats based on castes seriously limits the prospects of their entering the institutions of higher education and getting government jobs.

Is it that there is total opposition to the policy of reservation amongst those who do not fall into the loop of 'protective discrimination'? Are they against social justice/equality *in toto*? It appears that not all of them stand so much against affirmative action in the form of reservations but it is the more articulate and vocal section among the upper castes which is largely opposed to the idea of reservations as a measure of uplifting the disadvantaged sections of society. Obviously, it is the middle and upper stratum of upper castes that is well educated and has high stakes in the field of education and in getting government jobs as well *(Figure 5.24)*.

The findings of the survey suggest that there is overwhelming support for reservation of seats for women in the Parliament and State Legislatures. Only 12 per cent of the youth are totally against this reservation for women. While 45 per cent of the youth supported reserving seats for all women, another 22 per cent supported reserving seats for women belonging to Dalit, Adivasi and OBC communities. However, 21 per cent did not express any opinion on this issue *(Figure 5.25)*.

**Figure 5.24**

**Lower stratum among upper castes are more likely to oppose reservation**

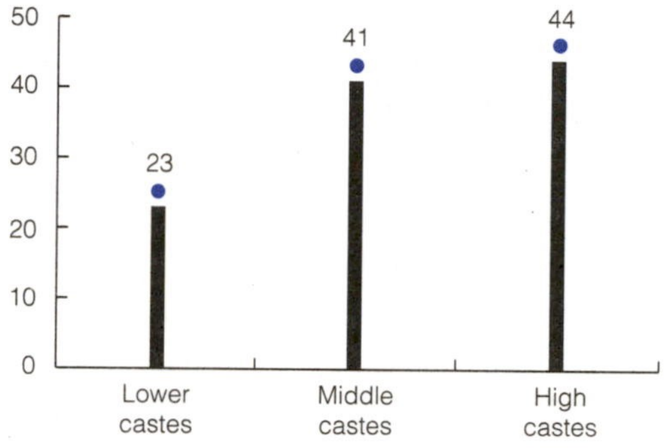


Affirmative action for SCs/STs in the form of reservation is one of the defining features of Indian Constitution. However, it turned out to be a contentious and hotly debated issue with the inclusion of Other Backward classes (OBCs) following the recommendation of Mandal Commission in early 1990s. The Commission had recommended for 27 per cent reservation for the OBCs in government jobs. There were protests in many parts of the country against it. The controversy resurfaced when there was a move by the Central government to reserve seats for the OBCs in elite institutions such as IIMs, IITs, AIIMS in 2006.

**Figure 5.25**

**Reservations and gender**

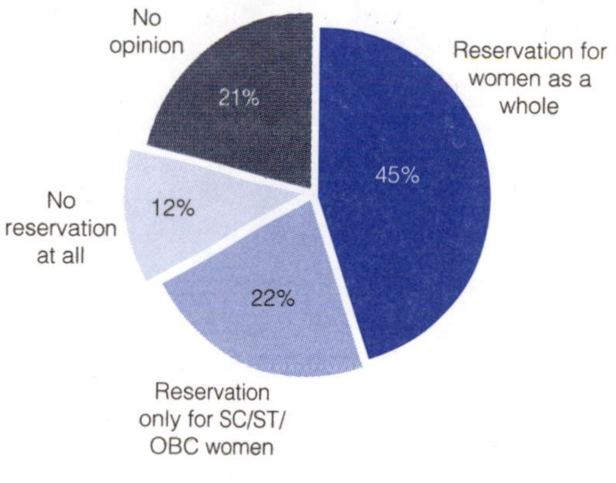


There is considerable difference between young men and women on the issue of reservation for women. As opposed to 66 per cent women, only about 51 per cent men support reservation for women as a whole. Among the men, those living in rural areas are slightly less likely to support women's reservation than those living in towns and cities *(Figure 5.26)*.

Men in towns and cities are slightly more likely to completely negate the idea of reserving seats for women in Parliament as compared to those living in rural areas. The highest support for reserving seats in Parliament comes from women in towns and contrarily women in cities are the least likely to support the idea of reservations for them in State Legislatures and Parliament.

**Figure 5.26**

**Support for reservation for women**

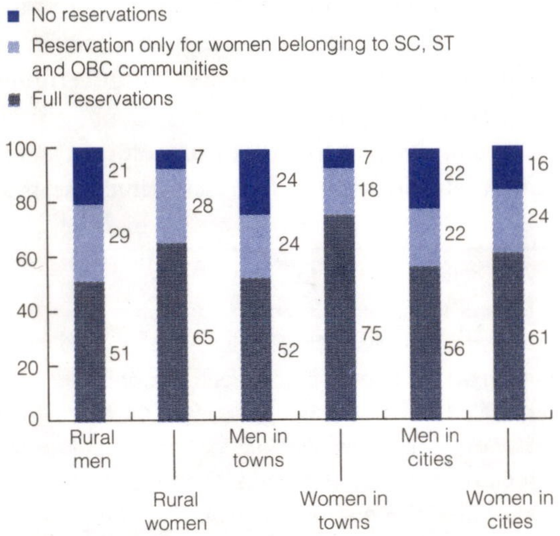


## Support for Idea of Reserving Seats for Youth in Parliament

Three-fourth of the youth seem to be supportive of the idea of reserving seats for youth in Parliament with only a very small number (4 per cent) opposed to this idea (21 per cent expressed no opinion on this issue).

Both, young men and women are equally enthusiastic about this proposal. Similarly, youth of all age groups seem to be excited about this proposal. The enthusiasm is more among the educated youth belonging to rich families as compared to those who are either illiterate or have managed to attain very low levels of education or those who belong to relatively poor or lower income families. There is hardly any caste divide on this issue and all youth, irrespective of their caste, seem to be committed to the idea of providing political reservations for the youth. While this opinion is more or less equally shared by the youth of all groups, there is slightly higher support for this idea among those from advantageous backgrounds *(Figure 5.27)*.

**Figure 5.27**

**Support for reservation of seats for youth in parliament and state legislatures**

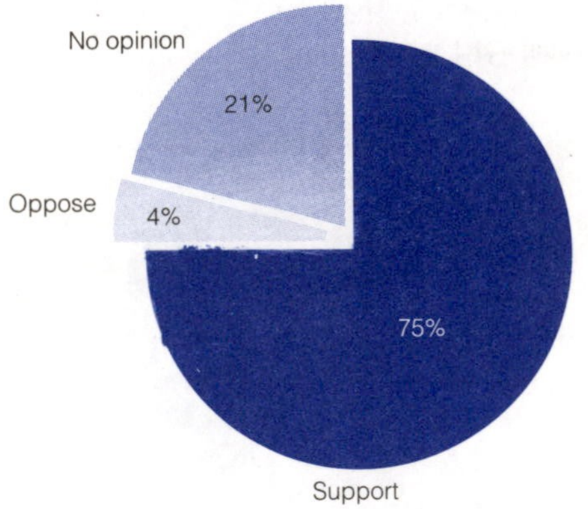


## Summing Up

The two main problems confronting the nation as identified by the youth are unemployment and poverty. The analysis in this chapter also shows that though there are minor differences among the youth living in different locations, they by and large want employment to be the first priority of the government.

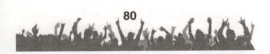

An interesting finding of the survey is that the youth attach less importance to problems of corruption and terrorism. This could perhaps be because they attach far greater importance to unemployment and poverty.

When it comes to other issues of national importance and what the priority of the government should be, the youth are in favour of the government tackling the problem of HIV/AIDS as the first priority, followed by maternal health and reducing child mortality rates.

Providing greater gender equality too is given priority by the youth, though this is a bigger priority for the women than it is for the men. Interestingly, the need for greater gender equality is seen to be lower among the educated women as compared to the uneducated ones. Further, while there is support for reservation of seats for women in Parliament and State Legislatures, this support is much less among the men living in towns and cities as compared to those living in the villages. The youth are on the whole more enthusiastic about reserving seats for all of them (men and women) in Parliament and State Legislatures.

SHAH RUKH KHAN
MADAME TUSSAUDS
YOU, YOUR FRIENDS
AND YOUR FAMI
SHAH RUKH KHAN
Stars in
MADAME TUSSAUDS
Co Starring
YOU, YOUR FRIENDS
AND YOUR FAMILY!

# CHAPTER 6: NATION AND THE WORLD

- About 29 per cent of the youth have heard about globalisation. The level of awareness about globalisation is positively associated with the educational level of the youth.
- A little over one-third of the youth who have heard about globalisation are of the opinion that it brings in more advantages than disadvantages. Educated youth are sharply divided on the advantages of globalisation.
- Youth from lower SES are skeptical about the availability of better and cheaper products in the market and employment opportunities abroad as a result of globalisation.
- The youth have a high level of awareness about the rest of the world.
- Most of the youth want India to treat her neighbours on an equal footing and are in favour of maintaining good relations with Pakistan.
- The youth are polarised on India's alliance with the US; they are opposed to the latter's hegemony over the rest of the world.

The world has seen tremendous changes in many areas of activity during the last two decades. It is widely claimed that the world is increasingly becoming a global village where geographical and political barriers are getting dismantled. There has been an unprecedented increase in international flow of capital, finance, productive assets and technology. The increased migration of people coupled with the flow of human resources from one country to another is also a feature of this new system. All this has produced a connectedness of the nation-states into a global village. Globalisation has resulted in the opening up of various opportunities across the world and the expansion of these opportunities across countries has ensured more equitable share of resources than ever with young people being the section which is best positioned to avail of these opportunities. However, the other side of the story presents a dismal picture. The classical notion of sovereignty (an essential attribute of the nation-state) of individual nation states, especially of those in the third world is under stress as they are losing their control over both domestic and external policies. Secondly, the benefits of globalisation are unacceptably unequal and skewed in favour of the rich (Western) countries. While the economies of advanced countries are globalised, they impose several restrictions on the movements of commodities and people from developing countries. Thirdly and finally, it is argued that the spread out of western life style through globalisation has produced socio-cultural tensions in non-western societies. All this has caused the emergence of counter currents against the processes of globalisation and reaffirmation of nation-state.

Given these contradictions and contestations, it would be worthwhile to examine issues such as:

- How aware are the youth about globalisation?
- What is the level of support for globalisation among the youth?
- What do they think of the neighbouring countries?
- What role do the youth visualise for India in the world?

## Awareness about globalisation

The findings of the survey show that about 29 per cent of the youth are aware of the term globalisation, while 71 per cent have not heard about it *(Figure 6.1)*. This lack of awareness about globalisation among Indian youth seems even lower when one considers the fact that in Germany 76 per cent of the youth are aware of globalisation (Shell Youth Study, 2006).

The youth in India are found to be marginally more aware of globalisation as compared to an average Indian. Viewed thus, the term globalisation has to still travel a long distance before it is heard and integrated in the lifestyles of the youth.

**Figure 6.1**

**Awareness about globalisation**

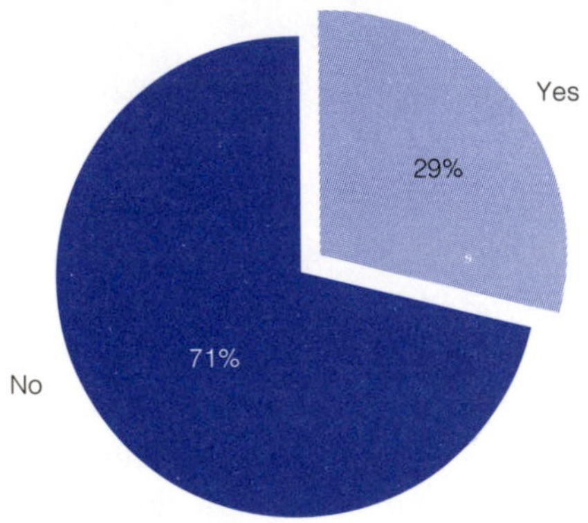


**Figure 6.2**

**Awareness about globalisation by locality and education**

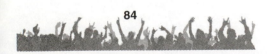

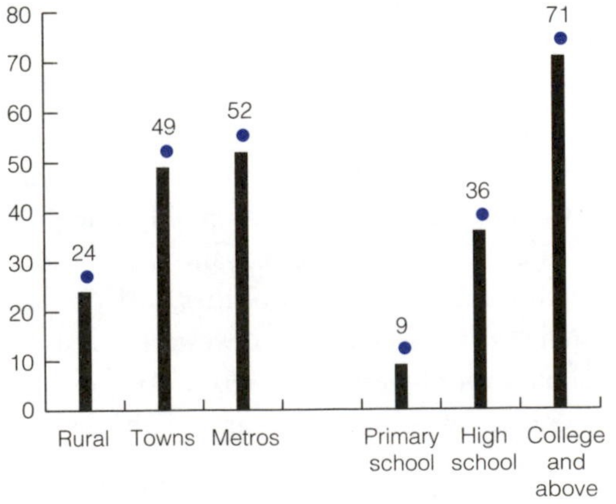


Awareness about globalisation is greatly influenced by the place of residence of the youth. While a majority of the youth living in the metros is aware of globalisation, only 24 per cent of those living in the villages are aware of it. Further, 49 per cent of those living in small and medium towns too have heard about globalisation *(Figure 6.2)*.

Awareness about globalisation is directly linked to the level of educational attainment. The higher the level of educational attainment, the greater is the awareness about globalisation. 71 per cent of those who have already completed their college education are aware of globalisation while only 9 per cent of those who have completed their primary education are aware of it *(Figure 6.2)*.

The level of media exposure appears to have a direct relationship with the level of awareness about globalisation. The higher the level of media exposure, the greater is the awareness about globalisation. A majority among the youth with high media exposure are aware of the term globalisation while among those with no exposure to the media, only 4 per cent are aware of it *(Figure 6.3)*.

> The level of awareness of globalisation among youth is much akin to that of the rest of the population. In a State of the Nation Survey held in January 2007, about 28 per cent of population (aged 18 years and above) had heard about globalisation. If this figure is compared with a previous study conducted 10 years ago (National Election Studies, 1998) when processes of globalisation had already set in the country, it appears that the rise in the level of awareness of globalisation is very slow. In 1998, about 26 per cent of people had heard about these processes. However, a caveat is in order. While the question on globalisation asked in NES 1998 and SONS 2007 was similar it was different in Youth Study 2007.

**Figure 6.3**

**Awareness of globalisation by media exposure**

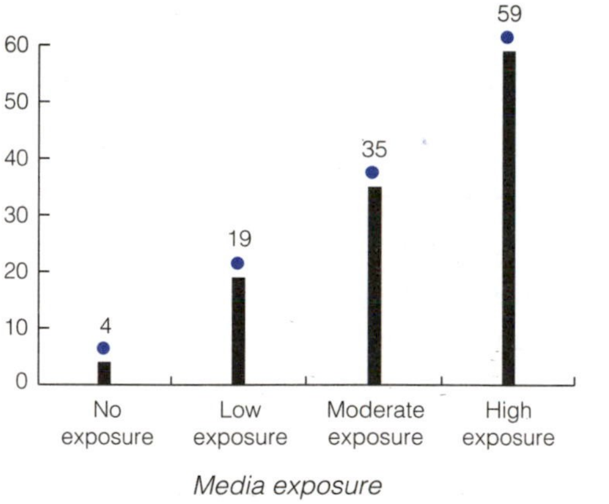


## Advantages of globalisation

The youth seem to be divided when it comes to supporting or opposing globalisation. Among those who have heard about globalisation, a little over one-third believe that it has benefited the country, while 24 per cent believe the opposite. Among those who are aware of the process of globalisation, 23 per cent believe that its advantages and disadvantages are more or less equal, with another 17 per cent having no opinion on this issue *(Figure 6.4)*.

While there is a great rural-urban divide when it comes to being aware about globalisation, this

**Figure 6.4**

**Opinions of youth on advantages and disadvantages of globalisation**

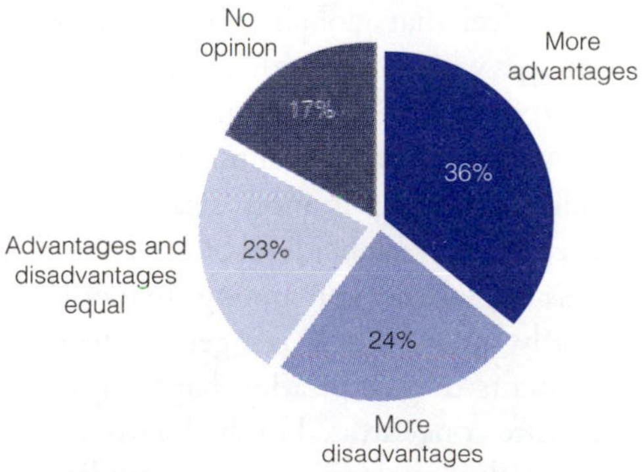


*Note: Figures pertain to those who have heard about globalisation.*

**Figure 6.5**

**Opinion about the advantages of globalisation by gender, locality and education**

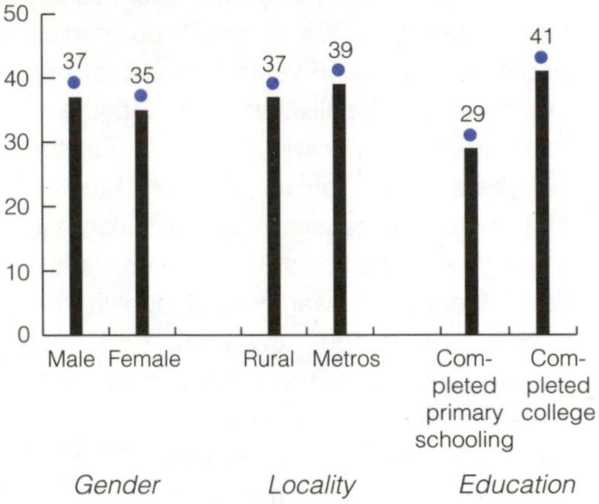


*Note: Figures calculated only from those who have heard about globalisation. All the figures are in percentages.*

difference vanishes when it comes to expressing opinions about the benefits of globalisation. The youth living in both the metros as well as the villages expressed more or less similar opinions about the benefits of globalisation. Further, there is hardly any difference of opinion about this even between genders.

Differences of opinion start surfacing with variation in the level of educational attainment. Education appears to be not only the most critical factor as far as awareness about globalisation is concerned but it also emerges as the dominant factor shaping one's attitude towards globalisation. Hence, those who are highly educated are more likely to have positive opinions about the effects of globalisation as compared to those who are either less educated or are illiterate. Of the highly educated (who have completed college education), about 41 per cent believe that globalisation brings in more advantages than disadvantages as against 21 per cent who believe in the opposite.

On the other hand, among those who have completed only primary school education, 29 per cent believe that globalisation offers more advantages than otherwise *(Figure 6.5)*. The findings of the survey suggest that those with higher socio-ecomomic status (SES) are more likely to feel that globalisation brings in more advantages while those with middle SES, feel that it brings in more disadvantages than advantages. Those with low SES are most likely to say that globalisation brings in more disadvantages.

The relatively higher level of opposition to the process of globalisation among the poor may be primarily because there is a general feeling that the benefits of globalisation hardly reach them as they are concentrated in the hands of the rich and with those belonging to the middle-income group *(Figure 6.6)*.

**Figure 6.6**

**Opinion on advantages and disadvantages of globalisation by SES**

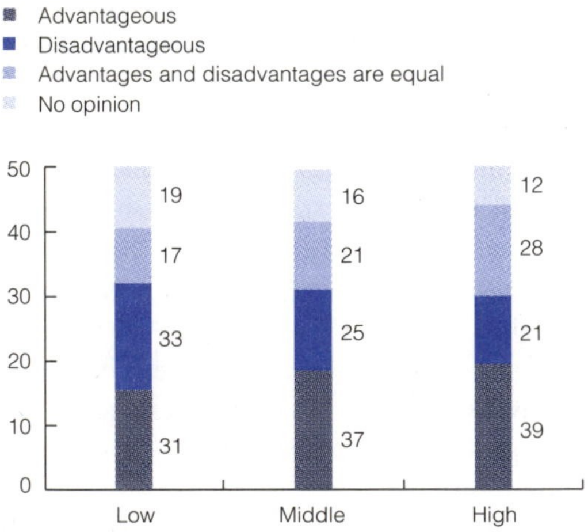

## Case Study 8

## *Shaping the Life: Kerala Youth Respond to Changing Socio-Economic Order*

by **Rajesh Komath** and **Rakkee Thimothy**

### Youth Perspectives

#### Farzania, female, 23 years (She is a Muslim from north Kerala)

I belong to Punnole, a village in Kannur district. I am presently pursuing Masters in Anthropology. I joined Anthropology after completing a Bachelor's degree in Chemistry. I wanted to pursue Chemistry for masters also. However, my marks were very less so I couldn't get admission. Moreover, my family was not very eager to send me to a far off place for further studies. Then I thought about joining the LLB course, but when I called the university law department, some how the phone call got wrongly transferred to the Anthropology department. After talking to me, some official from the Anthropology department told that even this is a good option. Then I thought about joining here and applied for this course. Neither was I very sure about the subject I had chosen nor any one from my family had any idea about it.

Now the things are changing even among our community. During earlier times, no one used to ask a girl about her interest in matters such as education and marriage. Nowadays at least they bother to ask. However, it is a different question whether some weight is given to her opinion or not. Since I was born and brought up in a very orthodox manner and that might be the reason that I never felt uncomfortable with all this. Some how, I feel that I have not thought very seriously about life or reflected upon whatever I get to know in my classroom. I feel that others in my class are also like that. Though it is a postgraduate class yet it is very rare to find serious discussions on various issues taking place in our classroom. Most of the times, their conversation revolves around popular TV serials or routine gossip. But my family does not own a TV and we don't go outside to watch movies etc.

I perform *namaz* five times a day. I used to wear veil also. After I get married, I may even wear a *burka* too. My sister and my mother also wear it. However, I don't find a problem with all this. Rather I am comfortable with it. I don't think that others are doing some thing wrong if they do not wear it. But I am not sure about the extent to which this decision of mine has been influenced by religion and society. All I can say is that I am comfortable with the idea. I come from a rural background. I am witnessing the so-called consumerist culture and modernity only after being drawn closer to an urban background. Yes, that way it is true that I and my family are traditional. If I tell my family that I need to go outside of the state for further studies, they might not be very much keen about it. However, they want me to be economically independent. It is only when some one asks me that how serious am I about my present course that I tend to think about it. I don't think that any one in my class seriously thinks about what we are learning here. They are doing it just like any other course. I don't know how students in other universities are taught or how they are approaching their subjects.

* * *

**Vijaya George, female, 19 years (She is Roman Catholic Christian from north Kerala)**

Globalisation is very much linked to the course I am presently pursuing degree in fashion technology. As the economy is growing globalisation of the market is inevitable. It is in a way a sign of the development of the economy. Forcing people to buy things is necessary for the existence of the market. But there are many negative effects of the globalisation and we have to be very cautious. May be because of the geographical peculiarity the impact of globalisation is very less in this region of the state. At my home I am considered to be modern. Because I do things according to my decisions, I don't know how to explain… but I lead a better life than many of my peers. I will have a good degree in my hand, wear jeans and casuals, got a mobile phone, own a computer and so on. I have a twin sister. She is studying for engineering. My father works in Gulf and my mother is a housewife. I don't have problem in wearing anything, I mean new kinds of dresses such as sleeveless blouse etc. But I restrict myself because I do not want to invite problem. However my sister is very shy by character and I cannot consider her to be modern. In my opinion what you wear and how you wear clothes or how you present yourself also gives a message. My family is also like that.

Now times have changed. Even in our class no girl wants to get married so quickly. Few years back this was not the situation. In a degree class it was difficult to find girls who were not married. Nowadays girls prefer to marry after post graduation preferably after getting a job. Another interesting thing which I observed is that the charm of marriage has diminished among the young people. No one is really excited to get married. I don't know the reason. But that doesn't mean that they don't get involved in relationships. But generally serious love affair is lacking in the campus. There may be affairs, but for the sake of it. But students now discuss sex more freely.

Relating the process of globalisation to the levels of media exposure it is interesting to note that not only is awareness about globalisation higher among those with high media exposure and vice versa, but that support for globalisation too follows the same route. The higher the level of media exposure, the greater is the support for globalisation and vice versa. Among those with high levels of media exposure, 40 per cent believe that globalisation brings about more advantages than disadvantages, while only 31 per cent among those with low media exposure share a similar opinion about the advantages of globalisation *(Figure 6.7)*.

**Figure 6.7**

**Higher the exposure to media, greater the support for globlisation**

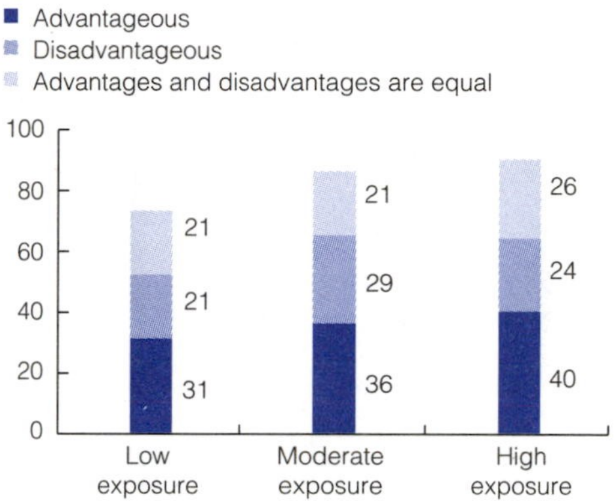


*Note: Figures pertain to those who have heard about globalisation (rest no opinion). All the figures are in percentages.*

## How has Globalisation Affected the Market?

It is a widely held view that the consumer market has expanded tremendously because of globalisation in recent decades due to which better products are available at cheaper rates. The survey sought to find out what the youth think about the consumer market in general and whether there was any difference of opinion among those who have heard about globalisation and those who are not aware of it.

The survey found that regardless of whether the youth have heard about globalisation or not, a majority of them (64 per cent) said that now better and cheaper products are available. Only 10 per cent of the youth hold the opposite view on this issue *(Figure 6.8)*.

This opinion is, however, much more sharply divided when we compare those who are aware of globalisation with those who have not heard about it. Among the youth who have heard about globalisation, an overwhelming 84 per cent believe that better and cheaper goods are available now while among those who have not

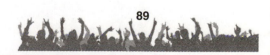

**Figure 6.8**

**Outcome of globalisation**

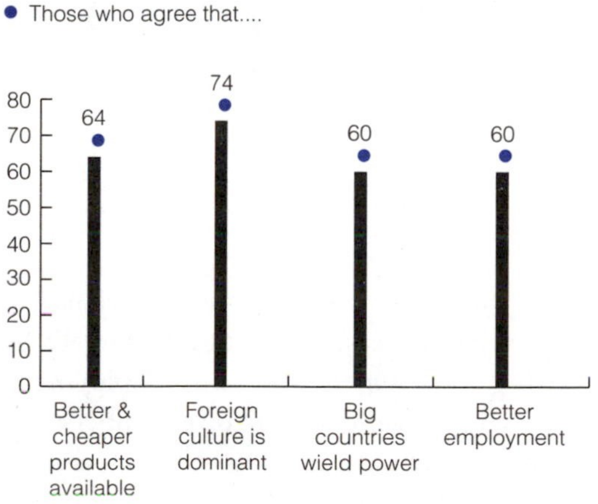


*Note: Rest no opinion.*

**Figure 6.9**

**Higher the SES of youth, greater the endorsement for cheaper goods being available**

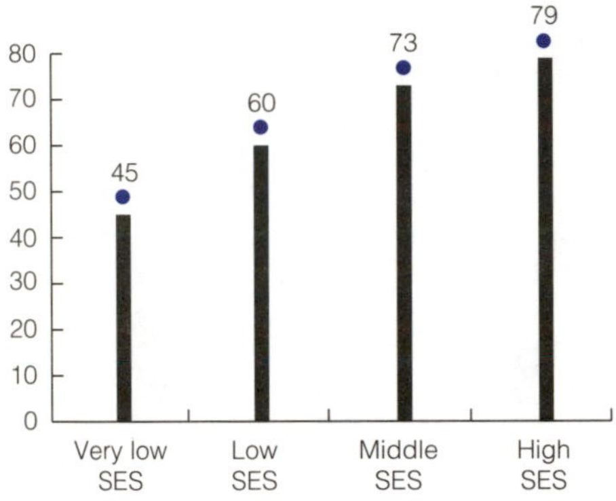


heard about globalisation only 56 per cent hold a similar view *(Figure 6.9)*.

The findings of the survey also suggest that though the benefits of globalisation are still somewhat unevenly spread among youth from families with different socio-economic backgrounds, it would be wrong to say that the poor have been completely left out of the process at least when it comes to benefits of cheaper and better goods. The benefits of the process of globalisation seem to have reached even the poorer sections of society, though in somewhat lesser degree. While among the youth belonging to high SES, 79 per cent believe that better and cheaper goods are available, only 45 per cent of those with low SES share this view *(Figure 6.9)*.

Though the benefits of globalisation still remain somewhat concentrated among the youth living in big and small towns, it would be incorrect to say that its benefits have not reached those living in the villages. The findings of the survey suggest that even among the youth living in villages, 62 per cent endorse the view that better and cheaper goods are available now *(Figure 6.10)*.

**Figure 6.10**

**Rural youth less likely to endorse cheaper goods being available**

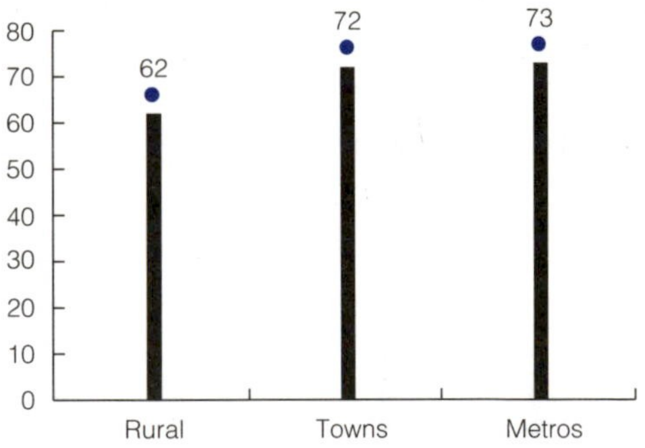


The pattern does not change very much when it comes to expressing opinions on the issues of increasing employment opportunities abroad among youth from different sections. Though opinions are sharply divided and tilted more in favour of those youth who would be considered as those belonging to the advantageous group, but the findings of the survey also suggest that this perception has started reaching the youth from the disadvantageous groups as well. It is neither unexpected nor surprising as these young people, being well educated and highly skilled, nurture a high ambition and are more likely to avail of various opportunities available abroad. On the other hand, the poor and those living in rural areas, being either illiterate or less educated and also unskilled can hardly think of getting employment abroad as employment opportunities abroad require certain amount of education and skill and also involve cumbersome documentation processes. Those who are well off meet the necessary requirements of going abroad easily and so have a promising world waiting for them beyond Indian shores.

The view that employment opportunities abroad have increased is perceived differently by those who have heard about globalisation and those who have not. Obviously, those who have heard about globalisation are educated and well informed about the happenings in and outside the country so it is natural for more of them to agree that there are better employment opportunities abroad than for those who have not heard about globalisation *(Figure 6.11)*.

**Figure 6.11**

**Awareness about globalisation and employment opportunities abroad**

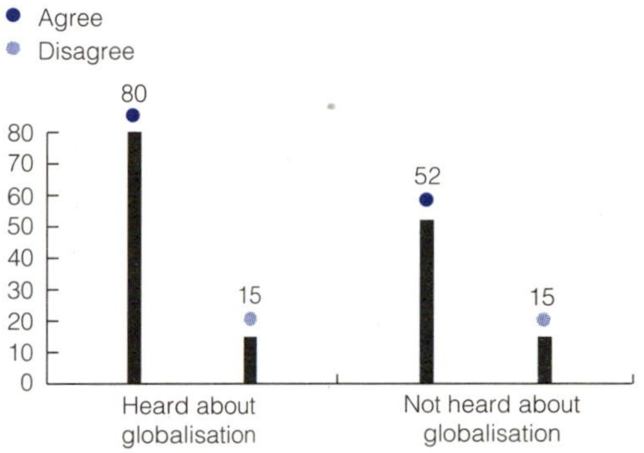


*Note: Rest had no opinion.*

The findings of the survey show that 60 per cent of the youth believe that the process of globalisation favours the rich nations at the cost of the poor ones and that the power equation between the rich and the poor countries gets tilted in favour of the rich countries. Only 13 per cent of the youth oppose this dominant view. While opinions with regard to greater employment opportunities abroad and cheaper goods being available have more to do with the actual experience with the process of globalisation, the question regarding poor and rich nations and the advantages of globalisation has more to do with the political beliefs that globalisation as a concept carries with it.

This belief finds stronger resonance among those who have heard about globalisation compared to those who are unaware of the process of globalisation *(Figure 6.12)*.

**Figure 6.12**

**Those aware of globalisation are more likely to agree that big countries wield all the power**

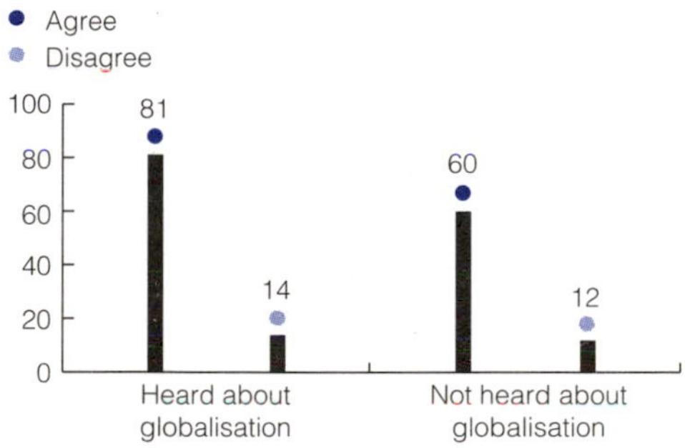


*Note: Rest no opinion. All the figures are in percentages.*

Educational attainment shares a direct relationship with agreement on this issue. The higher the level of educational attainment, the greater is the belief that bigger countries wield more power and vice versa.

However, it is also important to note that across educational categories, the youth are more likely to agree than to disagree with the statement that big countries wield all the power *(Figure 6.13)*.

**Figure 6.13**

**Higher educational attainment greater is the agreement that big countries wield all the power**

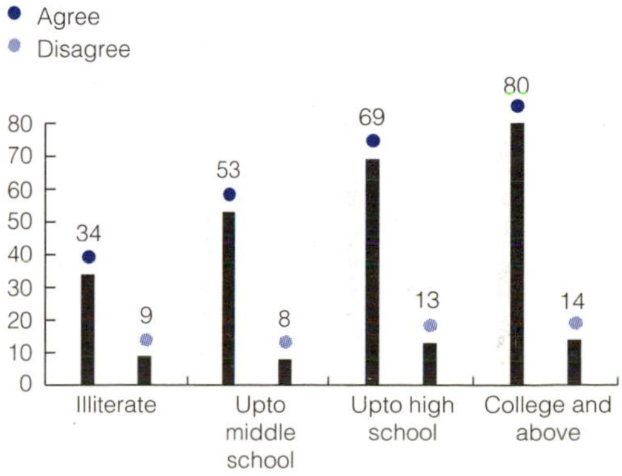

**Figure 6.14**

**Higher the level of media exposure, greater is the agreement that big countries wield all the power**

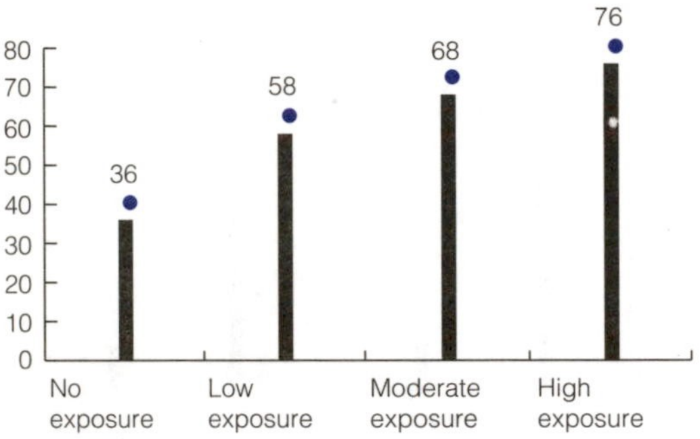


*Note: Figures pertain to those who agree that big countries wield all the power*

People with higher media exposure strongly support the statement that globalisation has led to bigger nations wielding all the power as compared to those with low media exposure *(Figure 6.14)*.

By virtue of territory, population and resource base, India acquires prominence in the world, especially in the South Asian region. Hence the study also aimed at finding out what the Indian youth think about India's neighbouring countries and also their views about those countries that are geographically not so close to it.

The findings of the survey show that among the Indian youth there is great awareness about four neighbouring countries—Pakistan, Bangladesh, Nepal and Sri Lanka. The maximum awareness is about Pakistan *(Figure 6.15)*.

Not only do the youth know about the neighbouring countries, but they also evaluate the relations that these countries share with India. On the relations that the four neighbouring countries have with India, a majority of the youth feel that India enjoys a friendly relationship with Nepal, Sri Lanka and also with Bangladesh. However, they do not feel the same about Pakistan. In fact, a majority of them (73 per cent) think

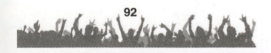

**Figure 6.15**

**Awareness about neighbouring countries**

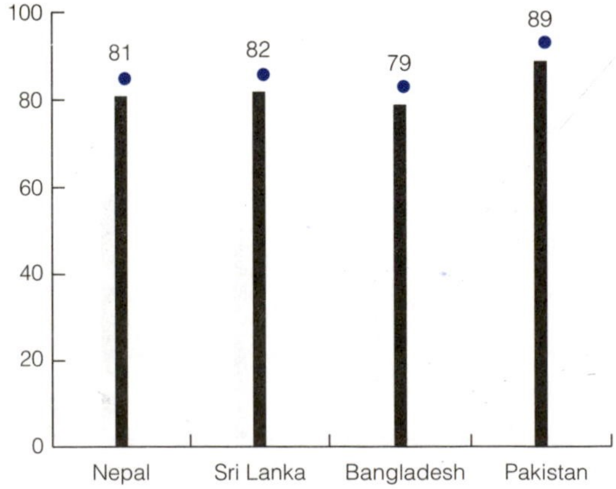


> During past few years, the level of awareness about the neighbouring countries seems to have increased. In 1999, overall 66 per cent of people had heard about Nepal, Sri Lanka and Bangladesh and 83 per cent about Pakistan. Except for Pakistan, all other neighbouring countries are considered to be having friendly relationship with India. However, if the perception of youth is the reflection of overall population, it is to be noted that in comparison to past few years, antagonism towards Pakistan has attenuated. In 1999, about 7 per cent people had considered Pakistan being friendly to India. As against this, about 23 per cent of youth in 2007 affirmed the same [Source: NES, 1999].

that Pakistan is not on good terms with India *(Figure 6.16)*.

The changing attitude of Indians in general, and the youth in particular towards Pakistan is reflected in their urge to have good relations

**Figure 6.17**

**How should India treat her neighbours?**

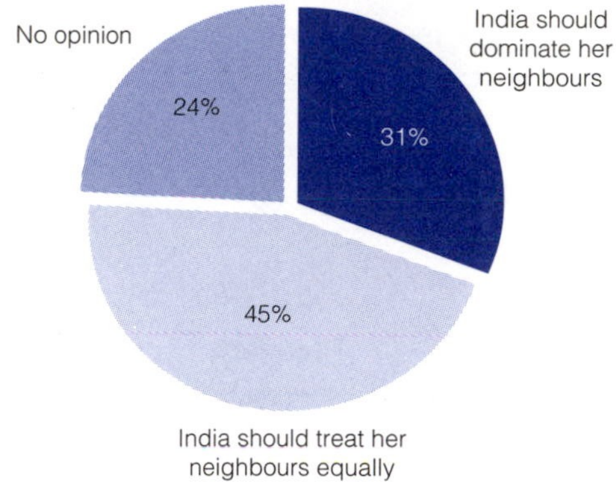


with neighbouring countries including Pakistan *(Figure 6.17)*. They put an additional emphasis on improving relations with Pakistan.

**Figure 6.18**

**Indo-Pak relationship: those who say...**

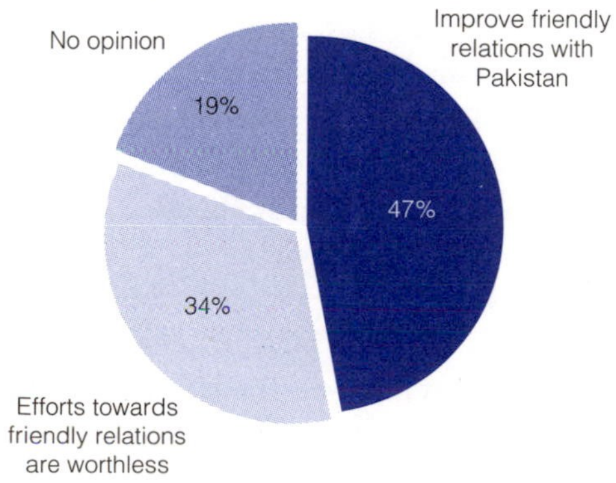


**Figure 6.16**

**Majority believe, India enjoys friendly relationship with her neighbours**

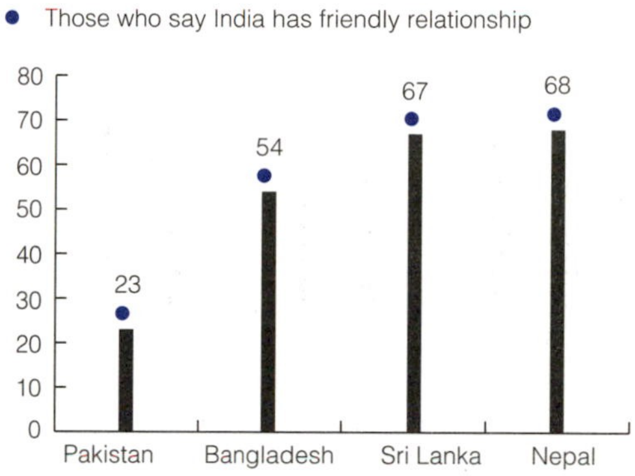


In a State of the Nation Survey (January 2006), about 25 per cent of the respondents (aged 18 years and above) stated that India should dominate over the neighbouring countries and 39 per cent were of the opinion that India should treat her neighbours equally, whereas rest had no opinion. Furthermore, about 47 per cent of respondents agreed that India should improve friendly relations with Pakistan as against 38 per cent who were against this. (Source: State Of the Nation Survey, January 2006)

In general, a majority of the youth would like the country to make efforts towards improving relations with Pakistan *(Figure 6.18)*. If the response of the youth is compared with that of the common people on this issue, it is clear that the views of the youth are in sync with the people in general.

Support for improving friendly relations with Pakistan however varies among the youth. Interestingly, those living in urban areas are more likely to support the efforts of friendly relations as compared to those living in the rural areas. This is

**Figure 6.19**

**Support for friendly relations with Pakistan by locality, religion and education**

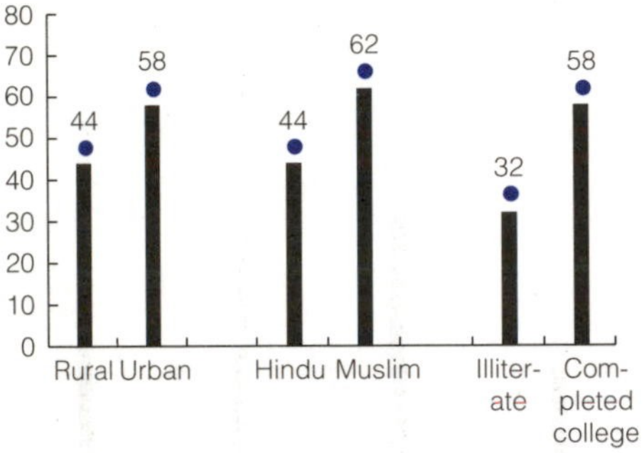


despite the fact that those living in the urban areas are considered to be more critical about Pakistan. It appears that the ongoing peace process and the various initiatives towards improving relations with Pakistan at various levels have significantly reduced antipathy towards Pakistan among the urban youth.

However, youth from different religions expressed different views when it comes to establishing friendly relations with Pakistan. Hence, as can be expected, the Muslim youth are more in favour of having good relations with Pakistan as compared to Hindu youth *(Figure 6.19)*.

## Relations with the US and Other Countries

The survey also sought to find out awareness levels about other countries among the youth. It was found that a large majority of the youth had heard about countries ranging from China to the US, Germany and Russia *(Figure 6.20)*. They know the US more than any other country except for Pakistan. Surprisingly, Russia gets a lower score among the youth compared to the US even though Russia has been the most trusted friend of India. This is probably a reflection of the decline of Russia and the dominance of the US in world politics and international affairs and India's recent increasing engagement with the US.

**Figure 6.20**

**Awareness about distant countries**

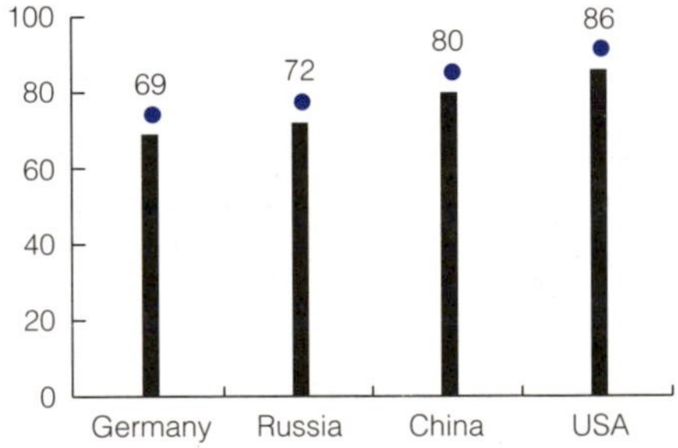


**Figure 6.21**

**Those saying India has friendly relation with...**

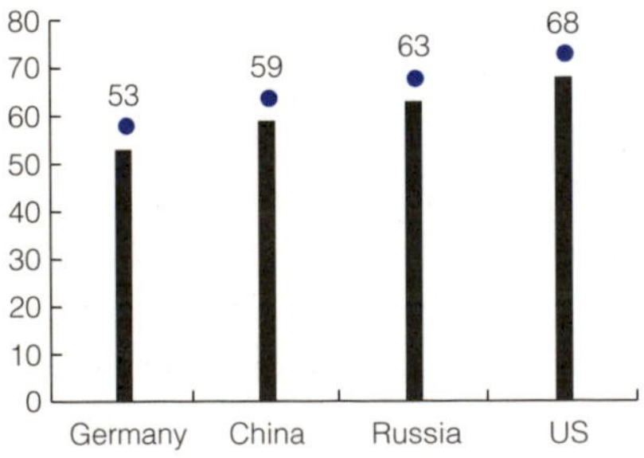


Again, the youth place high premium on the US for her friendly relations with India as compared to other countries. Of those who have heard about the US, about 68 per cent say that the US and India enjoy friendly relations. The corresponding figure for Russia is slightly lower than that for the US *(Figure 6.21)*.

While a majority of the youth recognise the US as a friend of India, they are sharply divided on her hegemony over the rest of the world. However, the US seems to be finding greater acceptability among the Indian youth as compared to what it was in the past. There is also a perception that engaging the US, in fact, serves larger national interests *(Figure 6.22)*.

There is, however, a slight difference of opinion when it comes to friendship with the US being in national interest, between the youth from rural areas as compared to those living in urban areas and also between the Hindu and Muslim youth. Further, those who have completed college education are far more likely to see friendship with the US as being in India's national interest.

**Figure 6.22**
**India and her relations with the US**

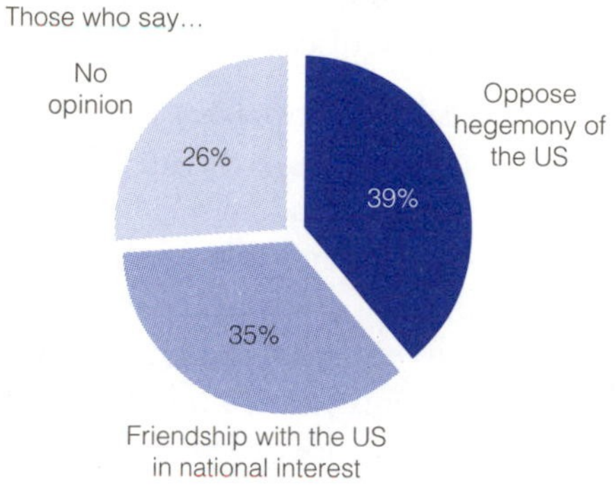


## Summing Up

Overall, there does not seem to be much awareness among the youth about the changes taking place in the contemporary world. A vast majority of them are not aware of globalisation. By and large the educated youth and those who live in cities know about globalisation. Further, it is the educated youth who tend to support the advantages of globalisation more than those who have either not heard about it or those who live in the rural areas.

Even though a majority of the youth have not heard about globalisation or are not convinced about its advantages, a large number of them do agree that better and cheaper goods are available today and that job opportunities abroad have increased. However, these youth do not know that this is happening because of globalisation. A major percentage of those youth who have low SES and those who live in the rural areas disapprove of the advantages of globalisation in the form of the expansion of consumer and labour markets.

Case Study 9

***Image and Identification among Indian Call Centre Workers***
by **Jonathan Murphy**

### Sites at which economic and cultural modernity is negotiated

Unsurprisingly, the Indian call centre workers who were surveyed were well connected to traditional and new technologies of mass communication. While in-depth interviews revealed that many were disinterested in and somewhat dismissive of formal 'politics', they were almost all regular internet users, television watchers, and newspaper readers, and a substantial proportion regularly read news and other magazines. Their awareness of the outside world is very high, supplemented, of course, by their experiences of dealing with international clients. Thus, this cohort is particularly susceptible to the predominantly pro-globalisation discourse of both the Indian and international mainstream media.

The call centre workers' attitudes towards their class status within Indian and international society provides mixed evidence on the hypothesis of an emergent transnational middle class. With regard to Indian society, an absolute majority of respondents described themselves as in the middle quintile of the population, although by income they would undoubtedly come in the top few per cent of the population. They clearly felt themselves 'in the middle', obviously not from the lower classes, but also not from the power elite. Ranking vis-à-vis foreign clients was illuminating. Almost all of the respondents worked in business processes where the majority of foreign clients would be expected to be of middle class or lower status (basic consumer finance, consumer good's product support, telecommunications service support, etc.) Although a plurality of respondents declared themselves 'equal to' their customers, a substantial proportion felt that their foreign customers were socially superior. However, as noted, there was a correlation between those perceiving themselves as in the upper two quintiles of the Indian population and a sense of being at least equal to the foreign clients. The responses to this question suggest that many respondents believe that India is still below Western countries in the global economic value chain, and thus that transnational middle class identity remains emergent rather than fully realised.

In contrast with the broader Indian youth population, the call centre group was very supportive of globalisation. Further, almost nine in ten were prepared to work overseas in order to further their careers, and a plurality were even prepared to give up the Indian citizenship for American in pursuit of their ambitions, which is again in stark contrast to the youth population as a whole. Usage of the English language was strikingly widespread. While most used Hindi or a vernacular language at home, English was almost as prevalent as Hindi when out with friends, and the majority stated that they mainly watch television in English. This is an important distinguishing factor for the call centre population (and the Indian elite population more generally) as compared to the general Indian population and a marker for transnationalising identity.

As might also be expected, the call centre group was well endowed with consumer goods, including items such as motorbikes, cellphones, stereo equipment, etc., befitting an international middle class status. In regard to aspiration, the call centre workers clearly favour ownership of a car, which is perceived as emblematic of an appropriate professional lifestyle. Most of the in-depth interview respondents not only indicated that they wanted to buy a car, but had set a specific and relatively short-term (within the next year) target to achieve this goal. Where a car had already been attained, purchase of a house was frequently mentioned. The centrality of consumerism as status identifier and personal motivator of the new middle class was observed.

The data collected on social attitudes reveal considerably more liberal perspectives and practices than the population as whole. Although the call centre workers share their compatriots' belief in the importance of family, in practical terms they appear to reject traditional beliefs regarding 'arranged' and 'love' marriages, the importance of marrying within caste, and the appropriateness of dating. While comparative data on sexual attitudes in India is scanty, the call centre group is certainly more tolerant of premarital sex than the prevailing social norm; indeed they were more liberal than American youth, though more traditional than Europeans.

The workers' commitment to their call centre careers was notable. Most respondents viewed their job as a career, and intended to stay in the business in the long-term. Somewhat contrary to popular media discourse, spouses and parents were generally supportive of the call centre career, despite the dislocation in social lives and physical health caused by night shift working. In common with Indians more generally, but to an even more marked extent, the call centre workers were very optimistic both about the country's future and about their own prospects. In the in-depth interviews, many interviewees said that 'nothing' could stop India, though a significant proportion did identify government and political corruption as a possible brake on growth.

Overall, the survey and interview data suggest that transnational identity, a global middle class habitus, is clearly present in at least an emergent form among India's international call centre worker population. This identity marks a rupture from earlier post-Independence middle class identity in terms of its identification with global consumer values, and focus on individual freedoms over earlier notions of collectivist nation-building.

The youth, however, show more awareness when it comes to India's friends and foes and are also suggestive of the path India should choose to deal with the world. Interestingly, a majority of the young people across the social spectrum want India to treat her neighbours on an equal footing and want India to have good relations with them, including Pakistan.

As the US is dominating the contemporary world, it is but natural that young people know more about her than about any other country. However, the young people seem to have mixed views on India's increasing engagement with the US. They are divided on whether India should oppose the hegemony of the US or ally with her for larger national interests. While the youth living in rural and urban areas differ slightly about whether India's alliance with the US is in national interest, the educated youth, especially those who have completed college education are more likely to believe that India's relations with the US are in national interest, compared to those who are less educated.

# CHAPTER 7: ANXIETY AND ASPIRATIONS

- The multi-level anxieties that the youth experience reflect the range of experiences that they are exposed to; these are significantly linked to their age, marital status, education and place of residence.
- The aspirations of the youth were diverse in their intensity and linked significantly to their SES, level of education and place of residence. The impact of SES, the benefits of education and exposure to urbanisation are clearly linked to what the youth look for in jobs/career.
- There was no direct co-relation between anxiety and the aspiration levels of the youth.
- Youth were by and large optimistic about their future. Those in the zone of uncertainty were basically those adversely affected because of their SES and educational attainment.

This chapter surveys the aims and aspirations of the youth along with identifying their anxieties and apprehensions. Some of the issues that are addressed in the chapter are:

- What hopes do the youth have for the future?
- What is their vision for the future?
- What trials and tribulations do the youth face?
- How do their perspectives differ across different spectrums and what causes this variation?

## Zones of Anxiety

To map the levels and intensity of anxiety among the youth, a series of questions were posed to them in order to construct a measure of the 'levels of personal anxiety' that they experience[1]. A set of five questions was selected to help measure anxiety from events over which the individual has some degree of control. Those questions were not included which sought to measure anxiety about events that the respondents had no direct control over. The rationale for the inclusion/exclusion was simple. A factor analysis and reliability test demonstrated that those zones of anxiety over which an individual has control hung together while those questions which involved anxiety over events that people had limited control over did not hang together. The items included levels of anxiety/ insecurity regarding employment/career, personal health, and prospects of marriage and family issues. A scale to measure the levels of personal anxiety was thus created. The responses were recoded on four dimensions—very high anxiety, high anxiety, low anxiety and very low anxiety.

**Figure 7.1**

**Levels of personal anxiety**

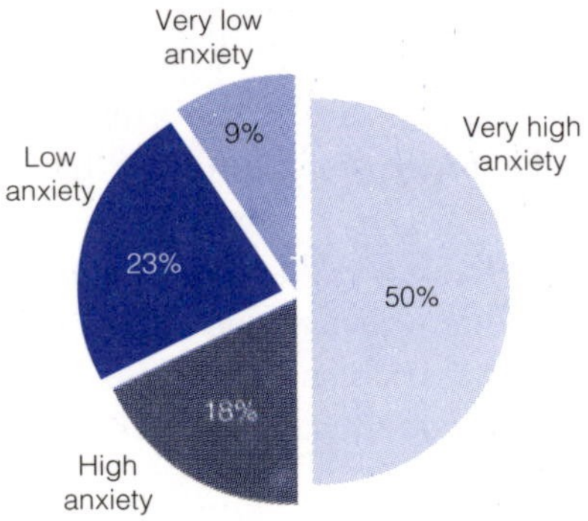


The study found that half of the youth reported very high anxiety. Two out of every ten youth experienced high anxiety while the remaining one-third fell in the low or very low anxiety category *(Figure 7.1)*.

The zones of anxiety that the youth fell into were influenced by age, caste, SES and education. Place of residence and religion do not appear to make a difference.

An analysis of the levels of anxiety across different age groups depending on the marital status of the youth shows that among the married youth, a large percentage have demonstrated very high anxiety at a young age (14 to 19 years) and at an older age (above 30 years) the same trend is observed. Among the unmarried youth, very high anxiety is reported by a significant number (52 per cent) in the 26 to 30 age band with the percentage of youth reporting very high anxiety declining after they crossed 30. At a younger age, married youth tend to report greater levels of very high anxiety. Once they cross the age of 30, the married youth again report a high per centage of very high anxiety. Unmarried youth in their twenties too tend to report higher very high anxiety levels *(Figure 7.2)*.

**Figure 7.2**

**Levels of anxiety by age and marital status**

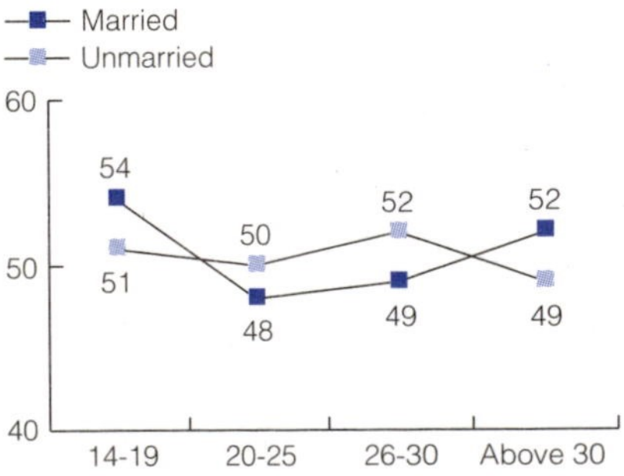

Very high anxiety levels among youth who are married and have no children tend to be lower than other youth who are unmarried or have children. There are important differences between anxiety levels of young people from different classes. Those in the middle-income range tend to report more very high anxiety levels. Those married youth who have children and are in the high-income group are least likely to experience very high anxiety levels. Youth from the high income bracket who are married but have no children as well as those who are married and have children report the same levels of "low" and "very low" anxiety taken together *(Figure 7.3)*.

**Figure 7.3**

**Levels of anxiety by marital status and SES**

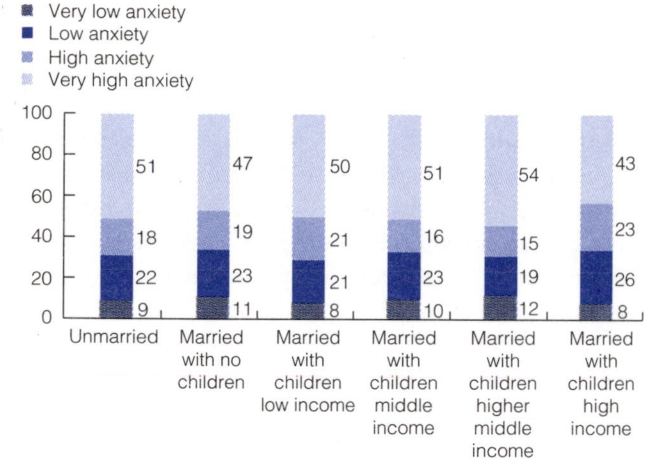


Some marginal differences in anxiety levels exist between the different age groups. In the case of married youth who have children and are from the low income group, the anxiety levels tend to increase with age. The same is true about married youth who have children and are in the middle income and higher middle-income categories. In the case of married youth with children in the high-income category, the anxiety levels tend to decline with age. In the case of this group (high income married youth with children) the reporting of "very high anxiety" is around 55 per cent in the 20-25 years age group.

Unemployed youth and students tend to report very high anxiety, more than those who are employed and those who are homemakers. There is hardly any difference among the professional categories when it comes to reporting high or low anxiety. Very low anxiety is reported by a smaller percentage of students and homemakers as compared to employed and unemployed youth. In the case of both the employed youth as well as the students, the percentage of those reporting very high anxiety increases with age. In the case of homemakers and unemployed youth it remains the same across age groups *(Figure 7.4)*.

**Figure 7.4**

**Levels of anxiety by occupational status**

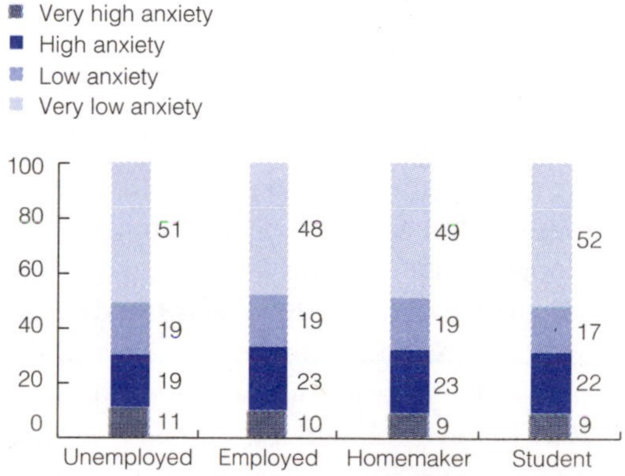

Case Study 10

## *Virtual Socialisation via Cyber Cafes: Narratives of Youth from Ranchi*

by **Shweta Jha**

### Sites at which economic and cultural modernity is negotiated

Cyber cafes in Ranchi have opened up a unique world to the youth of the city. They have not only become an important part of the online community but also active participants in overall content development in cyberspace. Despite global exposure through Internet, most of the youth are deeply rooted in their local traditions and value systems. They are better informed after being exposed to the Internet. Many of them are using their new position to empower fellow youth. Many others are introspecting and trying to find solutions to the age-old problems of their communities. Thus, contrary to the popular notion, cyber cafes are not merely shady joints promoting all sorts of vices. Rather these small Internet hubs provide a storehouse of knowledge and information especially in small cities where the youth lack the right kind of exposure that is easily available in large metropolitan cities.

Features of cyber cafes are however a little different form those in large cities. Cyber cafes in Ranchi combine several things: as a training centre, trading spot, DTP centre, meeting place for young people and above all, a unique venue where the poor and the rich share the fruits of the internet revolution. Most of the youth of the city started going to the cyber café mainly to learn and have hands on experience especially to complete their project work. Despite initial inhibitions, they have displayed significant interest in the cyber world by actively participating and connecting to the online communities across the globe. Even the girls have come forward in a big way to become a vibrant segment of virtual socialisation taking place in the city. Alongside virtual socialisation, the youth of the city find ample opportunities to socialise in person at the numerous cyber cafes in Ranchi. Their common interests, profiles and socio-economic background augment such off-line interaction among the youth. Cyber cafes in Ranchi have led to an increased level of awareness about the corporate world, society and politics amongst the youth. A large number of youth do not see any negative side effects of surfing the net. Instead, they view the Internet as a powerful platform for virtual socialisation. The youth of Ranchi have become a vibrant segment of global online communities. The worldview of young cyber café users has also undergone a sea change. For example, their trendy e-mail addresses speak a lot about their fast changing attitude and intention to take on the world. The number of young people having their personal web-pages is also increasing by the day. A number of young cyber café users in Ranchi have graduated from being content users to content creators.

The levels of anxiety appear to differ depending upon the place of residence of the youth. While two-third of the youth across locations are in the high anxiety or very high anxiety bracket, in the cities a smaller percentage of youth fall in the very high anxiety bracket *(Figure 7.5)*.

**Figure 7.5**

**Level of anxiety by locality**

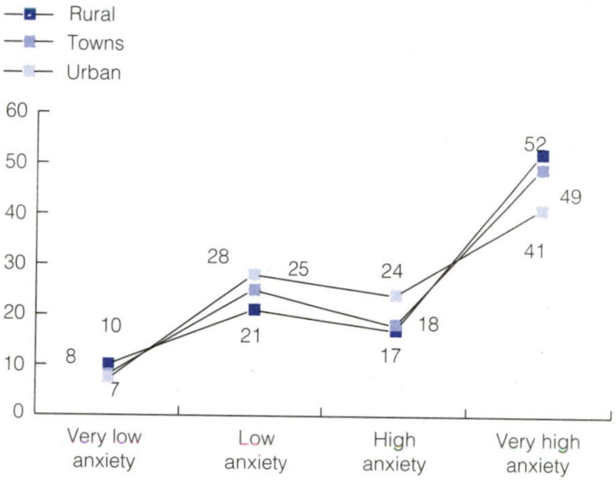


## Levels of Aspiration

An attempt was also made in this survey to tap the levels of aspiration among the youth. Two questions asked in the survey were used to prepare the index[2]. These questions dealt with the importance of achieving one's goals, success and doing better than others. When the responses to both these questions were analysed it was found that they had a strong correlation. Five categories of responses were created—very low aspirations, low aspirations, moderate level aspirations, high aspirations and very high aspirations.

Three out of every ten youth have very high aspirations while one-fourth have high aspirations. Two out of every ten have moderate aspirations and more or less the same number have low aspirations. A very small percentage of the youth (7 per cent) have very low aspirations. This implies that more than half the youth have very high or high aspirations. Less than one-third has low or very low aspirations and less than 20 per cent have a moderate level of aspirations *(Figure 7.6)*.

**Figure 7.6**

**Levels of aspiration among youth**

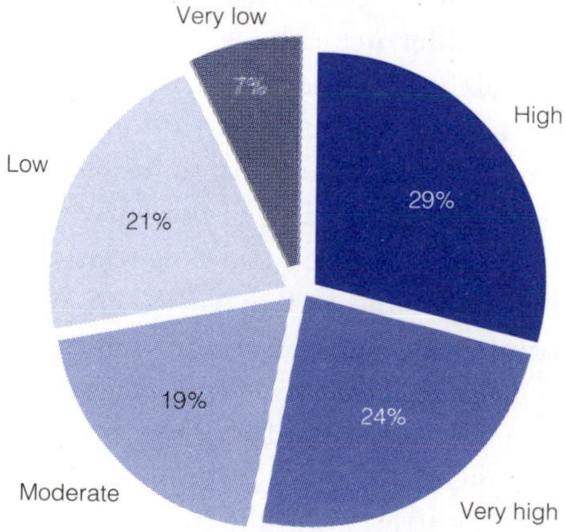


It was found that an important variable that defined and determined the nature of youth aspirations was their place of residence. The youth in small towns appear to have the highest level of aspirations. Further, a comparatively lower number of youth in towns have low or moderate aspirations as compared to those living in villages and metropolitan areas. Interestingly, those living in villages have higher aspirations as compared to those living in cities. It could be argued that in cities, the exposure that young people have and the environment that they live in results in higher levels of contentment and thus there are limited aspirations. The youth living in towns are located in spaces, which are on the threshold of growth and progress *(Figure 7.7)*. They are exposed to the elements of big cities and aspire for the lifestyle, opportunities and progress available in the cities. The same appears to be true for those living in the villages, though with a lesser degree of intensity as compared to those living in the towns *(Figure 7.7)*.

**Figure 7.7**

**Levels of aspiration among youth by locality**

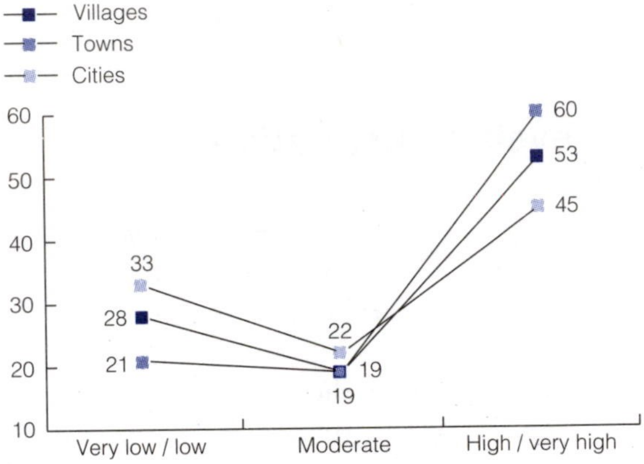


Caste also appears to be an important variable when it comes to the aspiration levels of the youth. A lesser number from among the Dalits and Tribals have very low aspirations when compared to those from the Other Backward Castes (OBCs) and Forward Castes *(Figure 7.8)*. A marginally higher percentage among the Dalits and Tribals appear to have high aspirations as compared to the Forward Castes.

**Figure 7.8**

**Levels of aspiration among youth by caste**

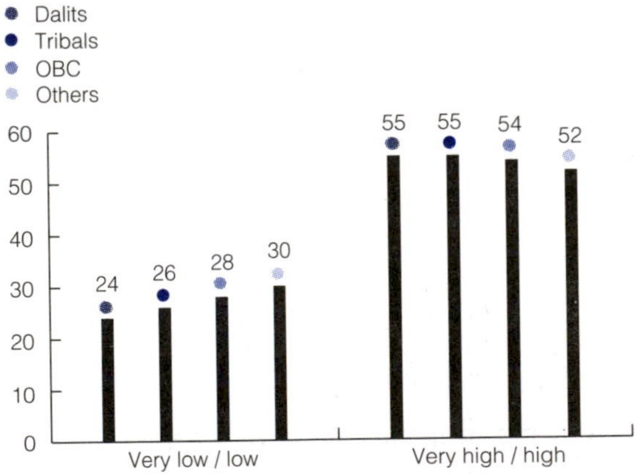


Given the continued experience of caste-based differences, the youth from Dalit and Tribal communities appear to have aspirations for a more fair and just life in which they have the opportunities to reach their full potential. In the case of the Forward Castes, the aspiration levels could be relatively lower because of the fact that they are already in comfortable socio-economic conditions and thus do not greatly aspire for a better life as much as those from the disadvantaged sections.

When the education levels of the respondents are taken into account, the trend which emerges is that those who have not had the benefits of education have limited aspirations. Nearly one-third

**These stars shone in the face of adversity**

She's as busy and hard working as the bees she looks after. Seventeen-year-old Anita from Bochaha village in Bihar's Muzaffarnagar is studying English Literature at Bhimrao Ambedkar University and it's all thanks to her beekeeping profession she took up six years ago. Anita is proud to claim that she is the 'first woman beekeeper in her state' and her honey is sold under the brand name Anita's Honey. She is also a UNICEF Girl Star along with Kiran from Patna, who runs the 'unladylike business' of a junkyard. Anita and Kiran, along with 12 others, have been selected as Girl Stars for educating themselves and becoming self-reliant in the face of extreme difficulties. Suryamani is an environmentalist who dons the garb of an activist while exhorting her fellow Oran tribesmen in Ranchi, Jharkhand. A Sanskrit graduate, Suryamani has refused several teaching job offers, as she does not want to 'be tied to a classroom'. The only woman-run computer institute in the remote village of Babina in Uttar Pradesh belongs to Sandhya. She took a loan and started off her institute with two computers. Seeing the plight of girls in Bardhunga village, 20 km from her own, she set up a computer there and helps girls with free advice on jobs. 'Doctorsaab' is how they address her whenever she visits her village in Nagpur, Rajasthan. For 19-year-old Anuradha Rathore, admission into the Medical College at Jodhpur was the fulfillment of a cherished dream. Afflicted with polio, Anuradha not only had physical disability to overcome but also societal pressure. She says she will go back to the village to practice.

Kavita Chawdhury, New Delhi, *The Indian Express,* May 9, 2007.

of those who could not read and write have limited aspirations *(Figure 7.9)*. Those who have completed college education have relatively higher aspirations.

The most significant variable that impacts an individual's aspiration levels is SES. A significant percentage of those with very low SES also have low aspirations. More than one-third of those in the low SES have low/very low aspirations. Among the middle and high SES only one-fourth have very low/low aspirations. On the other hand, a high percentage of those in the middle and high SES have very high/high aspirations. Nearly six out of every ten in the high SES have high/very high aspirations. In the low SES, this comes down to four in every ten *(Figure 7.10)*.

**Figure 7.9**

**Higher the education, greater the level of aspiration among youth**

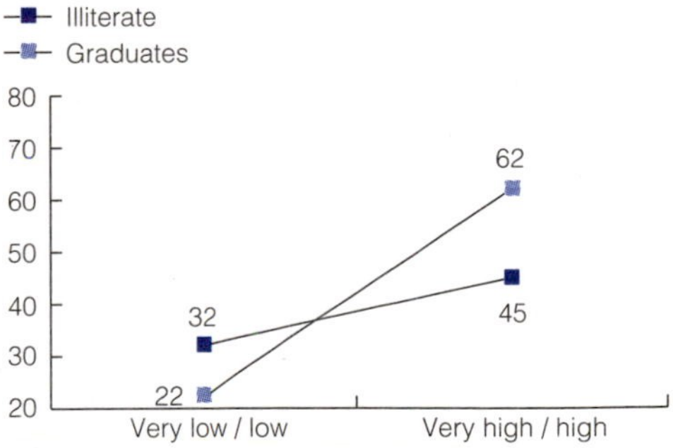


**Figure 7.10**

**Higher the SES of youth, greater the level of aspiration among them**

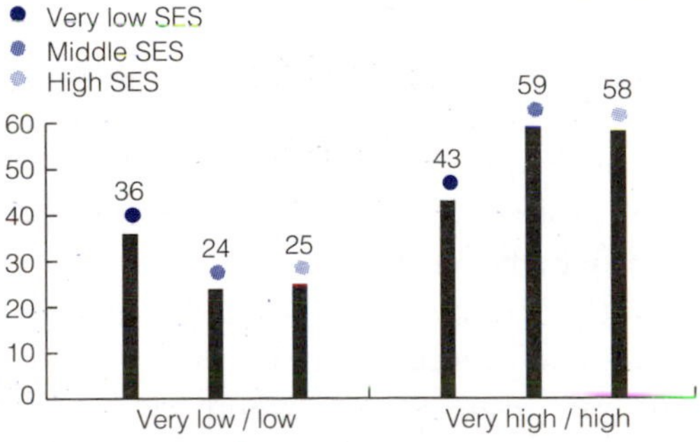

An attempt was made to link the aspiration levels of the youth with the importance that they attach to higher education. The results show a direct link between high aspirations and an intense desire to secure the benefits of higher education. Nine out of every ten youth who have very high aspirations feel that gaining access to higher education is extremely important. Just half the youth who have very low aspirations feel that access to higher education is extremely important. Less than 2 per cent of those, who have high or very high aspirations thought that gaining access to higher education is not at all important. Among those with very low aspirations this percentage shoots up eight times (16 per cent) *(Figure 7.11)*.

**Figure 7.11**

**Higher the level of aspiration, greater the desire for higher education among youth**

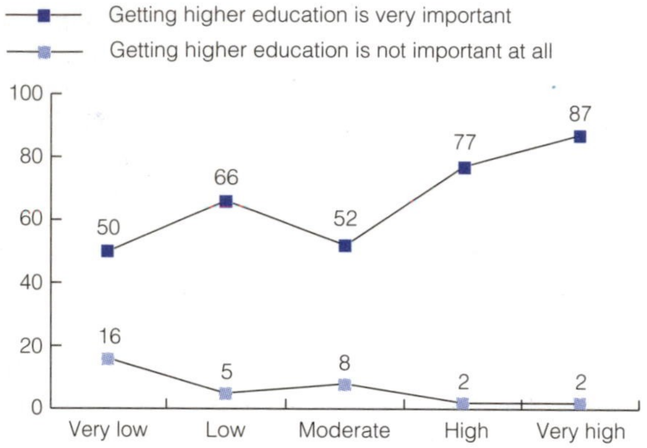


As a part of the survey the youth were also asked what would be the most important factor that they would look for when finding a job. This was asked irrespective of their employment status. They were offered four options: a) A job with good income; b) A job with security even if it meant a lower salary; c) A job with an opportunity to work with people of your choice and; d) A job that gives you a feeling of accomplishment/satisfaction.

While one-third of the youth opted for the good income option, another one-third opted for the secure job option. Less than 10 per cent say that they would prefer a job that allows them to work with people of their choice and less than 20 per cent stated that they would look for a job that gives them a sense of accomplishment/satisfaction.

The percentage of those opting for a high salary job is higher among those living in cities and who have a lower SES. Job security is not a major concern for the youth living in the cities and seeking a job that gives them satisfaction is very important for graduates and those from high SES.

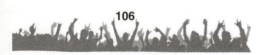

On the basis of the discussion above, it can be concluded that when it comes to the aspiration levels of the youth the most significant variable is SES. The next most critical variable is the educational level of the youth. The higher the educational level, the greater is the level of aspirations. What is important to reiterate here is that the aspiration level of the youth in small towns and in newly emerging urban settings is significantly higher than the aspiration levels of those living in villages and in big cities. This is linked to the 'promise of opportunity' that life exposes them to which in turn gives rise to high aspirations and expectations. However, a caveat needs to be added here. The aspirations are in significant ways relative to the 'worldview' of any individual. They are a by-product of social encounters, peer interactions and the window with which one views the world and the future.

**Figure 7.12**

**Higher the level of aspiration, greater the level of anxiety among youth**

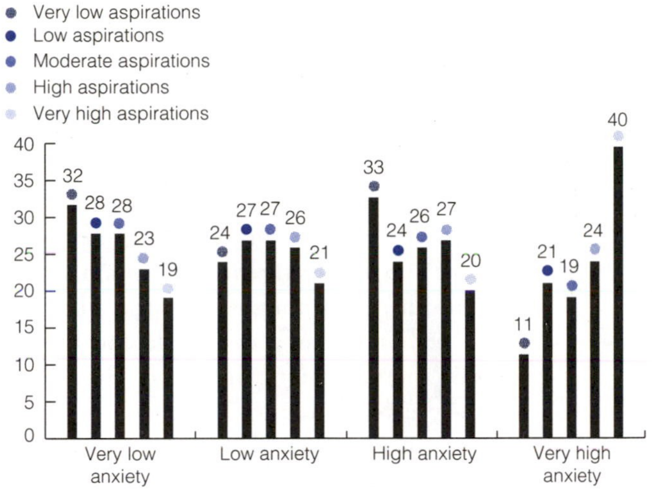


If an attempt is made to co-relate the Index of Anxiety with the Index of Aspirations, it is found that high anxiety is not directly linked to high aspirations or vice versa. While there is a tendency for those with very low aspirations to have low/very low anxiety, there is a significant percentage of exceptions. Similarly, those with very high expectations may increasingly have high or very high anxiety but in this bracket too there is a major chunk (40 per cent) that has low or very low anxiety *(Figure 7.12)*. A statistical analysis demonstrates that SES of the youth seems to be the true indicator of high or low anxiety/aspirations.

## Perceptions about the Future

Two questions in the survey sought a response to how do the youth perceive developments in the future in their own lives and in the lives of their children? Based on the responses, an index on 'Youth Perceptions about the Future' was created[3]. Furthermore three categories of answers were created—optimistic about the future, uncertain about the future and pessimistic about the future.

One finds that more than eight out of every ten youth are optimistic about the future. Thirteen per cent are uncertain and just 3 per cent are pessimistic about the future *(Figure 7.13)*.

Is there a pattern among those who are uncertain about their future? Among the youth,

**Figure 7.13**

**Overwhelming majority of youth are optimistic about future**

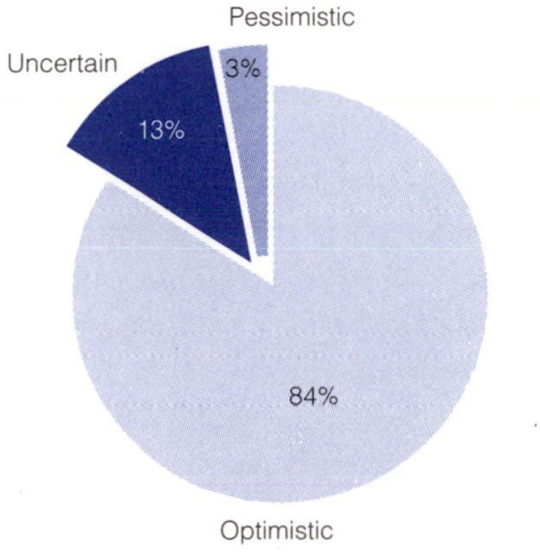

**Figure 7.14**

**Uncertainty about future by age, caste and SES**

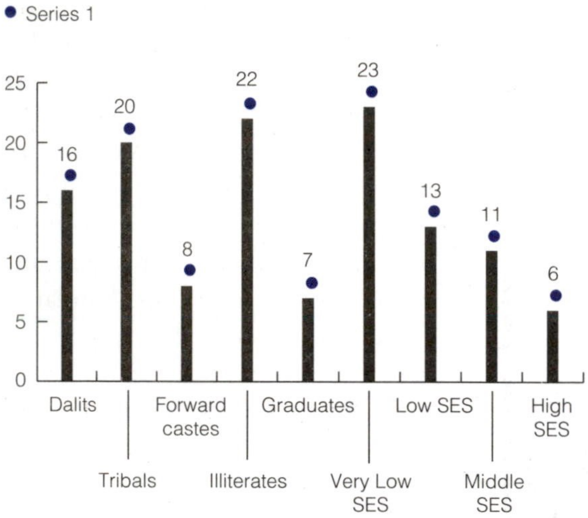


there is a marginally higher degree of uncertainty about the future among the 18+ years age group as compared to those in the 14 to 18 years age group *(Figure 7.14)*. Those in towns are more optimistic about the future and less uncertain as compared to those living in villages and cities. There is greater anxiety about the future among the Tribals and Dalits as compared to the Forward Castes. The less educated are clearly more agitated and uncertain about the future as compared to those who have access to higher education. Those with lower SES are clearly more uncertain about their future. Among the youth who are married and belong to middle and higher SES, there is more optimism about the future as compared to the others.

It is clear that certain sections among the youth have serious anxieties about how their future and that of their children is shaping up. The most critical factor appears to be SES.

An attempt was made to cross tabulate the perceptions of the youth about their future and their aspirations. It was found that those who were uncertain about the future were more likely to have low/very low aspirations. As the aspiration levels increased the uncertainty about the future reduced *(Figure 7.15)*.

**Figure 7.15**

**Those having higher levels of aspiration are least likely to be uncertain about future**

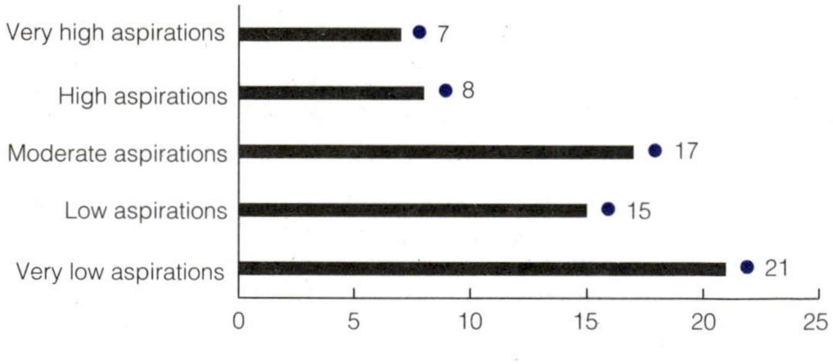


Among the different variables, the one that appears to best explain the variations in perceptions about the future is socio economic status (SES). This variable influences the direction of all other variables. As the SES of the youth improves, uncertainty about their future reduces. The next most important variable is the level of education. The better the access to education, less are the levels of uncertainty about the future. Marital status is the next predictor of the perception on the future. Married people tend to be less uncertain about the future. The index also included the respondents' position on whether they think that their children would have a better life than theirs. Those married and with children are more positive about this 'real' situation as compared to those who are unmarried and have to imagine the future of those who are not yet born.

## Summing Up

The aims and aspirations and anxieties and apprehensions of the youth are clearly linked to three variables. The first is SES and on all the issues analysed in this chapter, it appears to be a critical marker. The second important variable is the educational status of the youth that also defines and determines their anxieties, anguish, aspirations and future. Finally, the place of residence too is seen to shape the perceptions of the youth. The aims and aspirations of the youth living in villages are often linked to the immediate world that they confront in their daily lives. Metropolitan India tends to present youth with a different set of anxieties and aspirations. Youth in small, emerging towns and cities seem to be at the threshold of real change. Not yet fully cut off from their rural roots but significantly influenced by the scent of urbanisation and all its trappings, the high level of expectations as reflected both in their anxieties and aspirations underscore this point.

### Endnotes

1) The questions that hung together included: Young people have various kinds of insecurities/anxieties in their lives. I will read out a few such insecurities. Tell me to what extent are you insecure about the following—to a great extent, somewhat or none at all a) Your employment/career; c) Personal health; d) Prospects of your marriage; and e) Issues within your family. Three elements which do not hang together and were thus excluded were: b) Riots and mob violence in the country; f) Road accidents; and g) Global terrorism. The responses to the four sub-sets of the question which hung together were recorded as ordinal variables ranging from 0 to 10, in which 0 denotes no anxiety and 10 denotes anxiety to a great extent. All these variables were turned into standardised z-scores. The z-scores were added and divided by the total number of variables (5). The new variable was then recoded into quartiles (4 categories with 25 per cent cut points).

2) The questions which were used to prepare the index were:

   Question 30a and e: Now I am going to read a few statements that deal with peoples' opinion towards life. Do you agree or disagree with these statements (Probe further if 'strongly' or 'somewhat' agree or disagree): a) It is important to achieve more than others; and e) I manage to achieve my goals and plans for success.

   Those who 'strongly agreed' with both the statements were given the value '10' denoting 'very high aspirations', while those who 'strongly disagreed' with both the statements were given the value '0' denoting 'very low aspirations'. 'No opinions' were excluded from the analysis. Five categories of response were created—very low aspirations, low aspirations, moderate level aspirations, high aspirations and very high aspirations.

3) The two questions that are used for the analysis are: Question 49: Few years from now, how do you foresee your future? Do you think your life will become very bright, somewhat bright or there will hardly be any change?

   Question 50: Do you think your children will have a better life than that of yours, worse than yours or that there will hardly be any difference?

Those who were optimistic about their and their children's future were labeled 'optimistic about the future'. Those who gave a negative answer to both the questions were labeled 'pessimistic about the future'. 'No opinions' were excluded from the analysis.

Based on the responses, three categories of answers were created—optimistic about the future, uncertain about the future and pessimistic about the future.

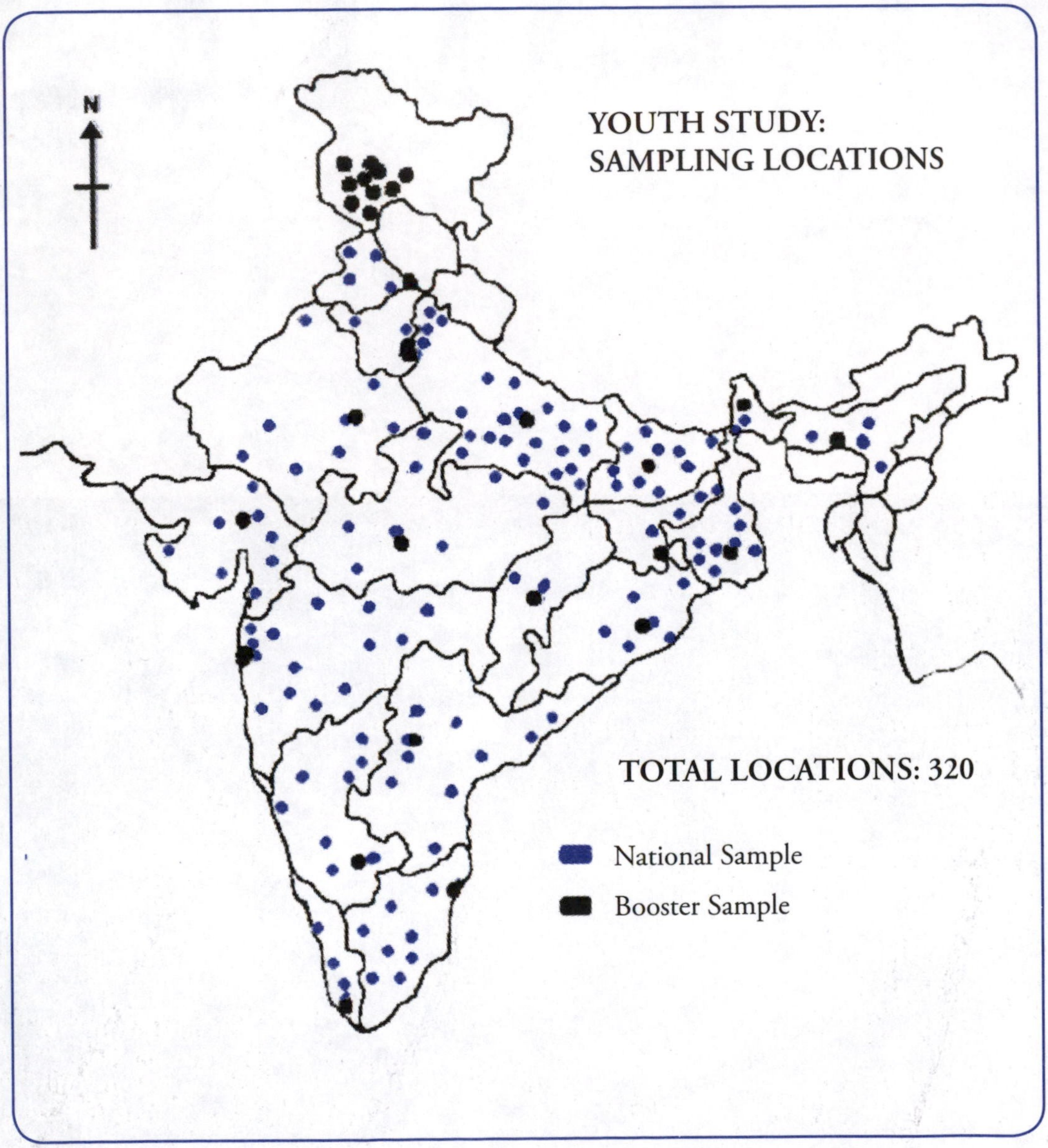
N
YOUTH STUDY:
SAMPLING LOCATIONS
TOTAL LOCATIONS: 320
National Sample
Booster Sample

# APPENDIX I
# Sampling for Youth Survey

## Target Group

**Those between age group 14–34 years**

The sample for the youth survey was drawn using the multi-stage systematic random sampling technique. The total target sample of 5,000 respondents was distributed in different states in proportion to their share in the youth population. Since distribution of the sample in proportion to the share of the youth in the population would have meant quota of few interviews in small states, many such states were removed from the universe from which the sample was drawn. The states which were removed from the sample were Goa, Himachal Pradesh, Uttarakhand, Manipur, Meghalaya, Mizoram, Tripura, Nagaland, Arunachal Pradesh and Sikkim. Taking into consideration the lower completion rate, a sample of 7,176 respondents in the age group of 18–34 years and 2,208 households for selecting respondents in the age group of 14–17 years were drawn from the electoral rolls. When the survey was completed, 5,000 youth from different age groups had been interviewed.

## Process of Sample Selection

The first stage in the sample selection was sampling of assembly constituencies in each state where the survey was to be undertaken. In each state the assembly constituencies were randomly selected using the Probability Proportionate to Size (PPS) technique.

The second stage in the sample selection was sampling the political unit—the polling booths. In each selected assembly constituency, two polling booths were randomly selected using the systematic random sampling technique. Since the polling booths represent locations in urban areas and villages, this helped in pointing out the locations at which the survey was undertaken. A total of 320 locations were randomly selected for the survey.

The third stage in the sample selection involved the sampling of respondents who were to be interviewed. For this the mix method of sampling the individuals as well as the households was used. Respondents in the age group 18–34 years were selected from the electoral rolls, but for the respondents in the age group of 14–17 years, the household where the survey was to be conducted among the youth were selected.

At the very beginning a sample of 34 respondents was selected using the electoral rolls. The universe for selecting the sample was freshly drawn by deleting the names of all those above the age of 35 years in the electoral rolls of all the sampled polling booths. The sample of 34 respondents was drawn using the systematic random sampling technique from this new universe with names of voters above 35 years deleted from the universe.

Once the sample of 34 respondents had been drawn the names of eight respondents were treated not as respondents but as selected household. In the list of selected individuals, respondent number 4, 8, 12, 16, 20, 24, 28, and 32 were not considered as selected respondents, but as selected households while the rest were treated as selected respondents. The quota for the proportion of households and individuals was decided keeping in mind the share of the youth in the population in the age group of 18–34 years and those in the 14–17 years age group.

## Selecting respondents from selected household

Now we had two lists: One of the selected respondents and the other of the selected households. The investigators tried to reach the selected respondents and conducted interviews with only those whose names figured in the selected respondents list. There was no substitution for those respondents who could not be contacted or interviewed for various reasons. Strictly only those respondents were interviewed whose names figured on the list of selected respondents.

From the list of selected households, the investigators had the liberty to choose the respondent. There were possibilities of investigator bias while selecting the respondents between ages 14–17 years in the selected households since the respondents had not been selected. While the overall mandate was to maintain a gender balance while selecting the respondents in the selected households, investigators followed a strict procedure for selecting the respondents in the selected household.

In some households the investigator could find both a boy and a girl in the age group of 14–17 years. In such cases, only one respondent was interviewed. While the investigator had the liberty to select either the boy or the girl from such a household, that decision was guided by the profile of interviews in other selected households. In case the investigator had already interviewed some girls in the other households, he selected the boy and vice versa. More than one interview in one household was not allowed.

## Achieving the target

While a sample of 24 respondents and eight households was drawn as the list which was to be targeted for the interviews, we ended up interviewing much less respondents than the number of sampled respondents. Of the total 24 respondents who were selected for the survey, on an average about 11–12 interviews were conducted at each polling booth. Amongst the selected households, about 4–5 interviews could be successfully completed under the specified parameters. Keeping in mind the shortfall in the rate of completion, an over sampling was done while drawing the sample both for the respondents as well as for the households.

There were rare occasions in a couple of localities where the investigators could not meet even one respondent in the 14–19 years age bracket in the selected household. In such cases he visited the house next to the one which was the selected household to interview any youth available between in the 14–17 years age group. Nearly 7 per cent of the total interviews were conducted in substituted households for meeting the respondents in the 14–17 years age group.

## Booster sample

While a national sample of 5,000 respondents is a good enough sample to draw conclusions about the youth at the national level, this would have constrained us in analysing the data in terms of levels of urbanity, i.e. village youth versus small town youth versus youth living in big cities. Since the sample of 5,000 was proportionately spread across towns and cities, the number of interviews from these small and big cities would have been small enough to not allow a me aningful analysis. Keeping this in mind a booster sample was drawn from the big cities in such a way so that apart from the metropolitan cities, the survey was conducted in all the capital cities of all the state where the survey was undertaken. The booster survey was conducted at 76 locations in the state capitals of the states where the survey was conducted.

The sample of 1,976 respondents in the 18–34 years age group and a sample of 608 households for interviews of those in the 14–17 years age group was randomly selected from the electoral rolls. The total number of booster interviews from the capital cities was 1,216.

The findings of the survey reported in this report are based on the findings of the national representative sample of 5,000 youth from different age groups, gender, castes and localities. The disaggregate analysis for towns and cities includes the booster sample collected from the cities and towns.

## Field work

Fieldwork for the youth survey was conducted during April–May 2007. The research investigators, mainly college and university students, were given special training in survey research techniques during a two-day workshop especially organised for this purpose in various states. All the respondents were interviewed in the face-to-face situation using the structured interview schedule.

# APPENDIX II
## CSDS-KAS Youth Survey 2007
## Questionnaire

**State Code** ☐☐ **Official A.C. No.** ☐☐☐ **Sample Type** ☐ **Official P.S. No.** ☐☐☐ **Respondent S.No.** ☐☐☐☐
As in Voter List

I have come from (name of the university if required) Centre for the study of Developing Societies, a research organisation located in Delhi. We are studying the opinion & attitudes of Indian youth for which we will interview hundreds of youths across the country. The findings of the research will be used for writing articles and academic purposes. The names of respondents interviewed in this survey will be kept strictly confidential. The survey is an independent study and is not linked with any political party or government agency. Kindly spare some time for this interview and answer my questions, as I need your active cooperation for making this study successful.

**Q1.** People have different opinions about the age at which young boys and girls should get married. Which according to you is an ideal age to get married for boys?

__________ **(Record exact age)** 88. No Opinion

☐☐

**Q2.** Which according to you is an ideal age to get married for girls?

__________ **(Record exact age)** 88. No Opinion

☐☐

**Q3.** Now I am going to ask you about activities which people generally do in their spare time. How regularly do you do the following in your spare time—mostly, sometimes or never? **(Read out options)**

| | Activities | Mostly | Sometimes | Never | No Opinion |
|---|---|---|---|---|---|
| a. | Listening to Music | 1 | 2 | 3 | 8 |
| b. | Going out with friends | 1 | 2 | 3 | 8 |
| c. | Reading books/magazines/Periodicals | 1 | 2 | 3 | 8 |
| d. | Playing some game/sport | 1 | 2 | 3 | 8 |
| e. | Watching films | 1 | 2 | 3 | 8 |
| f. | Watching Television | 1 | 2 | 3 | 8 |

a ☐ b ☐ c ☐ d ☐ e ☐ f ☐

**Q4.** **(If watches Television.)** How regularly do you watch the following on Television—is it daily, more than once a week, rarely or never? **(Read out the programmes listed)**

| | **T.V. Shows** | **Daily** | **More than once a week** | **Rarely** | **Never** | **N. A.** |
|---|---|---|---|---|---|---|
| **a.** | Religious and spiritual programmes | 1 | 2 | 3 | 4 | 9 |
| **b.** | Films | 1 | 2 | 3 | 4 | 9 |
| **c.** | News/political debates | 1 | 2 | 3 | 4 | 9 |
| **d.** | Sports/Matches/tournaments | 1 | 2 | 3 | 4 | 9 |
| **e.** | Business news/channels | 1 | 2 | 3 | 4 | 9 |
| **f.** | Songs/Music Videos | 1 | 2 | 3 | 4 | 9 |
| **g.** | Soaps/T.V. Serials | 1 | 2 | 3 | 4 | 9 |
| **h.** | Reality Shows | 1 | 2 | 3 | 4 | 9 |

a ☐ b ☐ c ☐ d ☐ e ☐ f ☐

**Q5.** If you recall your childhood days, how would you describe your upbringing - would you say that your upbringing was very strict, strict, not so strict or not at all strict?

1. Very strict 2. Strict 3. Not so strict 4. Not at all strict 8. No opinion

☐

**Q6.** If you think about the way you would like to bring up your children, you would bring them up—exactly the same way your parents brought you up, more or less the same way, differently or very differently?

1. Exactly the same way 2. More or less the same way 3. Differently 4. Very differently 8. No Opinion

☐

**Q7.** How many times have you participated in any protest, demonstration, struggle or movement—Several times, Once or twice or Never

1. Several times 2. Once or twice 3. Never 8. No opinion

☐

**Q8.** If you recall the number of times you have voted since you became eligible for voting, how would you best describe yourself—have you voted in every election, voted in most elections, voted in some elections, hardly ever voted.

1. Voted in every election 2. Voted in most elections 3. Voted in some elections
4. Hardly ever voted 8. No answer 9. N.A. [Not Eligible or eligible only once]

☐

**Q9.** Do you think your vote has effect on how things are run in this country or do you think your vote makes no difference?

2. Has effect 1. Makes no difference 8. No Opinion

☐

**Q10.** How interested are/were your parents in politics - are/were they very interested, interested, not interested or not at all interested?

1. Very interested 2. Somewhat interested 3. Not very interested 4. Not at all interested
8. No response

☐

**Q11.** Do you study in school/college or have you completed your school/college studies?

1. Studying in school 2. Studying in College 3. Completed school
4. Completed college 5. School drop out 6. College drop out
7. Never went to school

☐

**Q11a.** (*If currently studying in school/college*) What is your opinion about attending School/College[*Choose whichever applicable* ]. Do you like to attend School/College- very much, somewhat, or you don't like going to school/college.

1. Like very much 2. Like Somewhat 3. Neither like nor dislike
4. Don't like going to school/college 8. No Opinion/Distance Education 9. N.A.

☐

**Q11b.** (*If studying or completed study*) Do you study/studied in government or private school?

1. Government 2. Private 3. Any other (Specify) ______________ 9. N.A.

☐

**Q11c.** (If studying or completed study) Where have/are you completed/continuing your schooling - village or city?

1. Village 2. Town 3. City 9. N.A.

☐

**Q12.** If you take into consideration the overall educational facilities available in India—do you think you are satisfied or dissatisfied with them? (Probe further if 'fully' or 'somewhat' satisfied or dissatisfied)

1. Fully Satisfied 2. Somewhat satisfied 3. Somewhat dissatisfied
4. Fully Dissatisfied 8. No opinion

☐

**Q13.** How would you describe your day-to-day life at school/college/workplace (ask the one applicable) like - is it very stressful, somewhat stressful, somewhat relaxed, or very relaxed?

1. Very Stressful 2. Somewhat stressful 3. Somewhat Relaxed
4. Very relaxed 8. No opinion 9. NA [Unemployed/Home maker]

☐

**Q14.** Now I am going to read out few things, you tell me how important are they for you – are they very important, somewhat important, somewhat unimportant or not important at all? (Read out options)

| | | Very important | Somewhat important | Not so important | Not important at all | No opinion |
|---|---|---|---|---|---|---|
| a. | Getting higher education | | | | | |
| b. | Being interested in politics | | | | | |
| c. | Taking on responsibility | | | | | |
| d. | Dressing up/dressing in latest styles/trends | | | | | |
| e. | Getting married | | | | | |

a ☐ b ☐ c ☐ d ☐ e ☐

**Q15.** Do you have children?

1 Yes 2 No

☐

**Q15a.** (If no) Would you like to have children in future?

1. Yes 2. No 8. Can't say 9 NA

☐

**Q16.** Would you want your husband/wife (choose whichever applicable) to earn—more than you or less than you?

1. Should earn more 2. Should earn Less 3. Does not matter.
4. Should not earn/work 5. Should earn equal 8. No opinion

☐

**Q17.** We often hear about people being discriminated on various accounts in their day-to-day life. Please tell me how often have you felt discriminated about the following - frequently, sometimes, or never? (Read out the reasons listed)

| | Reason | Frequently | Sometimes | Never | No Opinion |
|---|---|---|---|---|---|
| a | Economic status/condition | 1 | 2 | 3 | 8 |
| b | Your Caste | 1 | 2 | 3 | 8 |
| c | Your Gender | 1 | 2 | 3 | 8 |
| d | Your Religion | 1 | 2 | 3 | 8 |
| e | Your state of origin/region | 1 | 2 | 3 | 8 |

a ☐ b ☐ c ☐ d ☐ e ☐

**Q18.** Do you watch/see films/movies?

2. Yes    1. No    8. No Answer

☐

**Q18a.** (If yes) Which type of films do you like the most? (Do not read out answer categories)

1. Action and adventure    2. Suspense/thrillers    3. Historical/Mythological/Religious
4. Musicals    5. Comedies    6. Films with a message
7. Dramas/Family/Social    8. Any other (Specify)________    9. No opinion 0. N.A.

☐

**Q19.** Now I will read out two statements on various issues. Tell me, do you agree with statement one (1) or statement two(2)?

**a** **1.** In matters of marriage boys and girls may be consulted, however final decision should be taken by parents
**2.** In matters of marriage though the parents may be consulted, final decision should be left to boys/girls themselves

1. Agree with first    2. Agree with second    8 No opinion

☐

**b** **1.** In our society, meeting/dating of boys and girls before marriage should be restricted.
**2.** There should be no restriction on meeting/dating of boys and girls before marriage

1. Agree with first    2. Agree with second    8 No opinion

☐

**c** **1.** In our society marriages must take place within one's own caste-community
**2.** There is nothing wrong if boys and girls of different castecommunity marry

1. Agree with first    2. Agree with second    8 No opinion

☐

**d** 1. Once married a couple must stay together even if it requires certain compromises.
2. If there are differences with ones partner, there is no harm in getting a divorce.

1. Agree with first    2. Agree with second    8 No opinion

☐

**Q20.** Do you use Internet?

2.Yes    1. No    8. No Opinion

☐

**Q20a.** (If yes) What do you use the Internet mainly for? (Do not read out answer categories)

1. E Mailing    2. Chatting/Social networking    3. For Information/Education    4. Gaming
5. Online Transactions    6. Any other (Specify)__________    8 No opinion    9. N.A.

☐

**Q20b.** (If yes to Q 20) How many hours a week do you spend on the Internet?
No of hours ______________________ (Record exract number of hours)

98. 98 and more          99. N.A

☐

**Q21.** Have you heard of the term 'globalisation'?

2. Yes          1. No          8. No Opinion

☐

**Q21a.** (If yes) Thinking of overall results/effects of globalisation, do you feel that globalisation leads to more advantages than disadvantages, more disadvantages than advantages or advantages and disadvantages are more or less same?

1. More advantages than disadvantages          2. More disadvantages than advantages
3. Advantages and Disadvantages are more or less same          8. No opinion          9 NA

☐

**Q22.** Now I will read out a few statements. You tell me for each do you agree or disagree with them? (Probe further whether 'fully' or 'somewhat' agree or disagree)

| | | Agree | | Disagree | | No opinion/ |
|---|---|---|---|---|---|---|
| | | Fully | Somewhat | Somewhat | Fully | D.K. |
| a. | Better and cheaper products are available as competition between different countries is increasing | 1 | 2 | 3 | 4 | 8 |
| b. | In society, foreign culture is becoming increasingly dominant | 1 | 2 | 3 | 4 | 8 |
| c. | The big countries wield all the power. | 1 | 2 | 3 | 4 | 8 |
| d. | Young people now get better employment Opportunities abroad | 1 | 2 | 3 | 4 | 8 |

a ☐     b ☐     c ☐     d ☐     e ☐

**Q23.** What according to you is the ideal age for a person to get employed (salaried job/self employed/start business)? (Record exact age) ______________________

98. Age no bar          99. No opinion

☐

**Q24.** There are various factors that motivate people to choose their occupation/work. I am going to read out a few considerations irrespective of whether you are seeking a job or not, which will be the most important consideration for your choice of occupation?[Read out options 1 to 4]

1. Job with good income.          2. Job with security even if it means lesser salary.
3. Job with an opportunity to work with people of your choice.
4. Job that gives you a feeling of accomplishment/Satisfaction.          8. Don't know/No Opinion

☐

**Q25.** Would you like to work in a government service, private service or take up own business/profession?

1 Government service 2 Private service 3 Own Business/Profession.
7. Any other (specify) ___________ 8 D.K/No opinion

☐

**Q26.** Now I am going to read out statements regarding the reservation of seats for SC, ST and OBC communities in higher education and professional courses. Tell me with which statement do you agree the most. (Read out option 1 to 4)

1. Seats should be reserved for SC, ST and OBC communities.
2. Seats should be reserved for SC, ST but not for OBC communities.
3. Seats should be reserved for SC, ST but only for economically weaker (poor) sections of the OBC communities.
4. There should be no reservation of seats for any community in higher education.
8. No Opinion

☐

**Q27.** I am going to name a number of institutions. For each one could you tell me how much trust you have in them. Is it great deal of trust, some trust, not very much trust or none at all?

| | | Great deal | Some | Not very much | None at all | No Opinion |
|---|---|---|---|---|---|---|
| a. | Central/National government | 1 | 2 | 3 | 4 | 8 |
| b. | State Government | 1 | 2 | 3 | 4 | 8 |
| c. | Local Government | 1 | 2 | 3 | 4 | 8 |
| d. | Civil Service | 1 | 2 | 3 | 4 | 8 |
| e. | Police | 1 | 2 | 3 | 4 | 8 |
| f. | Army | 1 | 2 | 3 | 4 | 8 |
| g. | Courts | 1 | 2 | 3 | 4 | 8 |
| h. | Parliaments | 1 | 2 | 3 | 4 | 8 |
| i. | Political Parties | 1 | 2 | 3 | 4 | 8 |
| j. | Election Commission | 1 | 2 | 3 | 4 | 8 |

a ☐ b ☐ c ☐ d ☐ e ☐ f ☐ g ☐ h ☐ i ☐ j ☐

**Q28.** Do you believe in God?

2. Yes 1. No 8. Can't say

☐

**Q29.** How often do you offer prayer/puja/namaj—daily, weekly, occasionally, only on festivals or never?

1. Daily 2. Once a Week 3. Occasionally 4. Only during festivals
5.Never 8 No opinion/answer

☐

**Q30.** Now I am going to read few statements that deal with peoples' opinion towards life. Do you agree or disagree with these statements? (Probe further if 'strongly' or "somewhat" agree or disagree)

| | | Agree | | Disagree | | No Opinion |
|---|---|---|---|---|---|---|
| | | Strongly | Somewhat | **Somewhat** | **Strongly** | |
| a. | It is important to achieve more than others | 1 | 2 | 3 | 4 | 8 |
| b. | Most decisions about my life are taken by others | 1 | 2 | 3 | 4 | 8 |
| c. | Nowadays one often has to do things that are not right | 1 | 2 | 3 | 4 | 8 |
| d. | I often feel alone/lonely | 1 | 2 | 3 | 4 | 8 |
| e. | I manage to achieve my goals and plans for success | 1 | 2 | 3 | 4 | 8 |
| f. | I cannot change anything about most things that disturb me | 1 | 2 | 3 | 4 | 8 |
| g. | Money is very important to remain happy | 1 | 2 | 3 | 4 | 8 |

a ☐ b ☐ c ☐ d ☐ e ☐

**Q31.** Thinking of 5 close friends, tell me how many of them are: (Record number)

| | Number | No Response |
|---|---|---|
| a. Boys/Girls [Ask for opposite sex whichever applicable] | ________ | 8 |
| b. From caste other than yours | ________ | 8 |
| c. From religious community other than yours | ________ | 8 |

a ☐ b ☐ c ☐

**Q32.** I am now going to read out a few things on which the young people generally spend money. Please tell me for each of these how much money do you spend in one month (Read out options and record in rupees)

| | **Activities** | **Amount Spent** | **N.A/D.K** |
|---|---|---|---|
| a | Watching movies (going to cinema/buying DVDs) | ..................... | 8888 |
| b | Eating out in restaurants and hotels | ..................... | 8888 |
| c | Buying Clothes/Shoes/Accessories | ..................... | 8888 |
| d | Buying Gadgets phones/I pods/Computer Softwares/ Watch/Music | ..................... | 8888 |
| e | Personal Mobile/Telephone Bills | ..................... | 8888 |

a ☐ ☐ ☐ ☐ b ☐ ☐ ☐ ☐

c ☐ ☐ ☐ ☐ d ☐ ☐ ☐ ☐

**Q33.** There are different opinions about drinking of alcohol. While some believe that a drinking of alcohol within limits is acceptable, while others say drinking alcohol is a bad habit and is not at all acceptable. There are still others who believe that though taking alcohol is not good but is necessary to maintain a social circle. What is your opinion about this?

1. Acceptable
2. Not at all acceptable
3. Necessary to maintain social circle
8. No opinion

☐

**Q34.** I am going to read out two statements about student unions in colleges, tell me whether you agree with statement 1 or with statement 2? (Read out options)

| | | |
|---|---|---|
| 1. There should be students union to protect | 2. Student unions should be banned as they disturb the rights and interests of the students. academic environment. | |
| 1. Agree with first | 2. Agree with second | 8 No opinion |

☐

**Q35.** Now I am going to read out a few statements about peoples' opinion about politics. For each of them you tell me, whether you agree or disagree. (Probe further if 'strongly', or "somewhat" agree or disagree)

| | Statements | Agree | | Disagree | | No Opinion |
|---|---|---|---|---|---|---|
| | | Strongly | Somewhat | Somewhat | Strongly | |
| a | Political parties are necessary in a democracy | 1 | 2 | 3 | 4 | 8 |
| b. | I think politicians do not care about people like me | 1 | 2 | 3 | 4 | 8 |
| c. | It is citizens duty to vote during elections | 1 | 2 | 3 | 4 | 8 |
| d. | I find understanding politics too complicated | 1 | 2 | 3 | 4 | 8 |
| e. | In India power rests with few people | 1 | 2 | 3 | 4 | 8 |
| f. | I find politics interesting | 1 | 2 | 3 | 4 | 8 |

a ☐ b ☐ c ☐ d ☐ e ☐ f ☐

**Q36.** I am going to read out 3 statements regarding reservations of seats for women in parliament and state assemblies. Tell me with which one do you agree the most? [Read out options]

1. Since women are underrepresented in parliament & state assemblies, seats should be reserved for them.
2. Seats should be reserved in parliament & state assemblies only for women who belong to SC, ST and OBC Communities.
3. There should be no reservation for women in parliament & state assemblies.
8. No Opinion

☐

**Q37.** If there is a proposal to reserve seats for youth in the parliament and state assemblies, would you support it or oppose it? (Probe further if "fully" or " somewhat" support or oppose)

1. Fully Support
2. Somewhat Support
3. Somewhat Oppose
4. Fully Oppose
8. No Opinion

☐

**Q38.** What according to you is the biggest problem faced by India? (Record the answer & consult codebook for coding) ______________________ 98. Can't say/No Answer
☐

**Q39.** There are various issues that a developing country like India needs to address. I am going to read out 3 such issues. What should the priorities of the government in addressing them: (Rank these issues from 1 to 3 in order of priority. 1 being the most important and 3 being the least important)

| | | No opinion |
|---|---|---|
| a. Reduce child mortality | ________ | 8 |
| b. Improve maternal health care facilities | ________ | 8 |
| c. Combat HIV/AIDS Malaria and other diseases | ________ | 8 |

a ☐ b ☐ c ☐

**Q40.** People sometimes talk about what should be the goals/aims of the country for the next 10 years. I am going to read out a few priorities of the government. How would you rank these 3 things in terms of their importance - 1 being the most important, 2 important & 3 being least important? (Rank these issues from 1 to 3 in order of priority)

| | | No opinion |
|---|---|---|
| a. Betterment of health services | ________ | 8 |
| b. Providing good education facilities | ________ | 8 |
| c. Guaranteeing employment for all | ________ | 8 |

a ☐ b ☐ c ☐

**Q41.** Now I would read out the names of a few countries. Have you heard the name of [Name of country]? (If Yes) How would you describe the relation of (Name of the country) with India - very friendly, friendly or not so friendly? (Read out options)

| Country | | Heard | | Government | | | | |
|---|---|---|---|---|---|---|---|---|
| | | Yes | No | Very friendly | Friendly | Not so friendly | No opinion | NA |
| a | China | 2 | 1 | 1 | 2 | 3 | 8 | 9 |
| b | America | 2 | 1 | 1 | 2 | 3 | 8 | 9 |
| c | Sri Lanka | 2 | 1 | 1 | 2 | 3 | 8 | 9 |
| d | Nepal | 2 | 1 | 1 | 2 | 3 | 8 | 9 |
| e | Pakistan | 2 | 1 | 1 | 2 | 3 | 8 | 9 |
| f | Russia | 2 | 1 | 1 | 2 | 3 | 8 | 9 |
| g | Germany | 2 | 1 | 1 | 2 | 3 | 8 | 9 |
| h | Bangladesh | 2 | 1 | 1 | 2 | 3 | 8 | 9 |

a ☐ ☐ b ☐ ☐ c ☐ ☐ d ☐ ☐ e ☐ ☐
f ☐ ☐ g ☐ ☐ h ☐ ☐

**Q42.** While deciding about career and academic options different families adopt different ways to take decisions. Among some families parents take all the decisions while in other families the parents and children discuss these matters together. Still there are some families in which children enjoy complete freedom in such matters. What has been your experience?

1. My parents decide everything
2. Parents and I discuss together
3. I enjoy complete freedom
8. No Opinion/Can't say

□

**Q43.** I am going to read out 3 statements about how people could remain happy. Tell me with which statement do you agree with the most? (Read out options)

1. To be happy in life one needs a family
2. One can be happy with or without family
3. One is happier alone, even without a family.
8. No Opinion

□

**Q44.** Now I would ask you how much trust do you have in people from various groups? I will show you a ladder with 1 to 10 steps (Show Card). If you place at step 1 those groups on whom you have a great deal of trust and at step 10 those groups on whom you have no trust then where would you place—

| | | No opinion |
|---|---|---|
| a. Your Friends | ________ | 88 |
| b. Your Relatives | ________ | 88 |
| c. People from your own caste | ________ | 88 |
| d. Your Neighbours | ________ | 88 |
| e. People from another religion | ________ | 88 |
| f. Your colleagues at work | ________ | 88 |
| g. People from caste other than yours | ________ | 88 |

a □ □ b □ □ c □ □ d □ □ e □ □

f □ □ g □ □

**Q45.** Different countries of the world play different roles in the global, socio-political and economic matters. In your opinion, what kind of role should India play in these international matters?

________________________________________

________________________________________

98. No Opinion

□ □

**Q46.** Now I will read out two statements on various issues. Tell me whether you agree with statement one (1) or statement two (2)?

| | |
|---|---|
| a. (1) The neighbouring countries of India should accept India as a big country and stop disagreeing | (2) By virtue of being big, it is the responsibility of India to treat all equally |

| | | |
|---|---|---|
| **1. Agree with first** | **2. Agree with second** | **8. No opinion** |
| b. (1) India should oppose bossism of America over the rest of the world even though it may render some harm to India | (2) America is the most powerful country of the world. It is in the interest of India to maintain good relationship with America | |
| **1. Agree with first** | **2. Agree with second** | **8. No opinion** |
| c. (1) The government of India should try to improve friendly relationship with Pakistan | (2) Efforts towards friendly relations with Pakistan are worthless | |
| **1. Agree with first** | **2. Agree with second** | **8. No opinion** |

a ☐ b ☐ c ☐

**Q47.** There are different opinions regarding government's handling of terrorism. Some people say that terrorist activities in India are a result of failure of the government. Others say that the government is doing its best to control terrorist activities. What is your opinion about it?

1. Terrorist activities in India are a result of failure of the government
2. Government is doing its best to control terrorist activities
8. No opinion

☐

**Q48.** How would you compare your family's financial condition with that of your relatives? Do you think your family's economic condition is better than most of your relatives, or your relatives are in a much better condition as compared to your family, or there is hardly any difference?

1. My family's economic condition is better than most of my relatives
2. My family's economic condition is worse than that of my relatives
3. No Difference
8. No response

☐

**Q49.** Few years from now, how do you foresee your future? Do you think your life will become very bright, somewhat bright or there will hardly be any change?

1. Very bright 2. Somewhat bright 3. No Difference
4. Dark future/bad future 8. No Opinion/Can't say

☐

**Q50.** Do you think your children will have a better life than that of yours, worse than yours or that there will hardly be any difference?

1.Live a better life 2.Live a worse life 3.No difference 8.No Opinion/Can't say

☐

**Q51.** I am going to read out a few statements. Tell me, whether you agree or disagree. (Probe further whether strongly or somewhat agree or disagree)

| | Statements | Agree | | Disagree | | No Opinion |
|---|---|---|---|---|---|---|
| | | Strongly | Somewhat | Somewhat | Strongly | |
| a | A viable democracy is not possible without political opposition. | 1 | 2 | 3 | 4 | 8 |
| b | Everyone should have the right to express their opinion, even if the majority is of a different opinion. | 1 | 2 | 3 | 4 | 8 |
| c | People should not be allowed to strike and demonstrate if they endanger public order | 1 | 2 | 3 | 4 | 8 |
| d | Conflict exists in every society and can only be resolved through violence. | 1 | 2 | 3 | 4 | 8 |

a ☐ b ☐ c ☐ d ☐

**Q52.** There are various issues that a developing country like India needs to address. I am going to read out 3 such issues. What should be the priorities of the government in addressing them: (Rank these issues from 1 to 3 in order of priority, 1 being the most important and 3 being the least important)

| | | No Opinion |
|---|---|---|
| a. Promote gender equality | ____________ | 8 |
| b. Ensure environment sustainability | ____________ | 8 |
| c. Strengthening our defence system | ____________ | 8 |

a ☐ b ☐ c ☐

**Q53.** I am going to read out few statements about the impact of Panchayat Raj tell me whether you agree or disagree with each. (Probe further whether 'fully' or 'somewhat' agree or disagree)

| | Statements | Agree | | Disagree | | No Opinion |
|---|---|---|---|---|---|---|
| | | Strongly | Somewhat | Somewhat | Strongly | |
| a. | Due to Panchayats delivery of benefits to people have improved | 1 | 2 | 3 | 4 | 8 |
| b. | Panchayats have led to increase in corruption | 1 | 2 | 3 | 4 | 8 |
| c. | Panchayats have resulted in reducing discrimination against Dalits | 1 | 2 | 3 | 4 | 8 |
| d. | Panchayats have empowered Women | 1 | 2 | 3 | 4 | 8 |

a ☐ b ☐ c ☐ d ☐

**Q54.** If you had an opportunity, would you like to settle in a foreign country?

2. Yes 1. No 3. Can't say

☐

**Q54a.** (If yes) If you get an opportunity, which country will be your most preferred choice for settling down? (Record the name of country) __________________

98. D.K/Can't Say 99 N.A.

☐ ☐

**Q55.** Young people have various kinds of insecurities/anxieties in their lives. I will read out a few such insecurities. Tell me to what extent are you insecure about the following- to a great extent, somewhat or not at all? (Read out options)

| | Insecurities | Great Extent | Somewhat | Not at all | No opinion |
|---|---|---|---|---|---|
| a | Your Employment/career | 1 | 2 | 3 | 8 |
| b | Riots and Mob Violence in the country | 1 | 2 | 3 | 8 |
| c | Personal Health | 1 | 2 | 3 | 8 |
| d | Prospects of your marriage | 1 | 2 | 3 | 8 |
| e | Issues within your family | 1 | 2 | 3 | 8 |
| f | Road Accident | 1 | 2 | 3 | 8 |
| g | Global Terrorism | 1 | 2 | 3 | 8 |

a ☐ b ☐ c ☐ d ☐ f ☐ g ☐

**Q56.** Considering all the people with whom you interact in your day-to-day life, who do you think are you influenced by the most in your own life. (Do not read out answer categories)

1. Parents 2. Siblings - brother/sister 3. Friends/Peers 4. Teachers
5. Colleagues 6. Neighbours 7. Seniors at office 8. Any other (Specify) ________
9. Not Influenced 0. No Opinion

☐

## BACKGROUND

**B1.** What is your age? (As mentioned by the respondent in completed years) __________________

☐

**B1a.** Age (According to the Voter List) __________________ (Not to be asked)

☐

**B2.** Gender: 1. Male 2. Female

☐

**B3.** What is your marital status?

1. Married
2. Unmarried
3. Living with someone, but unmarried
4. Divorced/Separated
5. Widowed

☐

**B4.** Till what level have you studied _______________ (Record exactly and consult code book)

☐

**B4a.** Till what level have your father and your mother studied?

Father _____________________________ Mother _____________________________

F ☐ M ☐

**B5.** What is your current education/employment status-

1. Student not seeking employment
2. Student seeking/doing part time employment
3. Unemployed
4. Fully employed
5. Homemaker/Housewife
6. Partly employed

☐

**B6.** (Even if partly or fully employed), What is your main occupation?[Read exactly and consult code book]

______________________________________________ 99 Unemployed

☐ ☐

**B6a.** (If the respondent is not the main earner) What is/has been the main occupation of the main earner of the family? _____________________________ (Record exactly and consult the code book)

☐ ☐

**B7.** How regularly do you read the newspaper - daily, frequently, rarely or never?

1. Daily
2. Frequently
3. Rarely
4. Never
8. No Opinion

☐

**B8.** What is your Caste/Jati-biradari/Tribe name? (Probe further, if Respondent mentions ambiguous surname) _____________________________ (Consult state code book, or master list)

☐ ☐

**B8a.** And what is your caste group? (Ascertain and consult SC/ST/OBC list in code book)

1. Scheduled Caste (SC)
2. Scheduled Tribe (ST)
3. Other Backward Caste (OBC)
4. Other

☐

**B9.** Which religion do you follow?

1. Hindu
2. Muslim
3. Christian 4. Sikh
5. Buddhist
6. Jain 7. Parsi
8. Other (Specify) ___________________

☐

**B10.** Generally, which language do you speak at home? ______________________
(Record exact answer & consult codebook for coding)

☐

**B11.** Area/Locality:

1. Village
2. Town (Below 1 lakh)
3. City (Above 1 lakh)
4. Metropolitan City (Above 10 lakh)

(If in doubt consult the electoral roll. If not stated on either then it is classed as a village)

☐

**B11a.** (If Town/City) Type of house where R lives (own or rented)

1. House/Flat/Bungalow with 4 or more bedrooms
2. House/Flat with 3 or 4 bedrooms
3. House/Flat with 2 bedrooms (With kitchen and bathroom)
4. House/Flat with 2 Pucca rooms (With kitchen)
5. House/Flat with 2 Pucca rooms (Without kitchen)
6. House with 1 Pucca room (With kitchen)
7. House/Flat with 1 Pucca room (Without kitchen)
8. Mainly Kutcha house
9. Slum/Jhuggi Jhopri/fully Kutcha 0. N.A.(Not applicable)

☐

**B11b.** (If Village) Type of house where R lives (own or rented)

1. Pucca (both wall and roof made of pucca material)
2. Pucca-kucha (Either wall or roof is made of pucca material and of other kutcha material)
3. Kutcha (both wall and roof are made of kutcha material other than materials mentioned in category 4)
4. Hut (both wall and roof are made of grass, leaves, mud, un-burnt brick or bamboo) 0. N.A

☐

**B 12.** Number of rooms in use in the household ______________________

☐

**B 13.** Total number of family members living in the household? (Adults __________Children __________)

a ☐ c ☐

**B14.** Do you or your family member have the following:

| | | Yes | No |
|---|---|---|---|
| a. | Car/Jeep/Van/Tractor | 1 | 0 |
| b. | Colour or B/W Television 2 Colour | 1 B/W | 0 B/W |
| c. | Scooter/Motorcycle/Moped | 1 | 0 |
| d. | Telephone/Mobile telephone | 1 | 0 |

| | | | |
|---|---|---|---|
| e. | Fridge | 1 | 0 |
| f. | Air Conditioner | 1 | 0 |
| g. | Washing machine | 1 | 0 |
| h. | Electric fan/cooler | 1 | 0 |
| i. | Bicycle | 1 | 0 |
| j. | Radio/Transistor | 1 | 0 |
| k. | Pumping set | 1 | 0 |
| l. | Cow/Buffalo (Record exact number of cow/buffalo together) ______________ | | 0 |

a ☐ b ☐ c ☐ d ☐ e ☐ f ☐ g ☐ h ☐ i ☐ j ☐ k ☐ l ☐

**B 15.** Do you personally have the following:

| | | Yes | No |
|---|---|---|---|
| a. | Mobile phone. | 1 | 0 |
| b. | Computer/Lap top | 1 | 0 |
| c. | Credit Card | 1 | 0 |
| d. | Debit card/ATM card | 1 | 0 |
| e | Home Loan | 1 | 0 |
| f | Vehicle loan | 1 | 0 |

a ☐ b ☐ c ☐ d ☐ e ☐ f ☐

**B 16.** Total monthly household income [Approx]:

1. Upto Rs. 1,000
2. Rs. 1,001 – Rs. 2,000
3. Rs. 2,001 – Rs. 3,000
4. Rs. 3,001 – Rs. 4,000
5. Rs. 4,001 – Rs. 5,000
6. Rs. 5,001 – Rs. 10,000
7. Rs. 10,001 – Rs. 20,000
8. Rs. 20,001 – Rs. 50,000
9. 50,001 and above

0. N.A

☐

## Other details

Name of the State ______________________________

Name of the Assembly Constituency ______________________________

Name of the Village/Locality ______________________________

Date of interview ______________________________

Name of the respondent ______________________________

Name of the investigator ______________________________

Name of the supervisor ______________________________

## APPENDIX III

# CSDS-KAS Youth Survey: Marginals for Appendix Basic Findings of all Questions

**Table 1**: Ideal age for boys to get married

| | Below 18 | 18 to 21 | 22 to 27 | 28 and above | Total |
|---|---|---|---|---|---|
| % | 1 | 36 | 50 | 13 | 100 |
| n | 71 | 1780 | 2489 | 659 | 4999 |

**Table 2**: Ideal age for girls to get married

| | Below 18 | 18 to 21 | 22 to 27 | 28 and above | Total |
|---|---|---|---|---|---|
| % | 10 | 69 | 19 | 2 | 100 |
| n | 495 | 3443 | 937 | 124 | 4999 |

**Table 3a**: Frequency of listening to music

| | Mostly | Sometimes | Never | Total |
|---|---|---|---|---|
| % | 36 | 46 | 18 | 100 |
| n | 1803 | 2301 | 895 | 4999 |

**Table 3b**: Frequency of going out with friends

| | Mostly | Sometimes | Never | Total |
|---|---|---|---|---|
| % | 23 | 47 | 30 | 100 |
| n | 1149 | 2355 | 1495 | 4999 |

**Table 3c**: Frequency of reading books/magazines/periodicals

| | Mostly | Sometimes | Never | Total |
|---|---|---|---|---|
| % | 21 | 38 | 41 | 100 |
| n | 1028 | 1907 | 2063 | 4999 |

**Table 3d**: Frequency of playing games/sports

| | Mostly | Sometimes | Never | Total |
|---|---|---|---|---|
| % | 15 | 30 | 55 | 100 |
| n | 757 | 1491 | 2752 | 4999 |

**Table 3e**: Frequency of watching films

| | Mostly | Sometimes | Never | Total |
|---|---|---|---|---|
| % | 24 | 51 | 25 | 100 |
| n | 1184 | 2530 | 1285 4999 | |

**Table 3f**: Frequency of watching television

| | Mostly | Sometimes | Never | Total |
|---|---|---|---|---|
| % | 39 | 39 | 22 | 100 |
| n | 1926 | 1956 | 1116 | 4999 |

**Table 4a**: Frequency of watching religious programmes on television

| | Daily | More than once a week | Rarely | Never | Doesn't watch TV | Total |
|---|---|---|---|---|---|---|
| % | 11 | 20 | 27 | 20 | 22 | 100 |
| n | 549 | 1000 | 1331 | 1003 | 1116 | 4999 |

Note: *Asked only to those who watch television.*

**Table 4b**: Frequency of watching films on television

| | Daily | More than once a week | Rarely | Never | Doesn't watch TV | Total |
|---|---|---|---|---|---|---|
| % | 19 | 36 | 19 | 4 | 22 | 100 |
| n | 959 | 1792 | 926 | 205 | 1116 | 4999 |

Note: *Asked only to those who watch television.*

**Table 4c**: Frequency of watching news/political debates on television

| | Daily | More than once a week | Rarely | Never | Doesn't watch TV | Total |
|---|---|---|---|---|---|---|
| % | 25 | 18 | 18 | 17 | 22 | 100 |
| n | 1240 | 920 | 898 | 824 | 1116 | 4999 |

Note: *Asked only to those who watch television.*

**Table 4d**: Frequency of watching sports on television

| | Daily | More than once a week | Rarely | Never | Doesn't watch TV | Total |
|---|---|---|---|---|---|---|
| % | 13 | 20 | 22 | 23 | 22 | 100 |
| n | 662 | 975 | 1117 | 1129 | 1116 | 4999 |

Note: *Asked only to those who watch television.*

**Table 4e**: Frequency of watching business news on television

| | Daily | More than once a week | Rarely | Never | Doesn't watch TV | Total |
|---|---|---|---|---|---|---|
| % | 8 | 12 | 18 | 40 | 22 | 100 |
| n | 404 | 578 | 915 | 1987 | 1116 | 4999 |

Note: *Asked only to those who watch television.*

**Table 4f**: Frequency of watching music vedios on television

| | Daily | More than once a week | Rarely | Never | Doesn't watch TV | Total |
|---|---|---|---|---|---|---|
| % | 28 | 24 | 15 | 11 | 22 | 100 |
| n | 1406 | 1189 | 730 | 558 | 1116 | 4999 |

Note: *Asked only to those who watch television.*

**Table 4g**: Frequency of watching TV serials/soaps on television

| | Daily | More than once a week | Rarely | Never | Doesn't watch TV | Total |
|---|---|---|---|---|---|---|
| % | 26 | 23 | 17 | 12 | 22 | 100 |
| n | 1303 | 1155 | 826 | 597 | 1116 | 4999 |

Note: *Asked only to those who watch television.*

**Table 4h**: Frequency of watching reality shows on television

| | Daily | More than once a week | Rarely | Never | Doesn't watch TV | Total |
|---|---|---|---|---|---|---|
| % | 7 | 12 | 17 | 42 | 22 | 100 |
| n | 367 | 582 | 829 | 2105 | 1116 | 4999 |

Note: *Asked only to those who watch television.*

**Table 5**: Way of being brought up

| | Very strict | Strict | Not so strict | Not at all strict | No opinion | Total |
|---|---|---|---|---|---|---|
| % | 16 | 35 | 33 | 13 | 3 | 100 |
| n | 786 | 1727 | 1667 | 656 | 162 | 4999 |

**Table 6**: Compared to their upbringing, the way respondents would like to bring up their children

| | Exactly the same way | More or less the same way | Differently | Very differently | No opinion | Total |
|---|---|---|---|---|---|---|
| % | 29 | 25 | 23 | 14 | 9 | 100 |
| n | 1437 | 1246 | 1167 | 711 | 438 | 4999 |

**Table 7**: Frequency of participating in protest, demonstration, struggle or movement

| | Several times | Once or twice | Never | Total |
|---|---|---|---|---|
| % | 6 | 16 | 78 | 100 |
| n | 287 | 787 | 3925 | 4999 |

**Table 8**: Frequency of voting in elections

| | Voted in every election | Voted in most elections | Voted in some elections | Hardly ever voted | Not eligible for voting | Can't say | Total |
|---|---|---|---|---|---|---|---|
| % | 38 | 20 | 13 | 10 | 16 | 3 | 100 |
| n | 1878 | 1018 | 662 | 496 | 798 | 147 | 4999 |

Note: *Asked only to those who are eligible for voting (above the age of 18 years).*

**Table 9**: Efficacy in vote

| | Makes no difference | Has effect | No opinion | Total |
|---|---|---|---|---|
| % | 25 | 49 | 26 | 100 |
| n | 1248 | 2424 | 1327 | 4999 |

**Table 10**: Parent's interest in politics

| | Very interested | Somewhat interested | Not very interested | Not at all interested | No opinion | Total |
|---|---|---|---|---|---|---|
| % | 11 | 26 | 24 | 31 | 8 | 100 |
| n | 554 | 1311 | 1181 | 1545 | 409 | 4999 |

**Table 11**: Status of education

| | Studying in school | Studying in college | Completed school | Completed college | School drop out | College drop out | Never went to school | Total |
|---|---|---|---|---|---|---|---|---|
| % | 15 | 10 | 17 | 11 | 28 | 5 | 14 | 100 |
| n | 731 | 500 | 827 | 577 | 1394 | 244 | 725 | 4999 |

**Table 11a**: Degree of liking to attend school/college

| | Very much | Somewhat | Doesn't like | No opinion | Currently does not attend school/college | Total |
|---|---|---|---|---|---|---|
| % | 16 | 7 | 1 | 1 | 75 | 100 |
| n | 828 | 285 | 59 | 9 | 3768 | 4999 |

Note: *Asked only to those who are studying.*

**Table 11b**: Type of school respondent studies or studied in

| | Government school | Private school | Other type of school | Dropped out, or never went to school | Total |
|---|---|---|---|---|---|
| % | 39 | 12 | 2 | 47 | 100 |
| n | 1391 | 618 | 86 | 2364 | 4999 |

Note: *Asked only to those who are studying or completed studies.*

**Table 11c**: Location of school respondent studies or studied in

| | Village | Town | City | Dropped out, or never went to school | Total |
|---|---|---|---|---|---|
| % | 27 | 14 | 12 | 47 | 100 |
| n | 1357 | 694 | 584 | 2364 | 4999 |

Note: *Asked only to those who are studying or completed studies.*

**Table 12**: Satisfaction with overall educational facilities available in India

| | Very satisfied | Somewhat satisfied | Somewhat dissatisfied | Fully satisfied | Dissatisfied | No opinion | Total |
|---|---|---|---|---|---|---|---|
| % | 23 | 40 | 13 | 5 | 20 | 100 | |
| n | 1147 | 1985 | 650 | 240 | 977 | 4999 | |

**Table 13**: Degree of daily stress at school/college/workplace

| | Very stressful | Somewhat stressful | Somewhat relaxed | Very relaxed | Don't know | Don't go to study/work | Total |
|---|---|---|---|---|---|---|---|
| % | 8 | 29 | 17 | 15 | 9 | 22 | 100 |
| n | 384 | 437 | 857 | 789 | 446 | 1085 | 4999 |

**Table 14a**: Importance given to higher education

| | Very important | Somewhat important | Not so important | Not at all important | Can't say | Total |
|---|---|---|---|---|---|---|
| % | 62 | 19 | 6 | 5 | 8 | 100 |
| n | 3107 | 931 | 318 | 267 | 377 | 4999 |

**Table 14b**: Importance given to being interested in politics

| | Very important | Somewhat important | Not so important | Not at all important | Can't say | Total |
|---|---|---|---|---|---|---|
| % | 15 | 31 | 27 | 19 | 9 | 100 |
| n | 726 | 1533 | 1366 | 933 | 442 | 4999 |

**Table 14c**: Importance given to taking responsibility

| | Very important | Somewhat important | Not so important | Not at all important | Can't say | Total |
|---|---|---|---|---|---|---|
| % | 56 | 30 | 6 | 2 | 6 | 100 |
| n | 2811 | 1478 | 274 | 119 | 318 | 4999 |

**Table 14d**: Importance given to dressing up according to latest trends

| | Very important | Somewhat important | Not so important | Not at all important | Can't say | Total |
|---|---|---|---|---|---|---|
| % | 28 | 32 | 22 | 11 | 7 | 100 |
| n | 1387 | 1590 | 1121 | 553 | 348 | 4999 |

**Table 14e**: Importance given to getting married

| | Very important | Somewhat important | Not so important | Not at all important | Can't say | Total |
|---|---|---|---|---|---|---|
| % | 53 | 27 | 7 | 5 | 8 | 100 |
| n | 2668 | 1363 | 371 | 224 | 73 | 4999 |

**Table 15**: Children

| | Have children | Don't have children | Total |
|---|---|---|---|
| % | 46 | 54 | 100 |
| n | 3211 | 2688 | 4999 |

**Table15a**: Aspiration to have children

| | Wish to have children | Don't want to have children | Can't say | Have children | Total |
|---|---|---|---|---|---|
| % | 35 | 2 | 15 | 48 | 100 |
| n | 1759 | 89 | 724 | 2428 | 4999 |

Note: *Asked only to those who do not have children.*

**Table 16**: Wanting spouse to earn

| | More | Less | Equal | Not work | Doesn't matter | No opinion | Total |
|---|---|---|---|---|---|---|---|
| % | 39 | 12 | 7 | 9 | 18 | 15 | 100 |
| n | 1944 | 622 | 329 | 429 | 888 | 787 | 4999 |

**Table 17a**: Frequency of being discriminated on economic status

| | Frequently | Sometimes | Never | Can't say | Total |
|---|---|---|---|---|---|
| % | 15 | 32 | 46 | 7 | 100 |
| n | 763 | 1613 | 2297 | 327 | 4999 |

**Table 17b**: Frequency of being discriminated on the basis of caste

| | Frequently | Sometimes | Never | Can't say | Total |
|---|---|---|---|---|---|
| % | 8 | 23 | 62 | 7 | 100 |
| n | 375 | 1167 | 3119 | 337 | 4999 |

**Table 17c**: Frequency of being discriminated on the basis of gender

| | Frequently | Sometimes | Never | Can't say | Total |
|---|---|---|---|---|---|
| % | 6 | 19 | 67 | 8 | 100 |
| n | 306 | 929 | 3349 | 415 | 4999 |

**Table 17d:** Frequency of being discriminated on the basis of religion

| | Frequently | Sometimes | Never | Can't say | Total |
|---|---|---|---|---|---|
| % | 5 | 13 | 73 | 9 | 100 |
| n | 241 | 665 | 3645 | 448 | 4999 |

**Table 17e:** Frequency of being discriminated on your state of origin

| | Frequently | Sometimes | Never | Can't say | Total |
|---|---|---|---|---|---|
| % | 5 | 13 | 71 | 11 | 100 |
| n | 253 | 654 | 3545 | 547 | 4999 |

**Table 18:** Watching films

| | Watch films | Doesn't watch films | Total |
|---|---|---|---|
| % | 75 | 25 | 100 |
| n | 3774 | 1225 | 4999 |

**Table 18a:** Types of films watched

| | Family drama | Action | Comedy | Thriller | Musical | Others | Can't say | Don't watch films | Total |
|---|---|---|---|---|---|---|---|---|---|
| % | 18 | 16 | 16 | 6 | 6 | 12 | 2 | 25 | 100 |
| n | 908 | 793 | 795 | 274 | 290 | 618 | 96 | 1225 | 4999 |

**Table 19a:** Opinion on marriage

| | The final decision about marriage should be taken by parents | The final decision about marriage should be taken by the girl and boy themselves | No opinion | Total |
|---|---|---|---|---|
| % | 65 | 32 | 3 | 100 |
| n | 3223 | 1621 | 155 | 4999 |

**Table 19b:** Opinion on dating

| | There should be a restriction on dating | There should be no restriction on dating | No opinion | Total |
|---|---|---|---|---|
| % | 63 | 32 | 5 | 100 |
| n | 3165 | 1586 | 248 | 4999 |

**Table 19c**: Opinion on inter-caste marriage

| | Marriages should take place within ones caste-community | There is nothing wrong if girls and boys from different caste-communities marry | No opinion | Total |
|---|---|---|---|---|
| % | 67 | 29 | 4 | 100 |
| n | 3349 | 1425 | 225 | 4999 |

**Table 19d**: Opinion on divorce

| | Once married a couple must stay together, even if calls for some compromise | If there are major differences between partners, there is nothing wrong in divorce | No opinion | Total |
|---|---|---|---|---|
| % | 74 | 18 | 8 | 100 |
| n | 3700 | 919 | 48 | 4999 |

**Table 20**: Internet usage

| | Use internet | Don't use internet | Total |
|---|---|---|---|
| % | 12 | 88 | 100 |
| n | 584 | 4415 | 4999 |

**Table 20a**: Purpose of using the internet

| | Email | Social networking | Information/ education | Others | Can't say | Don't use internet | Total |
|---|---|---|---|---|---|---|---|
| % | 3 | 2 | 4 | 1 | 2 | 88 | 100 |
| n | 144 | 91 | 223 | 46 | 78 | 4415 | 4999 |

Note: *Asked only to those who use the internet.*

**Table 20b**: Weekly hours spent on the internet

| | Up to 10 hours | 11 to 20 hours | More than 21 hours | Can't say | Don't use internet | Total |
|---|---|---|---|---|---|---|
| % | 7 | 1 | 1 | 3 | 88 | 100 |
| n | 328 | 69 | 55 | 131 | 4415 | 4999 |

Note: *Asked only to those who use the internet.*

**Table 21**: Awareness about Globalisation

| | Heard about globalisation | Not heard about globalisation | Total |
|---|---|---|---|
| % | 29 | 71 | 100 |
| n | 1456 | 3543 | 4999 |

**Table 21a**: Opinion on Globalisation

| | Overall advantageous | More disadvantageous | Equally advantageous & disadvantageous | No opinion | Not heard about globalisation | Total |
|---|---|---|---|---|---|---|
| % | 11 | 7 | 6 | 5 | 71 | 100 |
| n | 526 | 360 | 333 | 237 | 3543 | 4999 |

Note: *Asked only to those who heard about globalisation.*

**Table 22a**: Opinion on whether better and cheaper products are available due to increasing global competition

| | Fully agree | Somewhat agree | Somewhat disagree | Fully disagree | No opinion | Total |
|---|---|---|---|---|---|---|
| % | 32 | 32 | 6 | 4 | 26 | 100 |
| n | 1603 | 1595 | 323 | 178 | 1301 | 4999 |

**Table 22b**: Opinion on whether foreign culture is becoming increasingly dominant

| | Fully agree | Somewhat agree | Somewhat disagree | Fully disagree | No opinion | Total |
|---|---|---|---|---|---|---|
| % | 43 | 31 | 5 | 2 | 21 | 100 |
| n | 2123 | 1565 | 248 | 98 | 964 | 4999 |

**Table 22c**: Opinion on whether bigger countries wield all the power

| | Fully agree | Somewhat agree | Somewhat disagree | Fully disagree | No opinion | Total |
|---|---|---|---|---|---|---|
| % | 31 | 29 | 9 | 4 | 27 | 100 |
| n | 1552 | 1423 | 465 | 175 | 1384 | 4999 |

**Table 22d**: Opinion on whether the youth have better emloyment opportunities abroad

| | Fully agree | Somewhat agree | Somewhat disagree | Fully disagree | No opinion | Total |
|---|---|---|---|---|---|---|
| % | 28 | 32 | 10 | 5 | 25 | 100 |
| n | 1403 | 1593 | 494 | 242 | 1265 | 4999 |

**Table 23**: Ideal age for getting employed

| | Below 18 | 19 to 25 | 26 and above | Can't say | Total |
|---|---|---|---|---|---|
| % | 14 | 59 | 7 | 20 | 100 |
| n | 710 | 2956 | 332 | 1001 | 4999 |

**Table 24**: Considerations while choosing a job

| | Good income | Job security, even if for a lesser income | Job satisfaction | To work with people of ones' choice | No opinion | Total |
|---|---|---|---|---|---|---|
| % | 34 | 33 | 18 | 8 | 7 | 100 |
| n | 1714 | 1669 | 878 | 415 | 322 | 4999 |

**Table 25**: Preferred sector to work in

| | Do a government sector job | Do a private sector job | Do business or practice a profession | Others | Can't say | Total |
|---|---|---|---|---|---|---|
| % | 64 | 10 | 15 | 2 | 9 | 100 |
| n | 3183 | 516 | 750 | 117 | 433 | 4999 |

**Table 26**: Opinion on reservations in higher education

| | Reservation for SC/ST & OBC | Reservation only for SC/ST | Reservation for SC/ST & poor OBCs | No reservations | No opinion | Total |
|---|---|---|---|---|---|---|
| % | 29 | 6 | 25 | 17 | 22 | 100 |
| n | 1471 | 316 | 1238 | 868 | 1106 | 4999 |

**Table 27a:** Degree of trust in central government

| | Great deal | Some | Not very much | None at all | No opinion | Total |
|---|---|---|---|---|---|---|
| % | 32 | 38 1 | 0 | 5 | 15 | 100 |
| n | 1573 | 1875 | 519 | 279 | 753 | 4999 |

**Table 27b:** Degree of trust in state government

| | Great deal | Some | Not very much | None at all | No opinion | Total |
|---|---|---|---|---|---|---|
| % | 27 | 41 | 14 | 5 | 13 | 100 |
| n | 1331 | 2065 | 676 | 263 | 664 | 4999 |

**Table 27c:** Degree of trust in local governement

| | Great deal | Some | Not very much | None at all | No opinion | Total |
|---|---|---|---|---|---|---|
| % | 26 | 38 | 16 | 7 | 13 | 100 |
| n | 1282 | 1927 | 810 | 352 | 629 | 4999 |

**Table 27d:** Degree of trust in civil services

| | Great deal | Some | Not very much | None at all | No opinion | Total |
|---|---|---|---|---|---|---|
| % | 16 | 31 | 25 | 13 | 15 | 100 |
| n | 798 | 1546 | 1246 | 650 | 758 | 4999 |

**Table 27e:** Degree of trust in police

| | Great deal | Some | Not very much | None at all | No opinion | Total |
|---|---|---|---|---|---|---|
| % | 15 | 29 | 23 | 23 | 10 | 100 |
| n | 773 | 1430 | 1148 | 1155 | 493 | 4999 |

**Table 27f:** Degree of trust in Army

| | Great deal | Some | Not very much | None at all | No opinion | Total |
|---|---|---|---|---|---|---|
| % | 59 | 20 | 6 | 4 | 11 | 100 |
| n | 2963 | 1011 | 306 | 189 | 530 | 4999 |

**Table 27g:** Degree of trust in courts

| | Great deal | Some | Not very much | None at all | No opinion | Total |
|---|---|---|---|---|---|---|
| % | 36 | 30 | 13 | 8 | 13 | 100 |
| n | 1788 | 1499 | 650 | 395 | 667 | 4999 |

**Table 27h:** Degree of trust in the Parliament

| | Great deal | Some | Not very much | None at all | No opinion | Total |
|---|---|---|---|---|---|---|
| % | 23 | 28 | 16 | 10 | 23 | 100 |
| n | 1156 | 1416 | 808 | 496 | 1123 | 4999 |

**Table 27i:** Degree of trust in political parties

| | Great deal | Some | Not very much | None at all | No opinion | Total |
|---|---|---|---|---|---|---|
| % | 9 | 25 | 23 | 27 | 16 | 100 |
| n | 446 | 1246 | 1171 | 1348 | 788 | 4999 |

**Table 27j:** Degree of trust in the Election Commission

| | Great deal Some | Some | Not very much | None at all | No opinion | Total |
|---|---|---|---|---|---|---|
| % | 33 | 27 | 10 | 7 | 23 | 100 |
| n | 1634 | 1333 | 509 | 356 | 1167 | 4999 |

**Table 28:** Belief in God

| | Believe in God | Don't believe in God | Total |
|---|---|---|---|
| % | 94 | 6 | 100 |
| n | 4719 | 280 | 4999 |

**Table 29:** Frequency of praying

| | Daily | Once a week | Occasionally | Only festivals | Never | Total |
|---|---|---|---|---|---|---|
| % | 53 | 18 | 16 | 8 | 5 | 100 |
| n | 2663 | 907 | 792 | 401 | 237 | 4999 |

**Table 30a**: Whether respondent gives importance to achieving more than others

| | Strongly agree | Somewhat agree | Somewhat disagree | Strongly disagree | No opinion | Total |
|---|---|---|---|---|---|---|
| % | 45 | 29 | 8 | 4 | 14 | 100 |
| n | 2267 | 1435 | 389 | 194 | 714 | 4999 |

**Table 30b**: Whether respondent's decisions in life are personal or taken by others

| | Strongly agree | Somewhat agree | Somewhat disagree | Strongly disagree | No opinion | Total |
|---|---|---|---|---|---|---|
| % | 14 | 28 | 25 | 20 | 13 | 100 |
| n | 676 | 1406 | 1254 | 1002 | 660 | 4999 |

**Table 30c**: Whether respondent feels that nowdays one often does things that are not right

| | Strongly agree | Somewhat agree | Somewhat disagree | Strongly disagree | No opinion | Total |
|---|---|---|---|---|---|---|
| % | 20 | 32 | 19 | 11 | 17 | 100 |
| n | 992 | 1621 | 959 | 557 | 869 | 4999 |

**Table 30d**: Whether respondent feels lonely

| | Strongly agree | Somewhat agree | Somewhat disagree | Strongly disagree | No opinion | Total |
|---|---|---|---|---|---|---|
| % | 15 | 25 | 25 | 21 | 14 | 100 |
| n | 765 | 1240 | 1258 | 1049 | 686 | 4999 |

**Table 30e**: Whether respondent thinks she/he manages to achieve goals and plans for success

| | Strongly agree | Somewhat agree | Somewhat disagree | Strongly disagree | No opinion | Total |
|---|---|---|---|---|---|---|
| % | 32 | 31 | 14 | 6 | 17 | 100 |
| n | 1602 | 1565 | 677 | 294 | 860 | 4999 |

**Table 30f**: Whether respondent feels that she/he cannot change anything about most things that disturb

| | Strongly agree | Somewhat agree | Somewhat disagree | Strongly disagree | No opinion | Total |
|---|---|---|---|---|---|---|
| % | 23 | 32 | 17 | 10 | 18 | 100 |
| n | 1163 | 1611 | 849 | 497 | 880 | 4999 |

**Table 30g**: Whether respondent thinks that money is very important to remain happy

| | Strongly agree | Somewhat agree | Somewhat disagree | Strongly disagree | No opinion | Total |
|---|---|---|---|---|---|---|
| % | 53 | 26 | 7 | 6 | 8 | 100 |
| n | 2667 | 1281 | 332 | 312 | 407 | 4999 |

**Table 31a**: Among five top friends, those from the opposite sex

| | One | Two | Three | Four | Five | None | Total |
|---|---|---|---|---|---|---|---|
| % | 12 | 17 | 8 | 4 | 7 | 52 | 100 |
| n | 616 | 828 | 396 | 219 | 348 | 2592 | 4999 |

**Table 31b**: Among five top friends, those from other castes

| | One | Two | Three | Four | Five | None | Total |
|---|---|---|---|---|---|---|---|
| % | 14 | 24 | 14 | 5 | 4 | 37 | 100 |
| n | 715 | 1216 | 714 | 266 | 239 | 1849 | 4999 |

**Table 31c**: Among five top friends, those from other religions

| | One | Two | Three | Four | Five | None | Total |
|---|---|---|---|---|---|---|---|
| % | 22 | 14 | 6 | 2 | 2 | 54 | 100 |
| n | 1104 | 688 | 292 | 100 | 85 | 2729 | 4999 |

**Table 32a**: Average monthly expenditure on watching films

| | |
|---|---|
| **Rs.** | 152 |

Note: *Average expediture computed from valid answers.*

**Table 32b**: Average monthly expenditure on eating out

| | |
|---|---|
| **Rs.** | 184 |

Note: *Average expediture computed from valid answers.*

**Table 32c**: Average monthly expenditure on purchasing accessories

| | |
|---|---|
| **Rs.** | 318 |

Note: *Average expediture computed from valid answers.*

**Table 32d:** Average monthly expenditure on purchasing gadgets and technology products

| | |
|---|---|
| **Rs.** | 175 |

Note: *Average expediture computed from valid answers.*

**Table 32e:** Average monthly expenditure on phone bills

| | |
|---|---|
| **Rs.** | 225 |

Note: *Average expediture computed from valid answers.*

**Table 33:** Opinion on drinking alcohol

| | Acceptable | Not acceptable | Necessary for social circles | No opinion | Total |
|---|---|---|---|---|---|
| % | 10 | 66 | 14 | 10 | 100 |
| n | 500 | 3288 | 720 | 491 | 4999 |

**Table 34:** Opinion on student's union

| | Student's unions are needed to protect the rights and interests | Student's unions should be banned as they disturb academic environment | No opinion | Total |
|---|---|---|---|---|
| % | 47 | 18 | 35 | 100 |
| n | 2357 | 904 | 1738 | 4999 |

**Table 35a:** Importance of political parties in a democracy

| | Strongly agree | Somewhat agree | Somewhat disagree | Strongly disagree | No opinion | Total |
|---|---|---|---|---|---|---|
| % | 41 | 25 | 5 | 3 | 26 | 100 |
| n | 20-40 | 1233 | 269 | 159 | 1298 | 4999 |

**Table 35b:** Opinion on whether politicians do not care about people like the respondent

| | Strongly agree | Somewhat agree | Somewhat disagree | Strongly disagree | No opinion | Total |
|---|---|---|---|---|---|---|
| % | 43 | 29 | 10 | 4 | 14 | 100 |
| n | 2154 | 1421 | 509 | 214 | 700 | 4999 |

**Table 35c:** Opinion on citizens' duty to vote during elections

| | Strongly agree | Somewhat agree | Somewhat disagree | Strongly disagree | No opinion | Total |
|---|---|---|---|---|---|---|
| % | 69 | 16 | 3 | 1 | 11 | 100 |
| n | 3472 | 778 | 145 | 47 | 557 | 4999 |

**Table 35d:** Whether understanding politics is too complicated

| | Strongly agree | Somewhat agree | Somewhat disagree | Strongly disagree | No opinion | Total |
|---|---|---|---|---|---|---|
| % | 28 | 29 | 16 | 9 | 18 | 100 |
| n | 1373 | 1458 | 812 | 436 | 920 | 4999 |

**Table 35e:** Opinion on whether in India power rests with few people

| | Strongly agree | Somewhat agree | Somewhat disagree | Strongly disagree | No opinion | Total |
|---|---|---|---|---|---|---|
| % | 36 | 30 | 8 | 5 | 22 | 100 |
| n | 1812 | 1446 | 411 | 226 | 1104 | 4999 |

**Table 35f:** Whether respondent find politics interesting

| | Strongly agree | Somewhat agree | Somewhat disagree | Strongly disagree | No opinion | Total |
|---|---|---|---|---|---|---|
| % | 15 | 25 | 19 | 23 | 18 | 100 |
| n | 729 | 1228 | 941 | 1162 | 939 | 4999 |

**Table 36:** Opinion on reservations of seats for women in Parliament and State Assemblies

| | Women are under-represented | Seats should be reserved for women | Seats should not be reserved | No opinion | Total |
|---|---|---|---|---|---|
| % | 45 | 22 | 12 | 21 | 100 |
| n | 2267 | 1074 | 592 | 1066 | 4999 |

**Table 37**: Support for reserving seats for the youth in Parliament

| | Strongly support | Somewhat support | Somewhat oppose | Strongly oppose | No opinion | Total |
|---|---|---|---|---|---|---|
| % | 56 | 18 | 2 | 3 | 21 | 100 |
| n | 2827 | 932 | 73 | 126 | 1042 | 4999 |

**Table 38**: Biggest problem faced in India

| | Unemploy-ment | Poverty | Over popula-tion | Corrup-tion | Terrorism | Illiteracy | Electri-city supply | Others | Don't know | Total |
|---|---|---|---|---|---|---|---|---|---|---|
| % | 23 | 21 | 9 | 4 | 3 | 2 | 2 | 16 | 20 | 100 |
| n | 1134 | 1028 | 432 | 207 | 136 | 112 | 92 | 860 | 998 | 4999 |

**Table 39a**: Priority of government in addressing to reduce child mortality

| | First | Second | Third | No opinion | Total |
|---|---|---|---|---|---|
| % | 20 | 33 | 36 | 11 | 100 |
| n | 977 | 1630 | 1816 | 576 | 4999 |

**Table 39b**: Priority of government in addressing to maternal health care facilities

| | First | Second | Third | No opinion | Total |
|---|---|---|---|---|---|
| % | 30 | 40 | 20 | 10 | 100 |
| n | 1486 | 1995 | 990 | 528 | 4999 |

**Table 39c**: Priority of government in combating HIV/AIDS, malaria and other diseases

| | First | Second | Third | No opinion | Total |
|---|---|---|---|---|---|
| % | 42 | 16 | 30 | 12 | 100 |
| n | 2117 | 787 | 1517 | 579 | 4999 |

**Table 40a**: Importance in terms of priority given to improving health services

| | First | Second | Third | No opinion | Total |
|---|---|---|---|---|---|
| % | 27 | 30 | 35 | 7 | 100 |
| n | 1370 | 1502 | 1759 | 367 | 4999 |

**Table 40b**: Importance in terms of priority given to providing good education

| | First | Second | Third | No opinion | Total |
|---|---|---|---|---|---|
| % | 28 | 41 | 23 | 8 | 100 |
| n | 1420 | 2056 | 1156 | 368 | 4999 |

**Table 40c**: Importance in terms of priority given to guaranteeing employment

| | First | Second | Third | No opinion | Total |
|---|---|---|---|---|---|
| % | 41 | 21 | 31 | 7 | 100 |
| n | 2053 | 1064 | 1531 | 351 | 4999 |

**Table 41a**: Awareness about China, and opinion on its relationship with India

| | Very friendly | Friendly | Not so friendly | No opinion | Haven't heard about China | Total |
|---|---|---|---|---|---|---|
| % | 8 | 38 | 13 | 18 | 23 | 100 |
| n | 379 | 1896 | 675 | 888 | 1160 | 4999 |

**Table 41b**: Awareness about America, and opinion on its relationship with India

| | Very friendly | Friendly | Not so friendly | No opinion | Haven't heard about America | Total |
|---|---|---|---|---|---|---|
| % | 10 | 47 | 9 | 18 | 16 | 100 |
| n | 524 | 2328 | 441 | 888 | 818 | 4999 |

**Table 41c**: Awareness about Sri Lanka, and opinion on its relationship with India

| | Very friendly | Friendly | Not so friendly | No opinion | Haven't heard about Sri Lanka | Total |
|---|---|---|---|---|---|---|
| % | 12 | 41 | 7 | 19 | 21 | 100 |
| n | 572 | 2069 | 361 | 944 | 1052 | 4999 |

**Table 41d**: Awareness about Nepal, and opinion on its relationship with India

| | Very friendly | Friendly | Not so friendly | No opinion | Haven't heard about Nepal | Total |
|---|---|---|---|---|---|---|
| % | 15 | 38 | 7 | 19 | 21 | 100 |
| n | 766 | 1903 | 326 | 936 | 1067 | 4999 |

**Table 41e**: Awareness about Pakistan, and opinion on its relationship with India

| | Very friendly | Friendly | Not so friendly | No opinion | Haven't heard about Pakistan | Total |
|---|---|---|---|---|---|---|
| % | 4 | 16 | 54 | 13 | 13 | 100 |
| n | 217 | 801 | 2676 | 676 | 629 | 4999 |

**Table 41f**: Awareness about Russia, and opinion on its relationship with India

| | Very friendly | Friendly | Not so friendly | No opinion | Haven't heard about Russia | Total |
|---|---|---|---|---|---|---|
| % | 15 | 28 | 5 | 20 | 32 | 100 |
| n | 757 | 1381 | 273 | 989 | 1599 | 4999 |

**Table 41f**: Awareness about Germany, and opinion on its relationship with India

| | Very friendly | Friendly | Not so friendly | No opinion | Haven't heard about Germany | Total |
|---|---|---|---|---|---|---|
| % | 5 | 29 | 7 | 23 | 35 | 100 |
| n | 270 | 1449 | 371 | 1138 | 1771 | 4999 |

**Table 41h**: Awareness about Bangladesh, and opinion on its relationship with India

| | Very friendly | Friendly | Not so friendly | No opinion | Haven't heard about Bangladesh | Total |
|---|---|---|---|---|---|---|
| % | 8 | 33 | 15 | 20 | 24 | 100 |
| n | 403 | 1645 | 749 | 997 | 1204 | 4999 |

**Table 42**: Way of taking decisions about career/academic options

| | Decisions taken by parents | Decisions taken along with parents | Completely individual decisions | Can't say | Total |
|---|---|---|---|---|---|
| % | 33 | 46 | 11 | 10 | 100 |
| n | 1654 | 2317 | 523 | 505 | 4999 |

**Table 43:** Role of family in personal happiness

| | Need a family to be happy | Can be happy with or without family | Happier alone without a family | No opinion | Total |
|---|---|---|---|---|---|
| % | 87 | 7 | 2 | 4 | 100 |
| n | 4353 | 362 | 103 | 181 | 4999 |

**Table 44a:** On a scale of 1 to 10 trust in friends

| | Step 1 | Step 2 | Step 3 | Step 4 | Step 5 | Step 6 | Step 7 | Step 8 | Step 9 | Step 10 | No Opinion | Total |
|---|---|---|---|---|---|---|---|---|---|---|---|---|
| % | 35 | 26 | 11 | 6 | 5 | 2 | 1 | 1 | 1 | 2 | 9 | 100 |
| n | 1766 | 1301 | 571 | 304 | 259 | 89 | 56 | 59 | 27 | 118 | 449 | 4999 |

**Table 44b:** On a scale of 1 to 10 trust in relatives

| | Step 1 | Step 2 | Step 3 | Step 4 | Step 5 | Step 6 | Step 7 | Step 8 | Step 9 | Step 10 | No Opinion | Total |
|---|---|---|---|---|---|---|---|---|---|---|---|---|
| % | 37 | 25 | 12 | 6 | 6 | 2 | 2 | 1 | | 2 | 7 | 100 |
| n | 1846 | 1262 | 612 | 284 | 284 | 89 | 78 | 60 | 22 | 107 | 353 | 4999 |

**Table 44c:** On a scale of 1 to 10 trust in people from own caste

| | Step 1 | Step 2 | Step 3 | Step 4 | Step 5 | Step 6 | Step 7 | Step 8 | Step 9 | Step 10 | No Opinion | Total |
|---|---|---|---|---|---|---|---|---|---|---|---|---|
| % | 10 | 15 | 24 | 16 | 13 | 4 | 3 | 2 | 1 | 3 | 10 | 100 |
| n | 506 | 735 | 1186 | 813 | 640 | 208 | 59 | 86 | 47 | 131 | 488 | 4999 |

**Table 44d:** On a scale of 1 to 10 trust in neighbours

| | Step 1 | Step 2 | Step 3 | Step 4 | Step 5 | Step 6 | Step 7 | Step 8 | Step 9 | Step 10 | No Opinion | Total |
|---|---|---|---|---|---|---|---|---|---|---|---|---|
| % | 8 | 13 | 17 | 20 | 15 | 6 | 4 | 2 | 1 | 4 | 10 | 100 |
| n | 400 | 674 | 829 | 1000 | 738 | 329 | 186 | 102 | 67 | 194 | 480 | 4999 |

**Table 44e:** On a scale of 1 to 10 trust in people from other religions

| | Step 1 | Step 2 | Step 3 | Step 4 | Step 5 | Step 6 | Step 7 | Step 8 | Step 9 | Step 10 | No Opinion | Total |
|---|---|---|---|---|---|---|---|---|---|---|---|---|
| % | 3 | 4 | 6 | 8 | 20 | 12 | 12 | 7 | 3 | 9 | 15 | 100 |
| n | 175 | 210 | 296 | 389 | 988 | 610 | 613 | 341 | 170 | 442 | 763 | 4999 |

**Table 44f**: On a scale of 1 to 10 trust in colleagues

| | Step 1 | Step 2 | Step 3 | Step 4 | Step 5 | Step 6 | Step 7 | Step 8 | Step 9 | Step 10 | No Opinion | Total |
|---|---|---|---|---|---|---|---|---|---|---|---|---|
| % | 8 | 10 | 9 | 10 | 14 | 13 | 7 | 5 | 2 | 3 | 19 | 100 |
| n | 383 | 523 | 472 | 485 | 681 | 667 | 361 | 239 | 103 | 149 | 936 | 4999 |

**Table 44g**: On a scale of 1 to 10 trust in people from other castes

| | Step 1 | Step 2 | Step 3 | Step 4 | Step 5 | Step 6 | Step 7 | Step 8 | Step 9 | Step 10 | No Opinion | Total |
|---|---|---|---|---|---|---|---|---|---|---|---|---|
| % | 4 | 5 | 5 | 6 | 11 | 12 | 16 | 8 | 6 | 10 | 17 | 100 |
| n | 193 | 238 | 240 | 294 | 547 | 632 | 797 | 413 | 289 | 501 | 856 | 4999 |

**Table 45**: Opinion on the role India should play in international matters

| | Focus on domestic issues | Focus on international issues | Other issues | Don't know | Total |
|---|---|---|---|---|---|
| % | 18 | 16 | 5 | 61 | 100 |
| n | 888 | 808 | 254 | 3049 | 4999 |

**Table 46a**: Opinion on role of India in the region

| | Neighbouring countries should accept India as a big country and stop disagreeing | By virtue of being big, it is the responsbility of India to treat all equally | No opinion | Total |
|---|---|---|---|---|
| % | 30 | 45 | 25 | 100 |
| n | 1530 | 2242 | 1228 | 4999 |

**Table 46b**: Opinion on America

| | India should oppose bossism of America, even if it brings harm to India | As America is the most powerful country, it is in interest of India to maintain good relations | No opinion | Total |
|---|---|---|---|---|
| % | 39 | 35 | 27 | 100 |
| n | 1949 | 1770 | 1280 | 4999 |

**Table 46c**: Opinion on Indo-Pak relations

| | GOI should try to improve friendly relations with Pakistan | Efforts towards friendly relations with Pakistan are worthless | No opinion | Total |
|---|---|---|---|---|
| % | 47 | 34 | 19 | 100 |
| n | 2337 | 1712 | 950 | 4999 |

**Table 47**: Opinion regarding government's handling of terrorism

| | Terrorism is a result of failure of Govt. | Govt. is doing best to curb terrorism | No opinion | Total |
|---|---|---|---|---|
| % | 35 | 40 | 25 | 100 |
| n | 1740 | 1991 | 1268 | 4999 |

**Table 48**: Opinion on respondent's family's financial condition to that of his/her relatives

| | Family's condition better | Family's condition worse | No difference | No response | Total |
|---|---|---|---|---|---|
| % | 27 | 26 | 38 | 9 | 100 |
| n | 1371 | 1295 | 1887 | 446 | 4999 |

**Table 49**: How does the respondent forsees his/her future

| | Very Bright | Somewhat bright | No Difference | Dark/Bad future | No opinion/ can't say | Total |
|---|---|---|---|---|---|---|
| % | 39 | 36 | 13 | 3 | 9 | 100 |
| n | 1964 | 1823 | 632 | 124 | 457 | 4999 |

**Table 50**: Opinion on whether's respondent's children will have better life

| | Live a better life | Live a worse life | No difference | No opinion/ can't say | Total |
|---|---|---|---|---|---|
| % | 66 | 7 | 13 | 14 | 100 |
| n | 3295 | 371 | 624 | 708 | 4999 |

**Table 51a:** A viable democracy is not possible without political opposition

| | Strongly agree | Somewhat agree | Somewhat disagree | Strongly disagree | No opinion | Total |
|---|---|---|---|---|---|---|
| % | 34 | 26 | 6 | 2 | 32 | 100 |
| n | 1708 | 1277 | 295 | 127 | 1592 | 4999 |

**Table 51b:** Everyone should have the right to express his/her opinion, even if the majority is of a different opinion

| | Strongly agree | Somewhat agree | Somewhat disagree | Strongly disagree | No opinion | Total |
|---|---|---|---|---|---|---|
| % | 49 | 25 | 4 | 1 | 21 | 100 |
| n | 2464 | 1222 | 213 | 62 | 1038 | 4999 |

**Table 51c:** People should not be allowed to strike and demonstrate if they endanger public order

| | Strongly agree | Somewhat agree | Somewhat disagree | Strongly disagree | No opinion | Total |
|---|---|---|---|---|---|---|
| % | 34 | 25 | 11 | 7 | 23 | 100 |
| n | 702 | 1251 | 560 | 328 | 1158 | 4999 |

**Table 51d:** Conflict exists in every society and can only be resolved through violence

| | Strongly agree | Somewhat agree | Somewhat disagree | Strongly disagree | No opinion | Total |
|---|---|---|---|---|---|---|
| % | 8 | 13 | 18 | 36 | 25 | 100 |
| n | 401 | 665 | 917 | 1771 | 1244 | 4999 |

**Table 52a:** Priority of government in promoting gender equality

| | Rank 1 | Rank 2 | Rank 3 | No opinion | Total |
|---|---|---|---|---|---|
| % | 35 | 25 | 28 | 12 | 100 |
| n | 1752 | 1237 | 1409 | 601 | 4999 |

**Table 52b:** Priority of government in addressing environment sustainability

| | Rank 1 | Rank 2 | Rank 3 | No opinion | Total |
|---|---|---|---|---|---|
| % | 22 | 36 | 9 | 13 | 100 |
| n | 1085 | 1811 | 454 | 649 | 4999 |

**Table 52c**: Priority of government in addressing to strengthen our defence system

| | Rank 1 | Rank 2 | Rank 3 | No opinion | Total |
|---|---|---|---|---|---|
| % | 35 | 26 | 28 | 11 | 100 |
| n | 1732 | 1303 | 1389 | 575 | 4999 |

**Table 53a**: Due to Panchayats delivery of benefits to people have improved

| | Strongly agree | Somewhat agree | Somewhat disagree | Strongly disagree | No opinion | Total |
|---|---|---|---|---|---|---|
| % | 36 | 36 | 6 | 4 | 18 | 100 |
| n | 816 | 1812 | 286 | 168 | 918 | 4999 |

**Table 53b**: Panchayats have led to increase in corruption

| | Strongly agree | Somewhat agree | Somewhat disagree | Strongly disagree | No opinion | Total |
|---|---|---|---|---|---|---|
| % | 24 | 32 | 17 | 5 | 22 | 100 |
| n | 1217 | 1598 | 836 | 270 | 1078 | 4999 |

**Table 53c**: Panchayats have resulted in reducing discrimination against Dalits

| | Strongly agree | Somewhat agree | Somewhat disagree | Strongly disagree | No opinion | Total |
|---|---|---|---|---|---|---|
| % | 25 | 33 | 13 | 4 | 25 | 100 |
| n | 1234 | 1676 | 644 | 216 | 1230 | 4999 |

**Table 53d**: Panchayats have empowered women

| | Strongly agree | Somewhat agree | Somewhat disagree | Strongly disagree | No opinion | Total |
|---|---|---|---|---|---|---|
| % | 33 | 32 | 9 | 4 | 22 | 100 |
| n | 1639 | 1591 | 470 | 216 | 1083 | 4999 |

**Table 54**: If respondent had an opportunity, whether he would like to settle in a foreign country

| | Yes | No | Can't Say | Total |
|---|---|---|---|---|
| % | 37 | 56 | 7 | 100 |
| n | 1865 | 2785 | 349 | 4999 |

**Table 54a:** Most preferred choice for settling down

| | USA | UK | Saudi | Arabia | UAE | Australia | Canada | Singapore | Japan | Others | Don't Know | Want to live in India | Total |
|---|---|---|---|---|---|---|---|---|---|---|---|---|---|
| % | 12 | 3 | 1 | 2 | 1 | 1 | 1 | 1 | 5 | 10 | 63 | 100 | |
| n | 580 | 128 | 65 | 117 | 69 | 57 | 49 | 62 | 227 | 511 | 3134 | 4999 | |

**Table 55a:** Extent of insecurity about employment

| | Great extent | Somewhat | Not at all | No opinion | Total |
|---|---|---|---|---|---|
| % | 44 | 24 | 17 | 15 | 100 |
| n | 2207 | 1216 | 847 | 728 | 4999 |

**Table 55b:** Extent of insecurity about riots and mob violence in the country

| | Great extent | Somewhat | Not at all | No opinion | Total |
|---|---|---|---|---|---|
| % | 22 | 42 | 21 | 15 | 100 |
| n | 1120 | 2106 | 1046 | 727 | 4999 |

**Table 55c:** Extent of insecurity about personal health

| | Great extent | Somewhat | Not at all | No opinion | Total |
|---|---|---|---|---|---|
| % | 37 | 36 | 18 | 9 | 100 |
| n | 1874 | 1778 | 910 | 437 | 4999 |

**Table 55d:** Extent of insecurity about prospects of respondent's marriage

| | Great extent | Somewhat | Not at all | No opinion | Total |
|---|---|---|---|---|---|
| % | 25 | 25 | 34 | 16 | 100 |
| n | 1231 | 1258 | 1722 | 788 | 4999 |

**Table 55e:** Extent of insecurity about issues within respondent's family

| | Great extent | Somewhat | Not at all | No opinion | Total |
|---|---|---|---|---|---|
| % | 18 | 34 | 10 | 38 | 100 |
| n | 905 | 1676 | 513 | 1906 | 4999 |

**Table 55f**: Extent of insecurity about road accident

| | Great extent | Somewhat | Not at all | No opinion | Total |
|---|---|---|---|---|---|
| % | 25 | 37 | 24 | 14 | 100 |
| n | 1251 | 1872 | 1169 | 707 | 4999 |

**Table 55g**: Extent of insecurity about global terrorism

| | Great extent | Somewhat | Not at all | No opinion | Total |
|---|---|---|---|---|---|
| % | 24 | 29 | 23 | 24 | 100 |
| n | 1211 | 1475 | 1139 | 1173 | 4999 |

**Table 56**: Influences in respondent's life

| | Parents | Siblings | Friends/ Peers | Teachers | Colleauges | Neighbours | Seniors at office | Others | Not influenced | No opinion | Total |
|---|---|---|---|---|---|---|---|---|---|---|---|
| % | 55 | 8 | 12 | 4 | 1 | 2 | 1 | 5 | 5 | 6 | 100 |
| n | 2774 | 385 | 618 | 189 | 81 | 109 | 30 | 235 | 277 | 300 | 4999 |

## APPENDIX IV

# List of Figures

## APPENDIX V

# Case Studies Commissioned for the KAS-CSDS Youth Study

| No. | Case Study Title | Name and Institution Affiliation of the Expert |
|---|---|---|
| 1. | Youth and the Entertainment Mall:<br>A Study of 'Prasads Imax' in Hyderabad | C. Ramachandraiah<br>Centre for Economic and Social Studies (CESS),<br>Hyderabad,<br>Andhra Pradesh. |
| 2. | Journey Towards Equality:<br>A Study of Enrolment Pattern of Muslim Girls at Undergraduate Level (General Stream Courses) in University of Mumbai | Suniti Nagpurkar<br>V.E.S. College of Arts, Science and Commerce,<br>Sindhi Society,<br>Chembur,<br>Mumbai. |
| 3. | Modern Youth and Embodied Work:<br>A Study in Kolkata | Swati Ghosh<br>Economics Department,<br>Rabindra Bharati University,<br>West Bengal. |
| 4. | Whither Formalism, Fundamentalism or Feminism? Sania Mirza, 'Sexy' Dressing and the Politics of Youth Perception | Surbhi Tiwari<br>Department of Sociology,<br>University of Pune. |
| 5. | Regimes of Control: Hindi Films and Political Cultures of Youth in Manipur | Yengkhom Jilangamba<br>Jawaharlal Nehru University,<br>New Delhi. |
| 6. | Spheres of Rage: Understanding Dalit Youth in Maharashtra | Gopal Guru<br>Centre for Political Studies,<br>Jawaharlal Nehru University,<br>Delhi. |

| No. | Case Study Title | Name and Institution Affiliation of the Expert |
|---|---|---|
| 7. | Youth Residing in Two Slum Areas of Mumbai | Rohini Kashikar Sudhakar<br>Department of Continuing and Adult Education and Extension Work,<br>SNDT Women's University,<br>Mumbai. |
| 8. | Shaping the Life:<br>Kerala Youth respond to changing Socio-economic Order | Rajesh Kumar Komath<br>School of Social Sciences, Mahatma Gandhi University,<br>Kerala.<br>&<br>Rakkee Thimothy<br>Centre for Economic Studies and Planning,<br>Jawaharlal Nehru University,<br>Delhi. |
| 9. | Image and Identification among the Indian Call Centre Workers | Jonathan Murphy<br>Cardiff University Business School, Cardiff,<br>UK. |
| 10. | Virtual Socialisation via Cyber Cafes:<br>Narratives of Youth from Ranchi | Shweta Jha<br>Apeejay Institute of Management & Information Technology,<br>New Delhi. |
| 11. | Youth in Violent Conflict in Jammu and Kashmir: A Case Study of Perceptions and Attitudes of Minority Community Students of Jammu University, Kashmir University and Migrant's Camp | Falendra K. Sudan<br>Department of Economics,<br>University of Jammu, Jammu,<br>Jammu and Kashmir. |
| 12. | Struggle for a Need-based Development: Life History of an Adivasi Youth in Chhattisgarh | Govinda Chandra Rath<br>G.B. Pant Social Science Institute,<br>Uttar Pradesh. |
| 13. | Illiterate and Semi literate youth in democratic India: Their Hopes, Struggles and Aspirations | Jasvir Singh<br>Independent Researcher. |

| No. | Case Study Title | Name and Institution Affiliation of the Expert |
|---|---|---|
| 14. | Child Marriage in Rajasthan—Coping with the Mephistopheles? | Pinki Solanki<br>Independent Researcher. |
| 15. | Youth and Student Politics:<br>A Case Study of Jamia Milia Islamia:<br>New Delhi | Pushkar Raj<br>People's Union for Civil Liberty,<br>Delhi. |

# APPENDIX VI
# Socio-economic and Demographic Profile of Indian Youth

**A3.1:** Proportion of Youth by Age, Gender, Residence, Caste/Tribe and Religion

| Background Characteristics | 15–19 | 20–24 | 25–29 | 30–34 | 15–34 |
|---|---|---|---|---|---|
| All | 9.7 | 8.7 | 8.1 | 7.2 | 33.8 |
| Male | 10.1 | 8.7 | 7.8 | 7.0 | 33.7 |
| Female | 9.3 | 8.8 | 8.4 | 7.4 | 33.9 |
| **Rural** | – | – | – | – | – |
| *Total* | 9.4 | 8.3 | 7.8 | 7.0 | 32.5 |
| Male | 9.9 | 8.2 | 7.4 | 6.7 | 32.2 |
| Female | 9.0 | 8.4 | 8.1 | 7.2 | 32.7 |
| **Urban** | – | – | – | – | – |
| *Total* | 10.5 | 9.9 | 9.0 | 7.8 | 37.3 |
| Male | 10.8 | 10.1 | 8.8 | 7.8 | 37.4 |
| Female | 10.3 | 9.7 | 9.3 | 7.9 | 37.2 |
| **SC** | – | – | – | – | – |
| *Total* | 9.7 | 8.4 | 7.9 | 6.9 | 32.9 |
| Male | 10.3 | 8.3 | 7.6 | 6.7 | 32.8 |
| Female | 9.0 | 8.5 | 8.2 | 7.2 | 33.0 |
| **ST** | – | – | – | – | – |
| *Total* | 9.3 | 8.0 | 7.9 | 7.1 | 32.3 |
| Male | 9.6 | 7.6 | 7.6 | 6.9 | 31.7 |
| Female | 9.1 | 8.4 | 8.2 | 7.3 | 32.9 |
| **Religion** | | | | | |
| ***Hindu*** | – | – | – | – | – |
| *Total* | 9.6 | 8.7 | 8.2 | 7.3 | 33.9 |
| Male | 10.0 | 8.7 | 7.9 | 7.1 | 33.8 |
| Female | 9.1 | 8.8 | 8.5 | 7.5 | 34.0 |

| | | | | | |
|---|---|---|---|---|---|
| ***Muslim*** | – | – | – | – | – |
| *Total* | 10.5 | 8.6 | 7.5 | 6.5 | 33.1 |
| Male | 10.8 | 8.7 | 7.2 | 6.3 | 33.0 |
| Female | 10.1 | 8.6 | 7.8 | 6.7 | 33.2 |
| ***Christian*** | – | – | – | – | – |
| *Total* | 9.9 | 9.1 | 8.6 | 7.5 | 35.1 |
| Male | 9.9 | 8.9 | 8.2 | 7.4 | 34.4 |
| Female | 9.9 | 9.3 | 9.0 | 7.6 | 35.8 |

Source: *Census of India, 2001, Office of Registrar General.*
Note: All figures in the table are in per cent and indicating the proportion of population in each segment of population. For example, the proportion of youth in the age group 15–19 to total population is calculated as:

$$\text{\% of youth } (15\text{–}19) = \frac{\text{Total population } (15\text{–}19) \times 100}{\text{Total population}}.$$

**A3.2:** Distribution of Youth by Age, Gender, Residence, Caste/Tribe and Religion

| | Of total population** | Of youth population (15–34)* |
|---|---|---|
| **Gender** | | |
| Male | 51.7 | 51.6 |
| Female | 48.3 | 48.4 |
| **Residence** | | |
| Rural | 72.2 | 69.3 |
| Urban | 27.8 | 30.7 |
| **Caste/Tribe** | | |
| SC | 16.2 | 15.7 |
| ST | 8.2 | 7.8 |
| **Religion** | | |
| Hindus | 80.5 | 80.6 |
| Muslims | 13.4 | 13.2 |
| Christians | 2.3 | 2.4 |
| Sikhs | 1.9 | 1.9 |
| Others | 1.9 | 1.9 |

Source: *Census of India, 2001, Office of Registrar General, Government of India.*

**A3.3:** Completed Levels of Education of Youth by Sex, Residence, Caste/Tribe and Religion

| | Literacy Rate | Below primary | Primary | Middle | Secondary | Higher Secondary | Graduate and above |
|---|---|---|---|---|---|---|---|
| **All Youth** | 71.0 | 7.4 | 15.6 | 15.4 | 15.3 | 8.1 | 6.0 |
| Male | 81.0 | 7.7 | 16.5 | 18.3 | 18.0 | 9.7 | 7.2 |
| Female | 60.4 | 7.0 | 14.7 | 12.4 | 12.4 | 6.4 | 2.3 |
| **Rural** | | | | | | | |
| Total | 65.1 | 8.4 | 16.3 | 15.2 | 13.0 | 5.9 | 3.1 |
| Male | 77.4 | 8.9 | 17.7 | 18.7 | 16.3 | 7.8 | 4.5 |
| Female | 52.2 | 7.9 | 14.9 | 11.5 | 9.6 | 3.8 | 1.7 |
| **Urban** | | | | | | | |
| Total | 84.5 | 5.0 | 14.1 | 16.0 | 20.5 | 13.1 | 12.4 |
| Male | 89.1 | 4.9 | 14.0 | 17.4 | 21.8 | 13.8 | 13.1 |
| Female | 79.4 | 6.3 | 14.2 | 14.4 | 19.1 | 12.3 | 11.6 |
| **SCs** | | | | | | | |
| Total | 60.8 | 8.4 | 16.2 | 14.7 | 10.8 | 5.0 | 2.7 |
| Male | 74.1 | 9.2 | 18.7 | 18.8 | 13.8 | 6.6 | 3.9 |
| Female | 46.7 | 7.6 | 13.6 | 10.5 | 7.7 | 3.2 | 1.5 |
| **STs** | | | | | | | |
| Total | 51.7 | 10.1 | 13.1 | 11.5 | 8.1 | 3.7 | 1.8 |
| Male | 65.8 | 12.2 | 16.4 | 15.1 | 10.7 | 5.1 | 2.6 |
| Female | 37.9 | 8.0 | 9.9 | 8.0 | 5.6 | 2.3 | 1.0 |
| **Religion** | | | | | | | |
| ***Hindu*** | | | | | | | |
| Total | 71.4 | 7.2 | 15.4 | 15.5 | 15.5 | 8.3 | 6.3 |
| Male | 82.1 | 7.4 | 16.3 | 18.5 | 18.5 | 10.1 | 7.6 |
| Female | 60.0 | 6.9 | 14.5 | 12.3 | 12.4 | 6.4 | 4.8 |
| ***Muslim*** | | | | | | | |
| Total | 63.9 | 9.4 | 17.9 | 14.0 | 11.5 | 5.0 | 3.0 |
| Male | 72.1 | 10.0 | 19.2 | 16.3 | 13.2 | 5.9 | 3.9 |
| Female | 55.3 | 8.7 | 16.5 | 11.5 | 9.6 | 4.0 | 2.1 |
| ***Christian*** | | | | | | | |
| Total | 85.4 | 6.1 | 13.9 | 18.1 | 20.2 | 12.5 | 9.3 |
| Male | 88.5 | 6.2 | 14.9 | 19.8 | 21.0 | 11.7 | 9.0 |
| Female | 82.3 | 6.0 | 13.0 | 16.4 | 19.5 | 13.4 | 9.5 |

Source: *Census of India, 2001, Office of Registrar General, Government of India.*
Note: All figures in the table are in per cent and indicating the proportion of population in each segment of population.

**A3.4**: Work Status of Youth by Sex, Residence, Cste/Tribe and Religion—2001

| Background Characteristics | Main worker | Marginal worker | Non worker |
|---|---|---|---|
| **All** | 40.4 | 13.4 | 46.2 |
| Male | 59.6 | 10.8 | 29.6 |
| Female | 20.0 | 16.2 | 63.8 |
| **Rural** | | | |
| Total | 42.7 | 17.5 | 39.8 |
| Male | 60.9 | 13.3 | 25.8 |
| Female | 23.9 | 21.7 | 54.4 |
| **Urban** | | | |
| Total | 35.1 | 4.3 | 60.6 |
| Male | 56.6 | 5.3 | 38.1 |
| Female | 11.1 | 3.2 | 85.7 |
| **SC** | | | |
| Total | 41.1 | 17.2 | 41.7 |
| Male | 58.2 | 14.6 | 27.2 |
| Female | 22.8 | 19.9 | 57.3 |
| **ST** | | | |
| Total | 49.0 | 24.9 | 26.1 |
| Male | 62.1 | 16.6 | 21.3 |
| Female | 36.1 | 33.1 | 30.8 |
| **Religion** | | | |
| ***Hindu*** | | | |
| Total | 41.2 | 14.0 | 44.8 |
| Male | 59.6 | 11.0 | 29.4 |
| Female | 21.5 | 17.3 | 61.2 |
| ***Muslim*** | | | |
| Total | 35.9 | 10.6 | 53.5 |
| Male | 60.2 | 10.5 | 29.3 |
| Female | 10.2 | 10.6 | 79.2 |
| ***Christian*** | | | |
| Total | 38.0 | 11.0 | 51.0 |
| Male | 51.3 | 10.2 | 38.5 |
| Female | 25.2 | 11.7 | 63.1 |

Source: Census of India, 2001, Office of Registrar General.
Note: All figures in the table are in per cent and indicating the proportion of workers, marginal workers and non-workers to total population of each category, viz rural, urban, etc.

**A3.5**: Projected Proportion of Youth in Selected Countries

| Country/Year | 2000 | 2005 | 2010 | 2015 | 2020 |
|---|---|---|---|---|---|
| India | 34.6 | 34.8 | 34.8 | 34.9 | 34.4 |
| Germany | 26.2 | 23.8 | 22.9 | 22.4 | 21.4 |
| Brazil | 36.5 | 35.9 | 34.5 | 32.4 | 30.5 |
| China | 34.4 | 32.4 | 29.9 | 29.3 | 28.5 |
| US | 27.5 | 27.3 | 27.2 | 26.5 | 25.7 |

Source: *World Bank, URL: http://devdata.worldbank.org/hnpstats/dp1.asp*
Note: Figures pertain to age group 15–34 years.

**A3.6**: Gross Enrolment Ratios in Selected Countries—2004

| Country | Secondary | | | Tertiary | | |
|---|---|---|---|---|---|---|
| | Total | Male | Female | Total | Male | Female |
| Brazil | 110 | 104 | 115 | 20 | 17 | 23 |
| China | 73 | 73 | 73 | 19 | 21 | 17 |
| Germany | 100 | 101 | 99 | – | – | – |
| India | 52 | 58 | 46 | 11 | 14 | 09 |
| Japan | 102 | 102 | 102 | 54 | 57 | 51 |
| US | 95 | 95 | 94 | 82 | 69 | 96 |

Source: *Global Education Digest, 2006, UNESCO.*

**A3.7**: Economic Activity Rate by Age Group and Sex—2000/2001

| Country | 15–19 | | | 20–24 | | | 25–29 | | | 30–34 | | |
|---|---|---|---|---|---|---|---|---|---|---|---|---|
| | Total | Male | Female | Total | Male | Female | Total | Male | Female | Total | Male | Female |
| Brazil | 55.8 | 66.1 | 45.1 | 71.1 | 90.7 | 51.6 | 73.6 | 96.0 | 51.6 | 75.7 | 97.1 | 54.9 |
| China | 58.6 | 55.8 | 61.7 | 91.6 | 92.4 | 90.8 | 95.3 | 97.9 | 92.5 | 95.7 | 98.6 | 92.6 |
| Germany | 34.2 | 36.3 | 31.9 | 76.8 | 78.2 | 75.4 | 83.1 | 87.9 | 77.8 | 86.8 | 96.4 | 76.3 |
| India | 44.4 | 52.6 | 35.4 | 65.9 | 86.2 | 43.9 | 71.8 | 96.1 | 45.1 | 76.8 | 97.5 | 54.0 |
| Japan | 15.8 | 16.8 | 14.7 | 71.9 | 71.9 | 71.9 | 83.1 | 95.3 | 70.3 | 79.5 | 97.6 | 60.7 |
| US | 38.8 | 40.1 | 37.4 | 75.5 | 78.5 | 72.4 | 85.4 | 90.9 | 79.8 | 86.5 | 93.1 | 79.8 |

Source: *United Nations Statistic Division.*
*http://unstats.un.org/unsd/cdb/cdb_dict*
Note: Age specific economic activity rate is defined as the ratio of the economically active population in a specified age group to the total population of the corresponding age group.

**A3.8**: Unemployment Rate among Youth (Aged 15–24)—2000/2001

| Country | Ref. Year | Total | Male | Female |
|---|---|---|---|---|
| Brazil | 2001 | 17.9 | 14.6 | 22.4 |
| China | 2000 | 3.1 | – | – |
| Germany | 2000 | 8.3 | 9.3 | 7.1 |
| India | 2000 | 10.1 | 10.1 | 10.2 |
| Japan | 2000 | 9.2 | 10.4 | 7.9 |
| US | 2001 | 10.6 | 11.4 | 9.6 |

Notes: 1. Figures are percentage of persons (aged 15+) unemployed.
2. Reference period: Average of monthly estimates.

Source: *United Nations Statistics Division http://unstats.un.org/unsd/cdb/cdb_dict*

Definition: Unemployment rate (15–24) is defined as the ratio of unemployed persons in the age group (15–24) to the economically active population of the same age group.

**A3.9**: Demographic Diversity in India: 2001

| | As % of total population |
|---|---|
| Male | 51.7 |
| Female | 48.3 |
| **Age Group** | |
| 0–14 | 35.4 |
| 15–34 | 33.8 |
| 35–59 | 23.1 |
| 60+ | 7.7 |
| **Residence** | |
| Rural | 72.2 |
| Urban | 27.8 |
| **Caste/Tribe** | |
| SC | 16.2 |
| ST | 8.2 |
| **Religion** | |
| Hindus | 80.5 |
| Muslims | 13.4 |
| Christians | 2.3 |
| Sikhs | 1.9 |
| Others | 1.9 |

Source: Census of India, Office of Registrar General,
Total population of India–1028610328 (Census 2001).

## PICTURES AND CONTRIBUTORS/COLLECTORS

1. Cover Page-Photograph courtesy Hindustan Times (www.hindustantimes.com)
2. Human Chain of Youth—Photograph contributed by Kinjal Sampat
3. Prove Your Identity—Photograph contributed by Rahul Verma
4. Graphics on overview page—contributed by Rajiv Kshetri
5. Graphic at the bottom of The Big Story: contributed by Rajiv Kshetri
6. Graphic at bottom of every page—contributed by Rajiv Kshetri
7. Chapter One: A Group of Youth—Photograph contributed by Kinjal Sampat
8. Chapter Two: Youth with Family Members—Photograph contributed by Vanita Leah Falcao
9. Chapter Three: Two different shoes of Youth—Photograph contributed by Naysa Ahuja
10. Chapter Four: Youth in Memory of Bhopal Gas Tragedy—Photograph contributed by Kinjal Sampat
11. Chapter Five: A Youth Throwing Remains of Used Flower in River—Photograph contributed by Vanita Leah Falcao
12. Chapter Six: Bollywood Picture at the gate of Madam Tausad, London—Photograph contributed by Banasmita.Bora
13. Chapter Seven: A Youth Walking Down the Pathways in a Desolate Forest—Painting Titled as 'Passing Through' by Rajiv Kshetri.